D1221070

From Durrow
to Kells

GEORGE HENDERSON

From Durrow to Kells

The Insular Gospel-books 650-800

with 263 illustrations

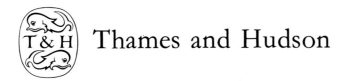 Thames and Hudson

© 1987 Thames and Hudson Ltd, London

First published in the United States in 1987 by
Thames and Hudson Inc., 500 Fifth Avenue,
New York, New York 10110

Library of Congress Catalog Card Number 86-71619

Printed and bound in the German Democratic Republic

Contents

Preface

As the crow flies over Ireland, Durrow, in County Offaly, is only forty miles from Kells, in County Meath. From the 'Book of Durrow' to the 'Book of Kells' is a longer journey, extended through many parts of the British Isles and involving more than a hundred years' worth of experience, thought, and practical endeavour.

The Insular Gospel-books are famous and popular in their own right, as works of art. As works of art they have been nodded-to in conventional histories of the early Church in Ireland and England. As books they have been catalogued, and as codicological entities they have been expertly described. Some individual Gospel-books have been the subject of thorough scrutiny and research by specialists from various disciplines, in connection with the publication of complete facsimiles. None the less, the date and provenance of all the major examples are still matters of dispute among scholars, who rely most heavily on the analysis of Gospel texts and of script.

The present book began life as a course of lectures, in Cambridge, to students specializing in the History of Art, and also to students of Anglo-Saxon and Celtic Literature and History. I wanted to provide my audience with a viewpoint which brought the great illuminated books of the Early Christian period in the British Isles truly into the domain of patronage and function, much of the literature on Insular art being exclusively concerned with questions of ornament and style. Some of my listeners were kind enough to suggest that the lectures were worth publishing. Thus the aim of *From Durrow to Kells* is to combine critical appraisal of the art and imagery of the Insular Gospel-books with a consideration of their specific historical context.

There are advantages in this dual approach. Through reference to the art and imagery – for example, to the strongly Pictish flavour of some of the designs – the implications of contemporary written records of political and ecclesiastical affairs can be more fully appreciated. Similarly through reference to the written records, facts may be discerned that could have significance both for the manufacture and for the historical distribution of the Gospel-books. All seven Insular Gospel-books surveyed here were made, in my opinion, outside Ireland, in the geographical sense. In spite of this, I do not regard the nomenclature 'Durrow' and 'Kells' merely as some broken tail-end of the history of those particular Gospel-books, but rather as essential facts, high among their credentials. At the centre of this book's thesis is the personality of Egbert (639–729), leader of international enterprises, English by birth, inhabitant of Ireland, Pictland, and Dál Riata. It is as some reflection of the integrated virtue and learning of men like Egbert that the religious imagery of the Insular Gospel-books is presented in the following pages.

It so happened that my course of lectures coincided with the publication of the first of a number of papers by Dr Dáibhi Ó Cróinín, who has been making a reassessment of some of the Gospel-books based on an historical reappraisal of the Anglo-Saxon mission to the Continent. His opinions have given the whole subject a useful jolt. There is some interesting overlap between us, particularly in respect of the role of Egbert. Dr Ó Cróinín, Dr Alfred Smith (another historian with strong convictions about the provenance of the Gospel-books), and I are at one in that we all think that the books' historical background is important.

6

But since, of the three, I am the only art historian, I hope that my particular angle complements their work. The crucial importance which I attach to Iona in my 'construct' of the history of the Insular Gospel-books is supported by Mr Ian Fisher's authoritative contribution to the recent Royal Commission volume on Iona; this has given us a much clearer picture of the early monastery and its artistic achievements.

Late in the twelfth century the scholar-priest Gerald of Wales wrote down a story, traditional in Kildare, about the creation of a now lost Insular Gospel-book. The story starts 'On the night before the day' when the scribe was to begin his work. In my book I have tried to view the Insular Gospel-books in this anticipatory way – to reconstruct the circumstances in which the individual books might have come into existence, and to envisage various factors which shaped and conditioned their contents, as we have them. Through wars and revolutions we have certainly lost major Insular Gospel-books and other relevant works of art. These losses must always haunt the theorizer. To pin-point the historical background of those that happen to survive may seem to some people over-ambitious or even pointless. But I believe that not to make the attempt isolates the Gospel-books artificially from the society which produced them, and in addition deprives us of vital evidence about that society. No one can dispute that the making of each of the surviving Gospel-books, which still evoke our unqualified admiration, was a profoundly conscious act, replete with specific intention. This view was propounded in the past in the sensitive and judicious writings of Dr Françoise Henry, and is currently being explored in more specific directions by such scholars as Professor Suzanne Lewis, Miss Hilary Richardson, and Professor Robert Stevick.

In considering the historical background, a difficulty of which I am only too aware is that important new investigations are now in progress into the history of the seventh- and eighth-century Irish Church. To trespass into that subject in an interdisciplinary way would always have been perilous, and I recognize that nowadays one enters a minefield. I am deeply grateful to Mr Richard Sharpe for saving me from basic errors, but in thanking him for reading Chapter 6 of this book I want to make it clear that I know that on many points of interpretation and chronology his views are very different from those expressed here. I am grateful for the encouragement of Dr Jennifer O'Reilly, who attended my lectures in 1983. Dr Isabel Henderson has generously given me information and advice throughout the entire process of shaping and completing this book. In preparing the index I have been greatly helped by the skill and patience of Miss Annabel Dainty.

Isle of Iona
September, 1985

G.H.

1 Map showing relevant sites in Scotland, Wales and England

I Introduction: the coming of the Gospel to Anglo-Saxon England

In 596 Pope Gregory I despatched a contingent of monks from Rome to preach Christianity to the pagan Anglo-Saxons.[1] The Britons, whose political power was confined by Anglo-Saxon encroachment to the west and north of the country, had been Christian ever since the original conversion of the Roman Empire, but the British Church deliberately took no interest in the spiritual welfare of the Anglo-Saxons, the sworn enemy.[2] In the fifth century Christianity had spread from Britain and Gaul to Ireland. By the late sixth century the ascetic zeal and missionary charity of the Church in Ireland had begun to turn outwards to mainland Britain and to the continent of Europe.[3] But just at this time Christ's charge to the Apostles, to carry salvation to the ends of the earth, was felt as a personal obligation by the great and enterprising Pope Gregory. The latest intelligence received from correspondents in Gaul suggested that a huge harvest of souls could be gathered in England. Aethelbert, King of Kent, had married a Christian, the daughter of the Merovingian King of Paris; her own bishop-chaplain was permitted to celebrate Mass in the royal city of Canterbury, in a church dedicated to the great missionary saint of northern Gaul, St Martin of Tours. Aethelbert was reported to be the ruler of a rich and stable kingdom, and to be the overlord of other client kingdoms; his own conversion could lead to the wholesale conversion of the English.

It was in these terms that Pope Gregory in due course addressed a letter to the King, referring to 'the English race over whom your Majesty is placed', and urging him to instil knowledge of the true God 'to the kings and nations subject to you'. This summons to share in the unity of the Christian faith had a tremendous political, propagandist, appeal. As formulated by the Pope, writing from Rome itself, it evoked the international society of the old Roman Empire. The Pope quoted the example of Constantine, who had led the Roman Empire to abandon the worship of idols and who had thereby, with God's blessing, surpassed his predecessors in fame and reputation. So also Aethelbert might exceed the ancient kings of his race in praise and merit.[4]

Aethelbert belonged to the royal family called Oiscingas, after Oisc, son of Hengist, and like other Anglo-Saxon rulers of his time was a reputed descendant of Woden.[5] It was a serious step to reject the old gods and along with them the social conventions and visible symbolism of traditional Germanic kingship. The benefits of Christianity had to be seen to be great, in material wealth and temporal influence, as well as in the reassurance of an eternal kingdom in the heavens. The Roman missionaries, led by their abbot, Augustine, at their first interview with King Aethelbert at Thanet declared that they brought the very best news from Rome. They displayed the culture as well as the message of the Gospel. In procession they chanted antiphons used in the churches of Gaul. They carried a silver cross as their standard (*pro vexillo*), and the likeness of Christ the Saviour painted on a panel.[6] (Afterwards the cathedral church established by Augustine in Canterbury was dedicated to Christ the Saviour, and must have housed the icon.[7]) As the mission prospered, the Pope sent very many different sorts of presents to the King (*dona in diversis speciebus perplura*), and to the churches of Canterbury sacred vessels, altar cloths and ornaments, vestments for the priests and clerks, and relics of the holy Apostles and Martyrs.[8] Canterbury's church of St Martin reflected a major

Gaulish cult.[9] Now by means of the relics it possessed, housed in its altars, it directly reflected and participated in the principal cults of Rome itself. A monastic church dedicated to the Apostles Peter and Paul was built to the east of the city. The Church of the Four Crowned Martyrs, Quattuor Coronati, on the Coelian Hill in Rome, had its counterpart in Canterbury.[10] Before 624, Mellitus, one of Augustine's companions and successors as Archbishop of Canterbury, dedicated a church at Canterbury to the Holy Mother of God. This also closely followed Roman precedent. In 611 Mellitus attended a synod in Rome, and must have visited the great Roman rotunda called the Pantheon, which only three years before had been handed over by the Emperor Phocas to the Church authorities and had been dedicated by Pope Boniface IV to the Holy Mother of God and All Martyrs.[11]

The personnel of the Roman mission, Augustine, Laurence, Justus, Mellitus and Paulinus, were evidently able practical organizers. But they brought with them from Rome an ideal concept of the English Church, based on the governmental structure of the old Roman province of Britain, with its two administrative centres at London and York.[12] Under the influence, and indeed control, of Aethelbert, Saberht, King of the East Saxons, accepted Christianity for his kingdom, the principal city of which was London. Another neighbouring king, Redwald of the East Angles, also received baptism out of respect for Aethelbert.[13] Paulinus appears to have been temporarily assigned to East Anglia, although not yet with full episcopal rights and duties. He was in fact destined for York, and it seems, reading between the lines of various narratives included in Bede's *Ecclesiastical History*, to have been his prime objective in and around Redwald's court to locate, impress, and achieve moral ascendancy over Redwald's client, the young exiled Prince Edwin, of the royal family of Deira, the province in which York lay.

What had first prompted Pope Gregory to set about the conversion of the Anglo-Saxons was the sight of fair-haired foreign boys, evidently pagans, for sale as slaves in the Roman market. When he asked where they came from, he was told that the men of that kingdom were called 'Deiri'. He immediately resolved that their nation should be snatched from the wrath (*de ira*) of Christ, and called to his mercy. He enquired who was the king of Deira, and was told 'Aelle'.[14] By the time

Augustine and his fellow-missionaries arrived, the ruler of England north of the Humber was Aethelfrith, of the rival, Bernician (Northumbrian) royal family, and the Deiran royal family was scattered, living in dangerous exile. Aethelfrith, a heroic war-leader of the pagan Germanic tradition, was remote from any influence the Roman mission might exert. British Christians knew him as the man who ordered the slaughter of over a thousand monks who had come from the monastery of Bangor-is-Coed to pray for his defeat on the eve of a battle near Chester. Aedán son of Gabrán, whom the Irish St Columba himself had inaugurated as King of the Irish of Dál Riata in Scotland, was utterly defeated in war by Aethelfrith.[15] Aethelfrith was consequently feared and obeyed by a wide circle of client kings. The British King of Elmet, at his bidding, poisoned Edwin of Deira's nephew who had taken refuge at his court.[16] In 616 messengers from Aethelfrith came to Redwald's court and put pressure upon him either to kill or to surrender Edwin.

In these apparently unpropitious circumstances, Edwin is reported by Bede to have been addressed, at dead of night, by a mysterious stranger who offered him royal power superior to that of all his ancestors, and indeed to that of any previous kings of the English, in exchange for a promise of obedience in the matter of religious belief.[17] Although Bede does not say so, the stranger was evidently Paulinus; the tempting bait of superior temporal dominion is exactly what was offered to King Aethelbert in Pope Gregory's letter. Aethelbert himself died in 616, and Redwald of East Anglia had already begun to rival him in power and prestige. Whether through the hidden persuasions and financial backing of the Roman missionaries and their friends abroad – Frankish coinage was found in the great ship-burial, probably Redwald's, at Sutton Hoo[18] – or by his own initiative, Redwald reacted positively to the threats of Aethelfrith, and backing Edwin, attacked and killed Aethelfrith in a decisive battle that scattered his family and followers, and placed Edwin on the throne of Deira and Bernicia.[19] From the battlefield or the wrecked encampment of Aethelfrith, Redwald could have commandeered as loot some of the more mysterious objects found in the Sutton Hoo burial – the ceremonial whetstone, of British manufacture, made of stone from southern Scotland, and the great bronze and enamel hanging-bowls, also of British or Irish manufacture. These are things

4

which Aethelfrith, victor over the British, and the Irish of Scotland, might himself have acquired in the very first years of the seventh century. They are at any rate oddly exotic in the East Anglian context, *37* in a sense more so than the Byzantine dishes from Sutton Hoo which speak of Redwald's diplomatic importance, or the Swedish heirlooms[20] which witness to his devotion to the heroic pagan past of his family, the Wuffingas, a devotion not altered by his acquaintance with Christianity. Bede reports that in the reconsecrated temple where a Christian altar had been erected, Redwald retained a small altar where pagan sacrifices were offered.[21] When Redwald died in 624, his funeral was marked by pagan rituals of the greatest splendour. He was laid in a ninety-foot ship, surrounded by treasure, *27-31* sumptuous personal equipment and all the symbols of heroic court life, and buried under a mound heaped up with immense labour.

Redwald's cautious and ambivalent attitude to Christianity or outright apostasy did not fundamentally affect the advancing fortunes of Christianity either in East Anglia or north of the Humber. He had played his essential part in promoting the cause of Edwin, and in Edwin's reign Roman Christianity moved north, to York.

The undertaking which Edwin had given, in duress, to Paulinus was not actually fulfilled until 628. Some years earlier, Edwin's marriage to Aethelbert's daughter Aethelberg brought Paulinus north as her bishop-chaplain.[22] Edwin acted circumspectly to achieve maximum popular support for the new faith and the new ethics. His kingdom would become Christian 'if it was judged by his wise men to be a holier religion and more worthy of God'. Edwin himself is reported to have learned the faith systematically from Paulinus in preparation for convincing his followers.[23] As a public display of the intellectual superiority of Christianity over pagan thought and practice, a letter, markedly theological in tone, was procured from Pope Boniface V (619–25) addressed to Edwin, annunciating the doctrine of the Trinity, the wonderful gift of eternal life which was the result of holy baptism, and setting out at length the traditional arguments against idolatry, with telling quotations from the Psalms. Pope Boniface's letter is written as if to persuade an obtuse or recalcitrant Edwin, but St Peter is already reckoned as Edwin's 'protector',[24] and the letter must have provided the King with ideas and language with which to sway his counsellors.

Edwin was now in a position openly to advocate Christianity. If his counsellors agreed with him, 'they might all be consecrated together in the waters of life'.[25] According to Bede, one of these counsellors made the useful contribution of likening the mystery of human consciousness to a sparrow which flies quickly through a lighted dwelling-hall, in from the dark at one end and out again into the dark at the other. To the uncertainty of life in seventh-century England the good news of Christianity, preached on the authority of the successor of St Peter in the city of Rome, must have brought an amazing sense of exhilaration and confidence. Christianity was a strikingly literate religion. Its body of primary written evidence, notably the Gospels, and its sophisticated expression of praise and worship, notably in the Psalms, made an inescapable impression. For the pitifully swift flight of the sparrow through the house, *passerum domum citissime pervolaverit*,[26] the Psalmist had the perfect antidote. In Psalm 83 he represents the coming of the faithful believer to the permanency and security of God's dwelling-place: 'Yea, the sparrow hath found itself an house, even thine altars, O Lord of hosts' (*Etenim passer invenit sibi domum . . .*).

King Edwin's systematic study of the faith reached its climax when as a catechumen in Easter week 628 he received final instruction and heard the scriptural lessons in preparation for his baptism on Easter Sunday. His careful education in the faith presumably involved the acquisition of a knowledge of Latin, the international language of Christianity. Edwin's literacy is taken for granted in a later letter from Pope Honorius in which he counsels the King to 'employ yourself with frequent readings from the works of Gregory, your Evangelist'.[27] Edwin was the first of a long line of literate Northumbrian kings, whose competence to rule was tested not only on the battlefield but also in ecclesiastical debate, and whose personal patronage of the Church was of major cultural importance.

Edwin's political power and prestige enabled him to persuade the new King of the East Angles, Eorpwold, Redwald's son and successor, to accept the Christian faith and sacraments.

Eorpwold's death, soon after his conversion, was followed by another short-lived pagan reaction, but in 630 or 631 Sigbert, Eorpwold's brother, returned from political exile to become King of the East Angles; Sigbert had been taught the Christian faith in Gaul, and he brought first-hand knowledge of the mature Frankish Church to bear upon the conversion of his people.[28] In collaboration with his Burgundian bishop, Felix, and with the help and blessing of the Church of Canterbury, Sigbert established a school where East Anglian boys were trained in Latin literature and in the rites of the Christian Church.[29] As well as promoting the Church in his kingdom as a cultural institution, consciously linked to Christian practice in Europe as a whole, Sigbert brought into the history of the conversion of the Anglo-Saxons a new level of personal commitment, in advance of the political and social realities of his time. He resigned his kingship, received the tonsure, and entered a monastery of his own foundation. Later, in the face of an attack by the still-pagan Mercians, the East Angles insisted that Sigbert take charge again of military affairs, and his precocious religious experiment ended in disaster on the battlefield.[30] Sigbert's idealism, however, underlines the importance in Christian teaching, for example in the papal letters to Aethelbert and Edwin, of a personal quest for salvation. The Christian had to believe and act, so as to escape the terror of God's judgment and earn the eternal life of the saints in heaven.

The attractions which King Sigbert saw in the monastic vocation must have been intensified by his official contacts in East Anglia in the 630s with Fursey and his brothers, an itinerant group of Irish missionary monks to whom Sigbert gave the derelict Roman fortress of Burgh Castle for their monastery.[31] Fursey and his company were highly characteristic of Irish monasticism from the late sixth century onwards, intent both on preaching the saving grace of Christ to others, and on the practice of a deeply devotional and ascetic life, often in voluntary exile in distant places, as pilgrims of Christ, *peregrini*, or as solitary hermits. The first of the great Irish monastic missionaries was St Columbanus, who left Ireland around the year 590 with twelve companions and sailed to Gaul.[32] He gained the support of the Merovingian ruler of Austrasia, who gave him a disused Roman fort at Annegray for a monastery. Later Columbanus founded the important monastery of Luxeuil.

The monastic rule which Columbanus established placed typical Irish emphasis on penance. The Irish Church, descended directly from the Early Christian Churches of Britain and Gaul, was of course orthodox in doctrine, but by the sixth century the Irish (and British) differed from the rest of Europe in some important customs, for example in the form of the monastic tonsure and in the method used to calculate the date of Easter.[33] Around 600 Columbanus in Gaul argued the Irish case against Frankish and Roman customs, and wrote apologias to Pope Gregory I and his successor Boniface IV. After being expelled by the Merovingian Theodoric II, he and a company of monks moved first to Metz, then into the province of Helvetia, and finally over the Alps into northern Italy. Under the patronage of Agilof, the ruler of Lombardy, Columbanus founded another major monastery, at Bobbio, where he died in 615.

The foundation of a series of monasteries, scattered over a wide geographical area and comprising a bulwark for secular society against the stern judgments of God, was the achievement also of St Columba,[34] who left Ireland in voluntary exile in 563 and established a monastery on the small island of Iona off the west coast of Scotland. From Iona he led preaching missions into Pictish Scotland to the north and east. Columba died on Iona in 597, the same year as Pope Gregory's mission arrived in Kent.

Fursey belonged to the next generation of Irish *peregrini*. After Sigbert's death Fursey left East Anglia and sailed to Gaul, where he founded among other monasteries Lagny-sur-Marne, east of Paris. In 654, four years after his death, Fursey's bones were translated into a shrine 'in the shape of a little house', at Péronne in Picardy, called *Perrona Scottorum* on account of its Irish origin.[35] Fursey literally joined the glorious company of the Apostles, for his shrine was made by St Eligius, the great Frankish goldsmith, administrator and bishop, who also made the shrines of the Apostles of France, St Denis and St Martin.[36] The outstanding reputation which St Fursey left behind him in the English Church derived from the record of his mystical and visionary life. In the midst of his intense study both of the holy Scriptures and of monastic discipline, he experienced ecstatic visions of the future state of the human soul. Like St Columba, who all his life carried on his side a livid scar where an angel was reputed to have chastised him with a scourge,[37] Fursey bore scars caused by an encounter with a soul burning in Purgatorial fire.[38] In another vision, of angels, he heard the angelic host singing the words: 'The saints shall go on from strength to strength, and the God of Gods shall be seen in Zion . . .'. This is a quotation from Psalm 83 which eloquently expresses the yearning of the soul for the direct perception of God, the Beatific Vision. The same Psalm (that of the homing sparrow) is consistently associated in the hagiographical writings of this period with the highest goal of the monastic life, 'the stillness of divine contemplation' as achieved by famous ascetics and hermits. We find the same experience recorded of the Anglo-Saxon Mercian prince Guthlac, who entered religion in the late seventh century and who lived as a hermit on a lonely island in the fenlands westwards from East Anglia. He, like Fursey, was carried up out of the body, confronted with Hell-mouth gaping, and consoled by meetings with saints and angels. At the climax of his vision he heard angels singing in chorus the same words: 'The saints shall go on from strength to strength . . .'.[39]

This same sense of close communion with the Church triumphant became a feature of Northumbrian Christianity after the death of Edwin in 632, in battle against the pagan enemy whom Sigbert of East Anglia also had to face, King Penda of Mercia.[40] Edwin had established the Church in Deira on the pattern of the Church in Kent. The seat of Paulinus's archiepiscopal see at York was a church of stone, begun in Edwin's time and dedicated to St Peter. Paulinus also built a stone church, 'of remarkable workmanship', at Lincoln.[41] Paulinus's evangelizing of Deira was supported by his deacon, James, a skilful teacher of liturgical chant. Edwin furnished his principal church in the grandest style, with a great gold cross and gold chalice. The design of this chalice might be guessed at by the recorded appearance of a chalice made by St Eligius a few years later for the monastic church of Chelles.[42] At Edwin's death, cross, chalice, and also Eanflaed, Edwin's daughter by his marriage with Aethelberg, were carried away by Paulinus to safety in Kent. He left behind in the church in York James the Deacon, who persevered in preaching and baptising.[43]

Meantime the changed political situation brought a fresh infusion of Christian teaching and practice from a different source. The sons of Aethelfrith, exiled during Edwin's reign among the Picts and Scots and reared on Irish Christianity, returned to their father's kingdom. After a series of defeats by Aethelfrith's traditional enemies the Britons his third son, Oswald, gained the upper hand and established a stable kingdom, in wealth and influence equal to Edwin's.[44] For clergy to man the Church in his kingdom and thoroughly to

Christianize his homeland of Bernicia, Oswald turned to the island monastery of Iona.[45] In the next chapter we shall look in more circumstantial detail at the establishment of Columban monasticism in Northumbria. Here we may note that from the mid-seventh century onwards Northumbrian Christianity became profoundly imbued with the best aspirations of Irish monasticism. From the Tweed to the Solway, hermits with English names but authentically Irish spirituality brought a general shift in the values of society and gave to northern England its 'Age of the Saints'. Like Fursey, the Englishman Dryhthelm witnessed with his spiritual eyes the pains of Purgatory and the promised joys of heaven.[46] The greatest of the Anglo-Saxon saints of the seventh century, St Cuthbert of Lindisfarne, laboured, as his biographer Bede tells us, to that pitch of excellence – the condition of those saints whom the Psalmist acclaims: 'they shall go on from strength to strength . . .'.[47]

The Columban Church followed the same customs that caused controversy in Gaul in the time of Columbanus's mission. The catechumens whom James the Deacon instructed in the faith at York might come to their baptism on Easter Sunday as determined by the Roman reckoning in a different week from the Easter Sunday calculated by Irish computation. Since the fasts of Lent and rites of Easter lay at the very heart of the Christian life, the divergence between the Roman and Irish parties, though it had no doctrinal implications, had about it the taint of schism. The matter became pressing when Oswald's brother and successor King Oswy married Eanflaed, Edwin's daughter. Her return to Deira strengthened the traditions of Roman Christianity established by her father, and brought the discrepancy between Irish and Roman observance right into the royal household, the King's chaplains celebrating Easter at one time and the Queen's chaplains at another.[48] In various provinces of the Irish Church, the Easter controversy was resolved at various times, throughout the seventh century and on into the early eighth, by conceding that old, venerated, but now evidently provincial customs should yield to the unity of custom promulgated on the supreme authority of the Roman See. As early as 633 the Church in southern Ireland generally shared the view expressed by Cummian, one of its abbots, that Ireland could not alone be right and Jerusalem and Rome be wrong.[49] Fursey's smooth path to canonization in mid-seventh-century Gaul suggests that he belonged to the first phase of South Irish *Romani*. On the other hand, Columbanus of Leinster and Bobbio, and Columba of Donegal and Iona, were independent traditionalists. The argument at the synod called by King Oswy at Whitby in 664 turned on the contrasting authority of the Apostolates of Columba and Peter. When it came *166* to a public debate, St Peter, Prince of the Apostles, Janitor of heaven, had indisputably the stronger claim to be obeyed.⁵⁰

Fortunately the unification of the Church in Northumbria after 664 on Roman lines did not essentially undermine or devalue the contribution of Columban monasticism. St Cuthbert belonged to the post-Whitby Northumbrian Church, and as Bishop of Lindisfarne took an active part in the diocesan organization established or confirmed by Theodore of Tarsus, the most active and creative of St Augustine's seventh-century successors as Archbishop of Canterbury.⁵¹

Theodore became archbishop four years after the Synod of Whitby, and lived until 690. Born in Cilicia and consecrated in Rome, literate in both Latin and Greek, he was heir to the totality of Christian tradition and citizen of a truly international society. The glamour and lure of that society was keenly felt by high-minded young men in Northumbria, Wilfrid and Benedict Bishop, students of James the Deacon and of the Kentish clergy introduced by Queen Eanflaed. By their frequent acquisitive journeys through Gaul and Italy, and by the amply endowed monasteries which they founded in Northumbria, at Hexham and Ripon, Wearmouth and Jarrow, Wilfrid and Benedict deeply influenced the physical, visual fabric of Northumbrian Christianity.⁵² The little Rome of early seventh-century Canterbury, with its relics, icons, vestments and music, was emulated and even surpassed in the late seventh century in the north of England. Christian treasures from Italy and Gaul came to the northern monasteries – Apostolic relics, panel paintings illustrating the Apocalypse, images of the Virgin and the Apostles, precious figured textiles and sacred vessels.⁵³ The teaching of liturgical chant in the Kentish manner, of which James the Deacon had been a master, was extended at Wearmouth and Jarrow by the presence, for a time, of John, choir master of St Peter's in Rome itself, and at Hexham by a famous musician, Maban, who had been trained in church music 'by the successors of the disciples of St Gregory in Kent'.⁵⁴ England might be at the frozen

edge of the world, as the early papal letters represented it, but distance was no obstacle. From the Roman point of view, the reputation and sanctity of Pope Gregory, who had by his own initiative constituted himself the Apostle of the English, gave permanent significance to the English Church. The sense of obligation felt by the English, the awareness of a special relationship with Rome, shines through the text of Bede's *Ecclesiastical History*, written in Jarrow before 731. Pope Gregory's overriding aim, however, was the unity of the Christian Churches, and that idea, too, was a positive and compelling one in the relations of the Northumbrian and Irish Churches in the period around 700.

In the late seventh century, therefore, Northumbria was highly charged, culturally and spiritually. The mixture, the wealth of ideas available from different sources, inevitably resulted in an outburst of original intellectual endeavour, prime examples of which are the illuminated Gospels-books which are the subject of this book. The cultural mix is represented in the person of Oswy's son Aldfrith, King of Northumbria from 685 to 705. Aldfrith succeeded his half-brother Ecgfrith after Ecgfrith's death in Pictland in the Battle of Nechtansmere.⁵⁵ *164* Like his grandfather Aethelfrith long before, Ecgfrith had waged war against his neighbours: against the Picts, ignoring the advice of St Cuthbert, and against the Irish, ignoring the advice of Egbert, a far-sighted English monk and bishop, permanently exiled for his soul's sake in Ireland – a Fursey or Columbanus in reverse.⁵⁶ Aldfrith on the other hand was perfectly in accord with the wise and conciliatory views of these great churchmen. He was educated in Ireland and Iona,⁵⁷ was half-Irish himself, and was friend and pupil of Adomnán, Abbot of Iona, the biographer of St Columba. He was equally open to the appreciation of Mediterranean culture. He gave eight hides of land (a considerable estate – by English reckoning the island of Iona itself consisted only of five hides) in exchange for a splendid book, a scientific compilation described as a *Codex Cosmographiorum*, brought back from Italy by Benedict Biscop.⁵⁸ This indicates the high value set on books by clerics and educated laymen alike. Through the book-collecting efforts of Ceolfrith, Benedict Biscop's successor as abbot of Jarrow-Wearmouth, the library of the joint monastery was enormous, stocked with major texts in important 'editions'. This library was the training-ground of Bede, the greatest historian of the early Middle Ages. At the beginning of the eighth century St Wilfrid's successor at Hexham, Bishop Acca, also built up 'a large and most noble library, assiduously collecting histories of the passions of the martyrs, as well as other ecclesiastical books'.[59] The participation of Aldfrith in the intellectual life of his time is at once more casual and more solidly based than the conscious efforts Edwin had had to make. Bede calls Aldfrith 'a most learned man in all respects'.[60]

The period around 700 was a high moment in English civilization generally. The transition to Christianity had been fully achieved, and England had settled down to enjoy its fruits. The comparative political stability and the widespread idealism of the time can be judged by the number of kings who, like Sigbert of East Anglia over half a century earlier, voluntarily resigned their kingdoms 'for the sake of the Lord'. In the narrowness of seventeenth-century political theory, the poet and polemicist John Milton could see no merits in this habit of the Old English kings. In his *History of Britain* he sneers at 'Kings one after another leaving their Kingly Charge to run their heads into a Monks Cowle'.[61] But just as Old English religious poetry is more 'first-hand' and truer to Holy Scripture than *Paradise Lost* and *Paradise Regained*, so also the fundamentally innocent opportunism of those who resigned their kingdoms seems above reproach.

One of these men was Caedwalla, King of the West Saxons, whose political career St Wilfrid had nurtured and advanced.[62]. At the height of his power in 688 he went to Rome, anxious, as Bede tells us, 'to gain the special privilege of being washed in the fountain of baptism within the threshold of the Apostles', that is, in the great Baptistry of St John Lateran. 'He hoped that soon after his baptism he might pass, cleansed as he was, to eternal joy.'[63] At his death, he had the honour to be buried in St Peter's Church, and his tomb was inscribed with an epitaph beginning:

220

Culmen, opes, subolem, pollentia regna, triumphos,
Exuvias, proceres, moenia, castra, lares;
Quaeque patrum virtus, et quae congesserat ipse
Caedval armipotens, liquit amore Dei;
Ut Petrum, sedemque Petri rex cerneret hospes . . .
Candidus inter oves Christi sociabilis ibit . . .

(The height of achievement, wealth, dynastic succession, royal power, victories, spoils, his chieftains, his stronghold, camp and home, and all that his own, and the valour of his ancestors, had amassed, warlike Caedwalla abandoned for love of God, so that as a pilgrim he might gaze upon the seat of Peter . . . washed white, he is become one of the company of Christ's sheep . . .)

Aethelred, King of Mercia, whose warlike temper Archbishop Theodore had moderated, likewise resigned his throne, in 704, and became first monk and then abbot of Bardney, a royal foundation in Lincolnshire.[64] His nephew and successor Coenred also resigned as king in 709, and went to Rome, where he received the tonsure from Pope Constantine and gave himself up to prayer, fasting, and almsgiving. With him to the holy places of Rome came a young prince of the East Saxons, Offa, who as Bede says, 'inspired by a like devotion, left his wife, his lands, his kinsmen and his fatherland on account of Christ and the Gospel' (*propter Christum et propter Evangelium*).[65]

Although the various centres of Christian life and scholarship mentioned briefly in this chapter were founded by churchmen and endowed by kings of many differing predilections, there is no doubt that universally it was the *Evangelium*, the text of the Gospels, which was the chief stimulus to faith and devotion. The especial significance of the Gospel-text in the British Isles is reflected in the remarkable fact that as many as half of all surviving Latin Gospel-books from the period AD 400–800 are associated with Insular centres.[66] The multiple meanings which the Gospel-book as a focus of devotion came, uniquely in this period, to bear, has not been fully appreciated. The contribution of art to this special function of the Insular Gospel-book is a subject which the present study explores.

In all Christian instruction, whether to clerical trainees or lay catechumens preparing for baptism, and equally in the celebration of the mystery of the Sacraments, the text of the Four Gospels had a central place. Above all other Scriptures the Gospels were pre-eminently the word of God. As the Psalmist says in Psalm 67, prophesying the coming dominion of God over all the kingdoms of the earth, 'the Lord will give his word to those who publish it' (*Dominus dabit verbum Evangelizantibus*). Since the subject of the Gospel narratives is Christ, the Word made flesh, the Gospels in a very particular sense intimated the presence of God among his people. When Pope Gregory was equipping St Augustine and his fellow-missionaries for their work of evangelizing

England, he sent them 'very many books', *codices plurimos*,[67] and among these books there must have been copies of the Gospels. A sixth-century Gospel-book, written in Italy and containing late seventh- or early eighth-century annotations in English handwriting survives in the Library of *173* Corpus Christi College, Cambridge (MS 286).[68] It came to Cambridge from Canterbury in the sixteenth century. It itself may have been one of the *codices plurimos*, and in recognition of this fact it is known as St Augustine's Gospels. The text of the Gospels in this manuscript is in Latin, in the version known as the *editio vulgata* or Vulgate. The Vulgate text of the entire Bible was devised in the late fourth century by the great scholar St Jerome, on the basis of older translations and of the original Hebrew and Greek texts.[69]

The Vulgate came to be accepted as the standard by the Church, on its slow journey towards unity of practice, and the pre-Jerome texts of the Holy Scriptures, known collectively as *vetusta translatio* or *vetus editio*, the 'Old Latin Bible', were gradually ousted. The Church of Ireland, older than the Anglo-Saxon Church, had long been accustomed to use the 'Old Latin' texts, but by the second quarter of the seventh century Irish scholars and churchmen were interested in obtaining copies of the Vulgate Bible. When the South Irish Abbot Cummian quotes from the Scriptures in a letter written in the 630s about the Easter controversy, he uses the Vulgate version.[70] The text of the Psalms in a manuscript known as the Cathach, traditionally ascribed to St Columba, is also the Vulgate.[71] On the other hand 'Old Latin' readings are a marked feature of Irish biblical manuscripts.[72] Anglo-Saxon England, although a late comer to the faith, was not exempt from the Early Christian, 'Old Latin' text of the Scriptures. The phraseology of the annotations added in England to St Augustine's Gospels echoes the 'Old Latin' Gospels.[73] Jarrow-Wearmouth was provided with the entire Bible text in the *vetusta translatio*, and was similarly provided, for purposes of scholarly comparison, with a pure and authentic Vulgate text, imported from Italy by Abbot Ceolfrith.[74]

To focus specifically on the Gospels, the difference between 'Old Latin' copies of the Gospels and Vulgate Gospels was not simply a matter of verbal variation. The 'Old Latin' version arranged the texts of the four Evangelists in a different order: Matthew, John, Luke, Mark.[75] In his tidying-up operation St Jerome preferred

Matthew, Mark, Luke, John; he also provided a scholarly apparatus to coordinate the four Gospel texts. Vulgate Gospel-books are prefaced by a letter which St Jerome addressed to Pope Damasus I (whose secretary St Jerome was in the 380s) about the new translation of the Gospels. The letter begins '*Novum opus me cogis ex veteri*' – 'The new *6, 99*, work which you commissioned me to make from *138* the old one'.[76] This letter served to introduce the so-called canon-tables, lists of parallel passages in the four Gospel narratives, indicated by numbers, which helped the reader to find his way around the Gospels and make cross-references, in the period before a system of chapters and verses had been invented.[77] These canon-tables were not St *140, 204* Jerome's creation; they were drawn up by Eusebius, Bishop of Caesarea in Palestine, early in the fourth century. But St Jerome approved of them and helped to promote their use. In order to make the canon-tables serviceable, the numbers which they contained, listed consecutively in columns, were set individually in the margins of the Gospels, to signal the relevant passage in the written text.[78]

'Old Latin' Gospel-books as well as Vulgate Gospel-books contained other prefatory matter, namely brief synopses of the contents of each separate Gospel; the synopses are known as *capitula*, 'little chapters', or alternatively as *breves causae*, that is, 'brief topics'. Traditionally each Gospel was provided with a short mystical treatise characterizing the author-Evangelist himself, called the *argumentum*. Although prefaces of these kinds feature in all early Gospel-books the actual texts employed in the prefaces in Vulgate Gospels differ from those in 'Old Latin' Gospels. 'Old Latin' Gospel Books have one extra feature, not favoured in the Vulgate, namely lists or glossaries of the Hebrew personal names found in the Gospels of Matthew, John, Luke and Mark. These Hebrew names are arranged in alphabetical order and interpreted by means of fantastic etymology.[79]

If they were planned not simply as texts for study but rather for liturgical use as the sacred repositories of God's word, Gospel-books might contain visual ornaments and images. The sixth-century St Augustine's Gospels, belonging to the still-unchallenged Classical naturalistic tradition of art, displayed portraits (only one survives) of the *173* Evangelists as authors seated within an architectural framework and surrounded by pictorial vignettes illustrating incidents from the Gospel.[80]

The Insular Gospel-books to which we are now about to turn do not seem ever to have favoured simple narrative illustration. Insular Gospel-books, however, do share features of the St Augustine's Gospels' prefatory pictures – the author-portrait, and above all the representation of the symbols of the Evangelists (man or angel, lion, eagle, and bull or calf) derived by Early Christian commentators from two great scriptural visions of the Majesty of God, that in the Book of Ezekiel in the Old Testament, and that in the Apocalpyse of St John, the last book in the New Testament.

Like so much else in the Insular Gospel-books, the handling of these sacred images, although rooted in conventional Early Christian usage, has an imaginative quality, a mental involvement and commitment which renders difficult the search for specific visual exemplars, and which amounts to a re-thinking of the entire genre. The Gospel-books made in honour of Christ and his saints by monks in Lindisfarne, Iona, and perhaps other places in between, during the period from around 650 to around 780, extended the scope of the written and illuminated codex in ways that had no precedent and no subsequent parallel. Acutely responsive to a remarkable range of cultural contacts, and animated by total religious conviction, they are among the greatest products and memorials of their time.

2 Cross carpet-page, the Book of Durrow, *f.* 1v

2 The Book of Durrow

Design

Trinity College, Dublin MS A.4.5 (alternatively MS 57), known as the 'Book of Durrow',[1] contains 248 folios measuring 24.5 cm by 14.5 cm. It is a copy of the Four Gospels in St Jerome's Vulgate version. As we might expect, there are shades and gradations of purity or impurity of text of the Scriptures in our period; unless a high standard of editorial accuracy was the conscious aim a scribe's rote memory of a text, or simply his occasional lapses of attention, could easily introduce discrepancies between his textual exemplar and his own copy. Nonetheless, the Book of Durrow is substantially Vulgate as opposed to 'Old Latin', and the four Gospels come in the familiar order, Matthew, Mark, Luke, John, not, as in the 'Old Latin' Bible, Matthew, John, Luke, Mark.[2]

The Durrow Gospels, like all Gospel-books of the early Middle Ages, is equipped with prefaces and scholarly explanatory matter, but before any text is reached the designer took a fundamental step towards decorative display in his book by placing at the opening of the whole volume, on its *f.* 1v, a formal carpet-like pattern, a tall, narrow rectangle containing a smaller rectangle of broader relative proportions, the inner field being framed down either side by tight segments of interlaced strands, continuous but changing from colour to colour, and framed across the top and bottom by other interlace, more widely looped and with few of the sharp angles apparent in the side interlace. Within these frames is placed a double-barred cross, each terminal and inner transection of which takes the form of a square block with short, narrow projections on each side, giving a reiterated cruciform pattern to the page. In each of the four corners of the inner rectangle is another detached square with projecting arms, filled with interlace,

and the entire series of patterns is set off on, in, or under (since spatial ambiguity is characteristic of these designs) a bed of interlace similarly arranging itself into cruciform patterns of interwoven cords. The projecting extremities of the upright and horizontal barred cross consist of neatly folded-in-upon themselves maze- or key-patterns. These form a continuous uncoloured border to the whole double-cross construction. Chequers and key- or step-patterns fill miniature squares within the squares of the main barred cross.

The design is complex, but we can say that its principal motif is the eight squares linked together by the upright and horizontal bars. The one and only surviving carpet-pattern page in the later Gospel-book of Kells consists similarly of a double cross with eight points of focus – in Kells medallions, not squares.[3] The vivid yellow in the Book of Durrow is the trisulphide of arsenic, or yellow arsenic, also called orpiment, often used as a gold substitute. The green, which is much decayed, is acetate of copper. The red is red lead. Throughout the book there is a limited but very effective bold colour-range.[4]

Folio 2 likewise contains a tall ornamental rectangle, framing a secondary squarer rectangle, the frame here being uniformly treated, as a sort of cell-system of diagonally placed cubes – really key- or maze-patterns but dominated by the plain cubic shape, so that the linking lines are subservient to the squares, making a spreading honeycomb effect. The inner rectangle is not abstract in treatment. Here we have the first show of overt iconography in the book, a cross with wide terminals, the quadrants filled with the symbols of the four Evangelists: man, eagle, bull and lion, reading the page clockwise.

19

4 Bronze, enamel and *millefiori* mount from the base of the large hanging-bowl, Sutton Hoo Ship-burial. *c.* 600

3 Carpet-page, the Book of Durrow, *f.* 3v

5 Bronze bowl, Jaatten, Norway. (?) Seventh century

We move after blank *ff.* 2v and 3 to *f.* 3v where *3* we find yet another patterned page, decorative, not figurative, emphasizing curvilinear patterns as enthusiastically as *f.* 1v featured stiff, straight lines *2* and right-angles. These are the patterns commonly called trumpet-spirals, the trumpet motif – the outer linking widening tubes with open vents or leaf-shaped ornaments laid across them – being on such a scale that the whole design seems articulated and active, like a kind of threshing-machine. These trumpet-spiral designs in the Book of Durrow are very intimately associated with metalwork designs, the escutcheons or ornamental discs at the bases or at the handles of bronze *4* hanging-bowls, of controversial date and function.[5] The closest analogy to Durrow *f.* 3v is not, however, an escutcheon (for these never reach this relative proportion of spiral to trumpet-lobe) but a bronze bowl entirely covered with spinning discs and trumpet-lobes, later adapted as a receptacle for a small pair of scales and weights, a common accompaniment of Viking burials. This particular bowl was found at Jaatten, in Norway, and is now *5* in Bergen University Museum. The bowl was carried off to Norway as loot, and reminds us that the civilization with whose luxury productions we are dealing was dislocated and destroyed by the Norse raiders and invaders of the ninth and tenth centuries.[6] The dispersal of works of art, both during the prosperous period of high civilization throughout the seventh and eighth centuries, and

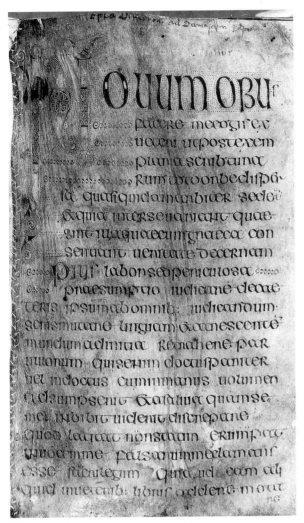

6 *Novum opus* prologue, the Book of Durrow, *f.* 4

7 Grid canon-tables (Canons IX, X), the Book of Durrow, *f.* 10

in the unsettled conditions which began around 800, gives rise to problems in determining the original provenance of most or all of these works. The Book of Durrow itself is a case in point. It is perhaps as likely to have reached Durrow in Ireland ready made, as a gift or in the hands of a refugee, as it is to have been manufactured on the spot.

6 On *f.* 4 we reach St Jerome's *Novum opus* prologue, the opening words being written in fancy capitals, the initial N in particular stretching through several lines of subsequent text. Although about half of St Jerome's prologue is concerned with Eusebius's canon-tables and forms an introduction to them, another item intervenes on *f.* 6v before the canon-tables begin, namely the glossary of Hebrew names, a traditional feature of 'Old Latin' Gospel-books. The later Lindisfarne

Gospels, whose structure is purely Vulgate, does not contain the glossary of Hebrew names. When it does occur in Insular Gospel-books it is significant of a shared outlook or shared textual exemplars, or even of direct dependence of one Gospel-book on another; like the Book of Durrow, the Book of Kells inserts a glossary of Hebrew names just before the opening of the canon-tables.[7]

In the Book of Durrow the canon-tables (*ff.* 8–10) are set out very simply in a ruled grid-system 7 of narrow columns, framed by narrow ornamental strips all round. After the canon-tables come the *capitula* or summaries of the content of the individual Gospels, first the *capitula* to Matthew on *f.* 11, beginning *Nativitas Christi in Bethlehem Judaea*, then *Magi munera*, etc. These are the 'Old Latin' summaries. The text is set out in two columns,

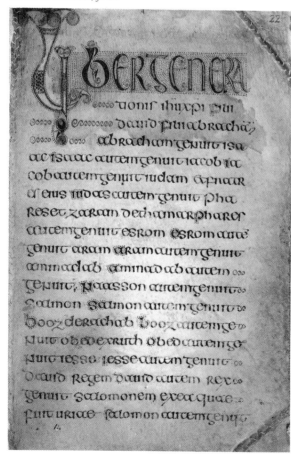

8 *Capitula* to St Matthew's Gospel, the Book of Durrow, *f.* 11

9 Beginning of St Matthew's Gospel, *Liber Generationis*, the Book of Durrow, *f.* 22

again with a fancy capital N to the first word, *8 Nativitas.*

Developments in display script and decorative handling of pages will lead us in due course to the much more sumptuous pages of the Book of Kells. Beside the elaborate fantasy of the *Nativitas* page of *208* Kells,[8] the *Nativitas* page of Durrow appears tentative or deliberately austere. The distance in form and content between these two pages is great, but there is in fact a close bond between the two books in their arrangement of the prefaces, the *capitula* and also the *argumenta.* The Gospel-books of Durrow and Kells agree in a very specific and curious heaping-up and dislocating of these prefaces.[9] In both, the *capitula* of Matthew is followed by Matthew's *argumentum.* Then, without introducing the relevant Gospel, we move to the *capitula* of Mark, beginning *Et erat Iohannis baptizans Jesum*, and then to the *argumentum* of Mark. Next, however, we move *not* to the *capitula* of Luke but to the *argumentum* of Luke, followed in Durrow by the *argumentum* of John, *Hic est Iohannis.* So also in the Book of Kells, we find on *f.* 15v the *argumentum* of Mark, and on *f.* 16v the *argumentum* of Luke, and then that of John. In Durrow the *capitula* of Luke and John are inserted at the end of the four Gospels, on *f.* 247v. In Kells they follow after the *argumentum* of John. So specific and idiosyncratic is this separation of the prefaces from the Gospel-texts themselves that use of a common model, or else the dependence of the Book of Kells directly on the earlier Gospel-book of Durrow, would be a reasonable conclusion. The fact that the anomalous order was not edited-out may suggest that it was of interest in itself. Perhaps some sanctity attached to the exemplar containing the prefaces in this idiosyncratic order, and the copyist wanted to preserve the whole unaltered. This is a pointer towards the origin and reputation of the Gospel-books as relics, or reflections of relics, of saints. In our consideration of the provenance of the Book of Durrow, it is useful always to remember that it or its model appears to have been available at a later stage in the history of Insular book-making to the designers of the Book of Kells.

The opening of the text of St Matthew's Gospel, Chapter 1 (*f.* 22), *Liber Generationis*, 'The Book of *9* the generation', is prefaced opposite (on *f.* 21v) by *53* an image of the symbolic man of St Matthew in a frame of flowing interwoven strands. Thirty-three leaves of the Book of Durrow are not each one-half of a folded-over double page – a *bifolium* – but are singles, stitched-in separately; consequently losses and displacements are likely to have occurred. There may have been a decorative carpet-page before the Gospel of St Matthew. It may be that the trumpet-spiral ornamental page – now, as we saw, *f.* 3v – was formerly in front of St Matthew's Gospel, between the symbol and the initial, on a scheme involving Evangelist symbol opposite blank recto, then carpet-pattern opposite initial and chapter opening. If not the *f.* 3v design, the carpet-page to Matthew is lost. There are carpet-pages before each of the three other Gospel-texts. *Liber Generationis* is not written larger than the *Novum opus* preface. It is followed on *f.* 23, at Matthew 1, 18, by the phrase, painted in brilliant yellow orpiment, *Christi autem generatio sic erat* ('the birth of Christ was in this wise'). The Greek monogram of Christ's name, Chi followed by Rho and Iota, a

80

11 Carpet-page, the Book of Durrow, *f.* 85v

10 Beginning of St Mark's Gospel, *Initium evangelii*, the Book of Durrow, *f.* 86

long-traditional formula in inscriptions, is given the glamour of large ornamental handling, a kind of second beginning to the Gospel when the mystery of the Incarnation is proclaimed.

The beginning of St Mark's Gospel is signalled by a painting of an eagle on *f.* 84v framed by tightly woven strands of interlace, followed on *f.* 85v by a carpet-page in which fifteen medallions formed of strands or ribbons are filled and linked by interlaced strands. The central medallion on the page contains a curved, splayed, equal-armed cross, set off against a step-patterned background. The first initial to St Mark's Gospel, *Initium evangelii*, is larger than its predecessors, the first downstroke of the N stretching three-quarters down the page.

61

11

10

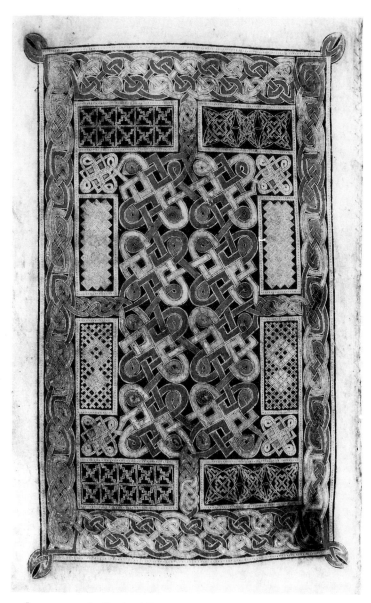

12 Carpet-page, the Book of Durrow, *f.* 125v

been retained when the 'Old Latin' order of the text was not followed. Another and more probable explanation is that the artist-designer of Durrow did not choose to follow the interpretation of symbols favoured by St Jerome, but followed instead the interpretation popularized by Irenaeus, a second-century Bishop of Lyons, and repeated by the fourth-century Spanish writer Juvencus in the poetic preface to his *Historia Evangelica*, whereby Mark is symbolized by an eagle and John by a lion. This interpretation was certainly known in Ireland in the late eighth to early ninth centuries, when a scribe named Macregol wrote an explanation of this symbolism in his Gospel-book (now in Oxford, Bodleian MS Auctor D.2.19).[11] The Juvencus poem was known to Adomnán, Abbot of Iona, who died in 704, and who visited Northumbria on two occasions.[12] The great Northumbrian scholar Bede was open-minded on the question of the linking of Evangelist symbols to specific Evangelists, and mentions a number of different permutations, defending this fluidity of interpretation against Acca, Bishop of Hexham, who had criticized any departure from the Jerome norm.[13] Essentially that norm holds good for all the Insular Gospel-books other than Durrow.

St Luke's Gospel is prefaced by a framed image of a calf walking in profile to the right (*f.* 124v), and a carpet-page (*f.* 125v) is opposite the initial words of the Gospel, *Quoniam quidem*, together with a second initial, to Luke 1, 5, when the narrative proper begins: *Fuit in diebus Herodis regis Iudeae*. The carpet-page displays a series of narrow rectangles, containing brittle and elegant variants of step-patterns, set within the main rectangle like a second segmented frame, around which, either relaxed or compressed, a set of looping and bent cords are allowed to flow or twist.

The text of St John's Gospel begins on *f.* 193, preceded by a picture of a wolf-like lion on *f.* 191v, in profile to the right, in a frame the side compartments of which respond to the proximity of the beast by opening a little the otherwise tightly woven interlace-strands. The carpet-page on *f.* 192v introduces animal-ornaments for the first time in the book, interweaving or queuing-up in six separate compartments soft, pliable-jawed, stylized creatures painted in alternate colours. These frame a square containing a medallion filled with interlace interspersed with small discs; three have symmetrical step-patterns within them, while in the fourth, central, disc is an equal-armed cross. The initial to

The representation of an eagle to symbolize St Mark, instead of the more familiar lion, has given rise to the suggestion that the artist of the Book of Durrow was paying tribute visually to the normal order of the pre-Jerome, 'Old Latin' Gospel-books, where, as we have noted, St John's Gospel is placed second and St Mark's last.[10] The order of the Evangelist symbols in Durrow is man, eagle, calf or bull, and lion, suggesting a sequence Matthew, John, Luke, Mark, by ordinary Jerome interpretation of the symbols. But it seems unlikely that the 'Old Latin' order of symbols would have

32 St John's Gospel is the most elaborate of the sequence, the downstroke of I in *In Principio* reaching to the base of the page of text. The enlargement of this letter may simply be a response to the peculiar sanctity of St John's Gospel, the most spiritually charged, most patently doctrinal of the four Gospels,[14] or it may be interpreted as evolution within the book, as the decorator elaborated on his own designs. The tendency to see the sequence of major initials in Durrow as in evolution is natural because of the scarcity of comparative material. We have to bear in mind that the context for these decorative forms is known to us now only in part. In addition, the artist's own taste and discretion may have curtailed or expanded his use of ornament, irrespective of the potentialities of the art-style as a whole. A final carpet-

14 page (*f.* 248) is decorated with interlace, with inset square crosses; crosses recessed in beds of interlace

13 are a favourite device in later Insular monuments.[15]

A number of decorated manuscripts have been brought into discussions of the date and pro-

13 Detail of a corner-post of the St Andrews Sarcophagus. Eighth century

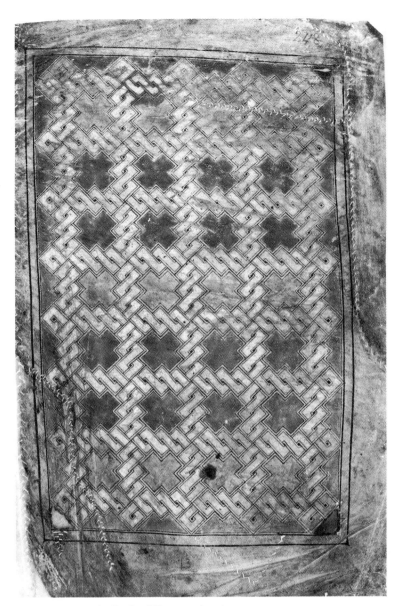

14 Carpet-page, the Book of Durrow, *f.* 248

venance of the Book of Durrow. It is uncertain whether they do more than very roughly indicate the chronology of tendencies into which that book may fit. All have Irish connections, but they belong themselves to independent sequences which do not necessarily interconnect. Nor are they all the same type of book, so that standards of display are not necessarily comparable. We can, however, say that the kind of small, rounded decorative letter used to start each Psalm in a fragmentary Psalter, the Cathach of St Columba, now in the Royal Irish Academy in Dublin, roughly matches the smallest

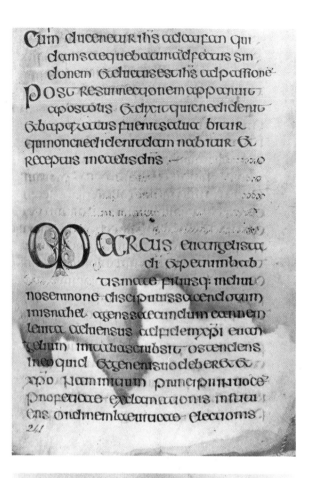

of the ornamental letters in Durrow, namely the initials to the glossary of Hebrew names and to *capitula* and *argumenta*. The Cathach's initial M to Psalm 55 (*Miserere mei*) splits the bars of the letter and terminates them in scrolls, much as does the letter M for Mark in Durrow's *argumentum* to Mark. The initial Q to Psalm 90 (*Qui habitat*) displays a cross appended, much like the attached cross in the Durrow M.[16] A striking resemblance between the Cathach and the Durrow letters is that they start big and lapse swiftly into the common scale of the text-letters. This is called the *diminuendo* motif. All this points to shared taught scribal practice. The Cathach was traditionally associated with St Columba, the text itself being credited to his own hand. As we shall see, a very similar association was traditionally established between St Columba and the Book of Durrow.

15 Beginning of the *argumentum* to St Mark's Gospel, the Book of Durrow, *f.* 17

16 Psalm 55, the Cathach of St Columba, *f.* 21. (?) Early seventh century

17 Psalm 90, the Cathach of St Columba, *f.* 48. (?) Early seventh century

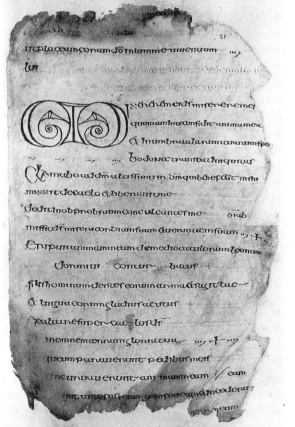

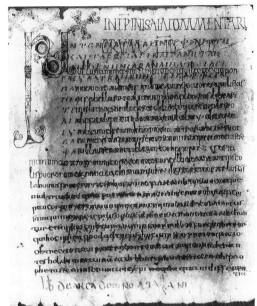

18 Carpet-page and text-page, Orosius's *World History*. Milan, Biblioteca Ambrosiana MS D.23 sup., *ff.* 1v, 2. Early seventh century

19 St Jerome's *Commentary on the Book of Isaiah*. Milan, Biblioteca Ambrosiana MS S.45 sup., p. 12. Early seventh century

Palaeographers regard the Cathach as an early survivor in the time-scale of Irish handwriting, but they tend to see it as representing Irish scribal practice more advanced than that displayed in a body of books associated with the continental mission of St Columbanus, Abbot of Bobbio. Books from the Bobbio library[17] have survived in the Ambrosian library in Milan, by chance rather than because they were regarded as important, and these may reflect the sorts of models that determined book-production back home in Ireland, or the sort of inventions and initiatives that were being made in any Irish scriptorium of the period, whether at home or abroad. Very interesting from our point of view is the use, in a *18* Bobbio copy of the *World History* written by the early fifth-century writer and theologian Orosius, of a carpet-page before the opening of the text. This consists of a thick border, the top and sides differentiated in pattern, round a large medallion with lesser discs in the corners. Opposite, the initial P of *Praeceptis* runs down the length of the text, and the R and E grade to a smaller size. Another Bobbio *19* text, Jerome's *Commentary on the Book of Isaiah*, is attributed by an inscription to Columbanus's successor as abbot, Atalanus, who ruled from 615 to 622. The initial N of *Nulla* integrates fishes into the form of the letter, like the dragon- or dolphin-head terminals which appear on the Cathach Q.

Sworls or spirals animate the curve of the linking stroke of the N, as in the Cathach M. The silhouette of the letter is reminiscent, on a lower level of design and calligraphy, of the N of *Novum opus* in Durrow. The scrolls or peltas at the base of the N, as well as the general outline, recall also the opening initial to St Mark's Gospel in a fragmentary manuscript in Durham Cathedral Library, MS A.II.10.[18] The latter initial is divided *20*

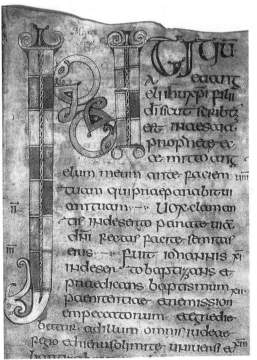

20 Beginning of St Mark's Gospel, *Initium*, Durham MS A.II.10, *f.* 2. Mid-seventh century

into segments along its length, like the Bobbio Jerome N. It has as the cross bar of the IN of *Initium* a motif of eared, roll-lipped dragons, like the head on the Cathach Q, with a similar collar-effect at the neck. The dragons on the IN change shape from curved to straight-sided, and change colour at the moment of the loop-crossing, effects reminiscent of tricks of design in the Luke carpet-page in Durrow. The dragons trooping up the sides of the St John *41* carpet-page in Durrow have hind legs which roll round and bend at an angle like the worms' bodies in the Durham MS A.II.10 initial.

21 Triple D-shaped frame containing *explicit* of St Matthew and *incipit* of St Mark, and the *Pater Noster*, Durham MS A.II.10, *f.* 3v. Mid-seventh century

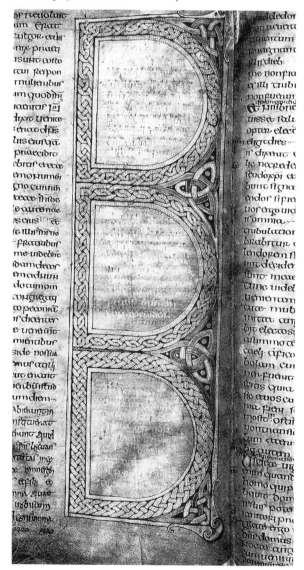

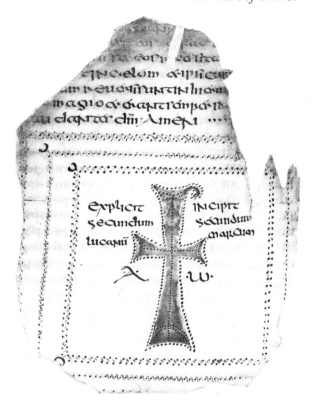

22 *Xp* monogram, Ussher Codex I, Trinity College MS A.4.15 (55), *f.* 149v. Early seventh century

There is one other ornamental page in Durham MS A.II.10, a framed *explicit/incipit* between St Matthew's and St Mark's Gospel. In the Book of Durrow the *explicit* (end) of one Gospel and the *incipit* (beginning) of another receives no decorative emphasis. But such emphasis is found in early Continental Gospel-books, for example in the sixth-century Valerianus Codex, an 'Old Latin' Gospel-book now in the Bavarian State Library in Munich, and also in an 'Old Latin' Gospel-book, the Ussher Codex I, in Trinity College, Dublin (MS A.4.15), which is palaeographically related to the early Bobbio books.[19] After Luke and before Mark (the 'Old Latin' order) the designer of the Trinity College manuscript introduced a square frame around the *explicit/incipit* and a red Chi-Rho *22* monogram, with the letters Alpha and Omega appended, and black dots around the cross. The *explicit/incipit* in Durham MS A.II.10 is much more elaborate, consisting of three D-shaped segments *21* framed with closely meshed interlace, and wider multi-coloured interlace, pelta and nearly-trumpet forms in the spandrels or interstices. The *explicit/incipit* is in the upper compartment, and in the lower is the text of the Lord's Prayer, written in Greek but transliterated in Latin characters.[20] The Greek text of the *Pater Noster*, here written in Greek letters, occurs at the end of the *Life of St Columba* by Adomnán, in a manuscript of that *Life* now in Schaffhausen in Switzerland, attributed to the scriptorium on Iona in the late seventh or early eighth century.[21] Again, a liturgical formula of Greek origin written in Greek letters occurs on the side of the so-called 'Cross of St Fahan' at Mura, near Derry, a major Columban foundation on the north coast of Ireland with direct sea-access to Iona.[22]

The style of colouring and interlacing, with strands of varied weight, which decorates the triple D of *f.* 3v of Durham MS A.II.10 comes close in skill and complexity to the Durrow Gospels.[23]

This brief look at tentative schemes or formulae of decoration relating to the Book of Durrow has already touched upon the vexed question of provenance. Bobbio, Iona, Ireland and Northumbria have entered the story.

Historical context

The Durrow Gospels reached the Library of Trinity College in Dublin in the seventeenth century through the good offices of Henry Jones, who served in the Protector Oliver Cromwell's army in Ireland and became Protestant bishop of Meath in 1661. Some years earlier Jones had assisted a great bibliophile, James Ussher, Archbishop of Armagh, to collate with the Vulgate the text of two manuscript copies of the Gospels, namely a Gospel-book then kept at Kells and a Gospel-book kept at Durrow in County Offaly, both associated locally with St Columba. The two Gospel-books were eventually taken charge of by Jones and deposited in Trinity Library, his gift being noted by a Fellow of the College, William Pallister, writing in 1681. Thus in the first half of the seventeenth century our 'Book of Durrow' *was* at Durrow. When it came to Trinity College Library it was contained in a metal cover, shrine or *cumtach*, which had an inscription on it, and that inscription was transcribed in 1677, after which the *cumtach* was lost. The transcription preserves, however, the important information that the *cumtach* was made at the order of King Flann of Ireland, who died in 916, in honour of St Columba.[24] Evidently there was belief in the specific Columbian association of the Book of Durrow during King Flann's reign. Much later, around 1100, documents relating to the church and monastery of Durrow were written at the end of the Book of Durrow (*f.* 248v), on the reverse of the last carpet-page.

Durrow Monastery was founded by St Columba himself. Bede mentions it in his *Ecclesiastical History* as 'the noble monastery in Ireland that from an abundance of oak trees is named in the language of

23 Iona, Tòrr an Aba from the south east

29

24 Christ treading on beasts and attended by angels, illustrating Psalm 90. Leaf from the Genoels-Elderen ivory Diptych. Late eighth century

the Irish *Dearmach*, that is, plain of oaks', and writes that Columba founded Durrow before he came to Britain in 563.[25] Columba may have had land for its foundation before he left Ireland, but Adomnán, Abbot of Iona, in his *Life of St Columba* written in the late 690s, says that St Columba went from Iona to found Durrow, and that on that occasion he was entertained at nearby Clonmacnois by Abbot Alither and his monks.[26] Alither became abbot in 585 according to the *Annals of Ulster*,[27] so Durrow would be after 585 – that is, after Iona. Adomnán represents St Columba as brooding over developments in the fabric of the monastery at Durrow while he himself was on Iona;[28] he was vexed in spirit because he knew that the Durrow monks, in the depths of winter, were labouring to the point of exhaustion on the construction of a large timber building.[29] On another occasion, St Columba was

sitting in his hut on Tòrr an Aba in the monastic [23] precinct on Iona and started up, crying 'Help! Help!' At this cry, to do his unspecified bidding, an angel who was standing in attendance nearby, flew with the speed of lightning from Iona to Durrow, south over the Irish Sea, and caught, before he could hit the ground, a monk, who, building the round monastic house, was falling from the highest point of the roof (*culmine monasterii rotundi*). 'Consequently he that fell was unable to feel any fracture or injury.'[30] This obedient angel was evidently required to act out the maxim of Psalm 90: 'He has given his angels charge over you, lest at [24] any time you should dash your foot against the stone.'[31]

According to Bede, Iona was Columba's chief foundation. He writes that from Durrow and Iona, 'very many monasteries are sprung which were established by his disciples in Britain and Ireland, over all of which the island monastery, in which his body lies, has pre-eminence'.[32] The only other specific foundation of Columba mentioned in Adomnán's *Life* is the neighbouring priory on the island of Hinba, which may be Colonsay or Jura, or one of the smaller islands. The site has not yet been identified.[33] An extensive missionary mandate, however, is made clear in Adomnán's *Life*. Columba is not simply spoken of as a leader of monks, 'leader of souls to the heavenly kingdom', but he is predestined also to be 'a leader of Nations into life'.[34] His conversion of a layman, head of a household, in Pictland is referred to by Adomnán. His presence and miracles made a powerful impression on the King of the Picts.[35] Monastic foundations must have been established on the mainland of Scotland, both in Dál Riata (Argyll) and in Pictland (on the east) in the sixth and seventh centuries. Adomnán notes at one point in the *Life* the outbreak of a terrible pestilence which afflicts all the inhabitants of Britain 'excepting two peoples only, the population of the Picts and the Irish in Britain. Although neither people is without great sins', says Adomnán, 'by which the Eternal Judge is often provoked to anger, yet until now he has spared both of them. To whom else can this favour conferred by God be attributed, but to Saint Columba, whose monasteries, placed within the boundaries of both peoples, are down to the present time held in great honour by them both?' So the Columban family of monasteries was clearly far-flung, by Adomnán's time, on the mainland of Scotland to the east and west.[36]

The extension of the Columban mission to Northumbria is described in vivid hagiographical terms by Adomnán and in a more sobre historical vein by Bede. In the reign of King Edwin his rivals the sons of Aethelfrith lived in exile, along with many of the Bernician nobility, in Pictland and on Iona. Political exile in Ireland and elsewhere is a significant cultural factor throughout the seventh century. In 632 Edwin was killed in battle against Penda of Mercia and Cadwallon, King of Gwynedd. The sons of Aethelfrith returned, and in 634 Oswald gained control of Bernicia and Deira by defeating Cadwallon.[37]

Adomnán represents this dynastic and political revolution as the fruits of a miracle wrought by St Columba:[38] 'In the terrible crashings of battles, by virtue of prayer, Columba obtained from God that some kings were conquered and other rulers were conquerors. This special favour was bestowed by God, who honours all saints, on him not only while he remained in this present life but also after his departure from the flesh, as a triumphant and powerful champion.' On the day before he fought Cadwallon Oswald saw a vision of a figure 'radiant in angelic form, whose lofty height seemed with its head to touch the clouds' – like the early sixth-century Boethius's famous vision of Philosophy personified, in *The Consolation of Philosophy*.[39] This figure was St Columba (how identified, we do not know), standing in the midst of the camp and covering it, 'all but a small remote part, with his shining raiment'. Columba declared that God had granted it to him that Oswald would return victorious and reign happily. Adomnán represents Oswald and his twelve companions as the only Christians in the army opposing Cadwallon. When Oswald reports his vision to his assembled troops, the entire army agrees to accept baptism. Adomnán claimed the authority of Oswald himself for this account of the matter. Ségené was abbot of Iona in Oswald's time, and his successor Failbe, who died in 679, told Adomnán that he had heard Oswald tell the miracle to Ségené. Evidently, then, after 634 Abbot Ségené visited Northumbria or King Oswald revisited Iona.

Bede gives a different account of the miraculous victory, and interestingly does not mention St Columba's part in it. 'The place is still shown today where Oswald came with his army, small in numbers, but strengthened by their faith in Christ. The place, called Heavenfield, on its north side is near to the Roman Wall. There before the battle

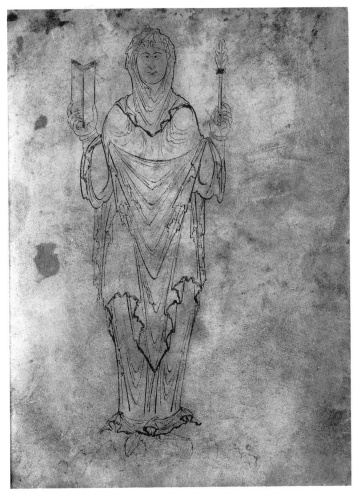

25 Philosophy, frontispiece to Boethius's *De Consolatione Philosophiae*, Cambridge, Trinity College MS 0.3.7, *f*. 1. Late tenth century

Oswald had the sign of the holy cross set up, holding it upright with his own hands while it was secured in the earth.' The entire army prayed on bended knees to God to send them heavenly aid.[40]

The setting up of a wooden cross suggests a connection with Iona, although Bede says nothing explanatory about it other than that it was unusual in Bernicia – 'it was the first time the sign of the holy cross had been seen there'. Adomnán's *Life of St Columba* – written later, however, than Oswald's time – refers to a cross standing on Iona beside the door of the shed where a kinsman of Columba, Prior Ernan of Hinba, died, and another cross, fixed in a millstone, at St Columba's own resting-place half-way between the cornfields on the west and the monastery on the east.[41] Even if these sites were marked posthumously, King Oswald might have seen these crosses before 633 or after 634.

31

26 Detail of ornamental panels, carpet-page, the Book of Durrow, *f.* 125v.

The Ionan connection with the religious and social establishment made by Oswald is not in doubt, and the story of Oswald's vision fits symbolically with his turning to Iona for church leaders for his kingdom. The priest Aidan came in 635 with monks from Iona, and was established as bishop on Lindisfarne Island, near the rock and royal fortress of Bamburgh.[42] The conversion of the kingdom and establishment of other monasteries and priories now proceeded, and continued into the eighth century.

Where in the monastic confederation (*familia*) of St Columba was the Book of Durrow made? The argument for England and Northumbria is supported by the resemblance between the objects in the pagan royal burial at Sutton Hoo in East Anglia[43] and the style of the decorations in the

27 Book of Durrow. The rectangular mounts and pyramidal mounts from the Sutton Hoo sword-belt are like the objects laid on a bed of interlace in the

26 Durrow carpet-page (*f.* 125v). The painted objects or ornaments are delicately decorated, like the interior of the irregular hexagon ornament on the purse-cover. The square blocks of the eight-

2 centred cross on *f.* 1v have minute panels of chequers, like the *millefiore* glass settings in the conical studs. We may compare the scabbard-

30 bosses from Sutton Hoo with the ornaments in the

41 centre of the St John's Gospel carpet-page. The symmetrically placed short and long ribbon-beasts on the St John's Gospel carpet-page are closely paralleled by the two varieties of creatures on the

28 Sutton Hoo purse-cover. The interlace strands on

31 the great buckle vary in width like the strap-work in the carpet-pages and initials. The idea of a carpet-page has a reasonable parallel in the rectangular,

framed, over-all treatment of the Sutton Hoo shoulder-clasps. The trumpet-spiral page (*f.* 3v) 29, 3 and various curvilinear initials can be understood as borrowing and developing an exotic element in the Sutton Hoo burial finds, represented by the hanging-bowls, a class of object made by 4 indigenous Pictish and British craftsmen.[44]

Precious metalwork is not all that we need invoke in characterizing the style of the Book of Durrow. The designs in the manuscript are 32 dominated by interlaces, of varying, contrasting weights and widths. This is not an outstanding feature of the Sutton Hoo regalia, apart from some wide and narrow interlaces in the great buckle. The most striking analogy to this feature of the Book of Durrow is in the reconstructed wrought-iron suspension-gear associated with the largest cauld- 33 ron, of which the chains show varied textures and patterns.[45] When hanging-bowls are invoked as analogies for the spiral patterns in Durrow, we also invoke by association suspension devices, perhaps chains or ropes.[46] According to Bede, bronze drinking-cups or bowls were hung on the public highways in King Edwin's time, before 632.[47] The smith's craft was highly regarded. In Germanic myth and folklore smiths are credited with magical powers. In early medieval Christian society their role remained vital.[48] In a story about the terrors of Judgment awaiting sinners, Bede mentions a smith belonging to a noble monastery in Bernicia, denigrating the smith, but not his craft.[49] The early ninth-century Northumbrian poem *De Abbatibus* celebrates a famous smith as one of the outstanding members of the community, a cell of Lindisfarne.[50] Adomnán picks out for mention a lay smith who was virtuous and gave large alms from his

27 Rectangular mounts of gold and garnets, and pyramidal mounts of gold, garnets and *millefiori*, from the sword-harness, Sutton Hoo Ship-burial

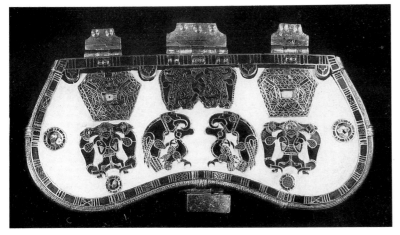

28 Purse-cover of gold, garnets and *millefiori*, Sutton Hoo Ship-burial

29 Pair of hinged shoulder-clasps of gold, garnets and *millefiori*, Sutton Hoo Ship-burial

30 Scabbard-bosses of gold and garnets, Sutton Hoo Ship-burial

31 Buckle of gold with niello inlay, Sutton Hoo Ship-burial

32 Beginning of St John's Gospel, *In Principio*, the Book of Durrow, *f.* 193

33 Reconstruction of wrought-iron suspension-gear of the great cauldron, Sutton Hoo Ship-burial

earnings.[51] Such people were socially important, and their technology, which was ubiquitous, was probably influential visually when it came to the ornament in other crafts and arts.

The Sutton Hoo master-jeweller designed his regalia for a context of clothes: for example, a mantle had been attached to the shoulder-clasps; the purse-cover argues a purse, and the sword-gear, a belt. Textiles and embroidery, much more ephemeral, have vanished while the regalia itself

survives. Fine textiles in high ecclesiastical or royal contexts are mentioned by Bede: the purple cloth woven with gold which decked the church of Ripon in Wilfrid's time, and King Oswald's purple and gold banner or *vexillum* over his burial place at Bardney in Lincolnshire.[52] So weaving-techniques and applied patterns of interlaced thread or cord may be assumed to have contributed to the aesthetic outlook and specific designs of the Durrow illuminator. A portion of elaborately

34

34 Detail of textile, called the *casula* of St Harlindis and St Relindis, of gold and silk on linen backing, in the Treasury of St Catherine's Church, Maeseyck. Ninth century

34 decorated textile preserved in the church treasury at Maeseyck in Belgium has been recognized as of English manufacture, a unique survivor of the high-class textiles of the early Anglo-Saxon period.[53] We hear from Bede's prose *Life of St Cuthbert* of the Abbess Verca's gift of linen, which St Cuthbert reserved for eventual use as a shroud. (At the saint's first disinterment the clothes on his body were found to have retained their original freshness and colour.[54]) When the pectoral cross of *174* St Cuthbert was discovered in 1827 it retained traces of a silk suspension-cord twisted with gold.[55]

Leather was also no doubt an important, creatively used material. The sword and the jewelled belt-ends and studs at Sutton Hoo presuppose elaborate leather harness.[56] Again, in an equestrian society, horse, cart, chariot-harness, must have taken many complicated forms. Bede reports that Bishop Aidan (died 651) gave away to a poor man a horse selected and equipped for the bishop's own use by King Oswine, and that the loss of the royal harness was no less regretted by the king than the loss of the horse.[57] If leather-working might be simple and crude, as in the making of the

calf-skin shelter of Aethelwold, the hermit of Farne, mentioned in Bede's prose *Life of St Cuthbert*,[58] it could also take more elaborate forms, as in the making of the elegant shoes with extra *60* tongues at the front and back of the ankle, found in seventh-century excavation-levels in Iona.[59]

The scraping, curing and even dyeing of vellum was a constant activity in the preparation of materials for writing Gospel-books. A unique survivor of what must have been a widely practised craft is the binding of the Stonyhurst Gospel, a relic of St Cuthbert originally preserved in his shrine. The red-leather binding is moulded on cord on one *35* side and drawn-on with a stylus on the other, and *36* then painted.[60] This work of art moves us perhaps too close to the Book of Durrow itself to offer independent witness to the growth of style via the skilful technology of leather-work in the period. The carpet-page and the binding of a book are obviously directly related. Beyond these, there are the techniques of comparatively ephemeral craft-materials such as thread and leather, which will have given a substantial context, lost to us, for Durrow's stylistic appearance.

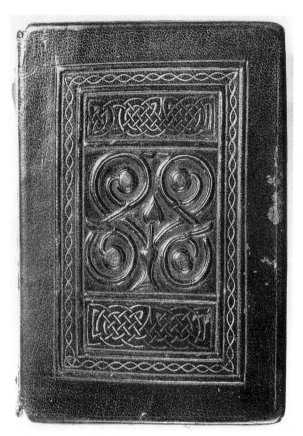

35 Front cover of the Stonyhurst Gospel. Eighth century

36 Back cover of the Stonyhurst Gospel. Eighth century

It seems likely that secular taste had a vigorous impact on religious ornament and on monastic crafts flourishing at the command of kings and noblemen. Adomnán reports that gifts of the people were deposited in the courtyard of the monastery at Iona for benediction. Columba was able to differentiate between specific people's gifts, and praised or blamed them. Some will have been gifts of kind, such as were deposited at Deathrib (Kilmore, Co. Roscommon) at the coming of Columba, but money and other treasure were presumably included.[61] Bede writes with great enthusiasm about the frugal and austere life led by the Iona monks who had settled at Lindisfarne. 'They had no money but only cattle . . . They were so free from avarice that none would accept land or possessions to build monasteries *unless compelled to by the secular authorities*' (my italics). Bede says of Aidan that he 'would never give money to powerful men of the world; on the contrary he distributed gifts of money which he received from the rich to the needy or for the redemption of those

unjustly sold in slavery'.[62] Thus Aidan and his colleagues and successors acted publicly to show the moral value of charity, but against a background of pressure of secular wealth, evidently flowing indiscriminately in their direction.

The clerical viewpoint is clearly represented by the praise with which Aidan greeted King Oswald's charitable Easter gesture of dismembering the great silver dish (*discus argenteus*) from his banqueting-table.[63] The status and value of such a vessel can be judged from the splendid Byzantine plates found in the burial at Sutton Hoo.[64] The giving away of Oswine's horse with its royal trappings is a similar case. While the clergy sought to inculate Christian values by their attitudes and actions, these stories show the availability of superfluous wealth which the secular power wished to bestow upon the Church.

Bede records that King Oswy offered 'a vast bribe of incalculable treasure' – called by Bede *ornamenta regia*, that is, regalia – to Penda, King of Mercia, to try to buy him off in war. Penda was bent

37

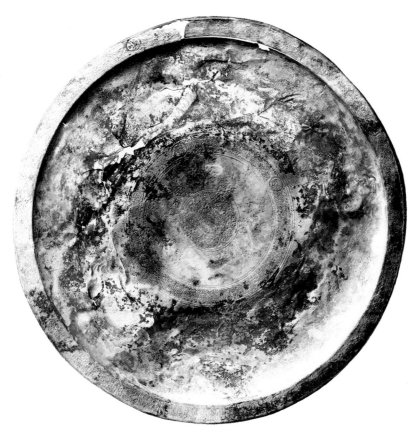

37 Silver dish bearing control stamps of the Emperor Anastasius I (491–518),
Sutton Hoo Ship-burial

on attacking Northumbria in 651, and the bribe was refused. Oswy then vowed to give to God what his pagan enemy would not accept.[65] This gift to God took a number of different forms, among them the vowing of his daughter Aelfflaed to perpetual virginity as a nun, and the handing over of twelve estates to monastic foundations, six each to Bernicia and Deira. But the loot, booty, regalia of British and Anglo-Saxon origin which Oswy had at his disposal could also go towards church decoration. Oswy sent gold and silver vessels to Rome, to Pope Vitalian, when he and his ally King Egbert of Kent dispatched Wigheard in 663 to be ordained Archbishop of Canterbury.[66] The enlargement of the Lindisfarne establishment by Aidan's successor Bishop Finan, also from Iona, must reflect the expansion of the number of religious centres after 655 under Oswy's patronage.[67]

Bede records that Lastingham in Yorkshire was established as a resort for King Oethelwald, where he might frequently come to pray and to hear the word, and where he might eventually be buried. Oethelwald believed that the daily prayers of those who served God would help him.[68] Although Lindisfarne's customs were not affected by the coming of great men – Bede says that no elaborate buildings were made for their reception, no splendid meals served[69] – the function of institutions like Lastingham in respect of the patron must be one of the reasons why secular decoration intruded into church use. This intrusion occurs even where we might not have expected it, in the stone entrance-portal of Romanizing Monkwearmouth, *38-9* where shallow-relief twin dragons, with eel-like bodies, interwoven tails and long pointed jaws, look like appliqué ornaments from Sutton Hoo, writ large.[70]

King Oswy endowed the church at Gilling in the North Riding as a penance for the murder of his co-king Oswine, and there prayers were offered for both men.[71] Alchfrith, Oswy's son, established Ripon for the salvation of his soul. Afterwards at Ripon, and for Ripon, Bishop Wilfrid had a

38–9 Ornamental jamb of the west doorway of St Peter's Church, Monkwearmouth, Co. Durham, with detail of dragon-heads. Late seventh century

Gospel-book written in gold for the health of his own soul.[72] That pattern could hold good, too, for the lay patron, who had the word and sacraments of the faith administered to him privately, as they were by Cedd's brother, the priest Caelin, in King Oethelwald's household.[73] The evidence for the practise of religion on kings' estates is plentiful. When Cedd, who was Oswy's nominee to the bishopric of the East Saxons, officiated at the baptism of King Swithelm, the baptismal ceremony took place at Rendelsham, the royal residence near Sutton Hoo in Suffolk, because the King of the East Angles was acting as Swithelm's sponsor.[74] It seems not unlikely that Rendelsham in 660 will have featured items of personal or other display related stylistically to the Sutton Hoo burial treasures. After only about thirty years, there could hardly have been total loss of continuity of artistic tradition, above ground.

Taste for Sutton Hoo-like objects could have travelled north specifically by means of Cedd's frequent returns to consult Finan at Lindisfarne. Cedd also presided over the monastic community at Lastingham.[75] Etheldreda, daughter of the King of the East Angles, married Oswy's son and successor Ecgfrith.[76] The royal seat at Rendelsham is paralleled in the north by the royal estate *Ad murum*, where King Penda's son Peadda was baptised, Oswy being sponsor, and where Sigbert, another King of the East Angles, was baptised by Bishop Finan.[77] In view of the precedent of King Edwin, whose large gold cross and chalice are mentioned by Bede,[78] it is inconceivable that Oswald and Oswy did not donate similarly luxurious objects for use on the altars of churches under their control or patronage.

A presumably sumptuous display-object in royal possession in Northumbria was the *loculus* or shrine of the arm and hand of King Oswald, 'venerated by many', says Bede, in the royal city of Bamburgh.[79] Oswald used to sit 'with the palms of his hands turned out', says Bede, 'because he was so accustomed to praying'. The division and distribution of the silver dish at Oswald's banquet took place immediately after Bishop Aidan and King Oswald had raised their hands to invoke a blessing
40 on their bread. Was the *loculus* a hand-shaped reliquary, with the hand spread in the *orans* position? The shrine of a king's hand, in a perpetual pose of intercession and itself sacred, marks a dramatic shift from the grave-goods interred with the pagan king a few years earlier. Aidan,

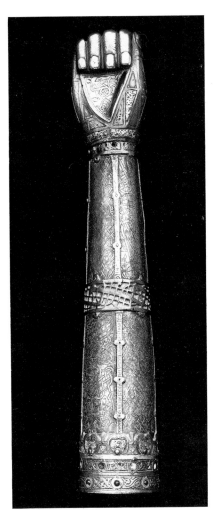

40 The Shrine of St Lachtin's Arm. Early twelfth century, bronze inlaid with gold and silver. This later Irish reliquary may help us to visualize the hand reliquary of St Oswald

responding publicly to Oswald's charity, said 'May this hand never perish'.[80] That was a prayer for the well-being of the king and for his soul's safety. In pursuit of the same ends the king might endow and equip and perpetually place on the altar the Word of God; that is, copies of the Scriptures. Adomnán records that intercession addressed to St Columba was emphasized by the placing of his holograph books on the altar at Iona.[81] Some such psychological promptings could have led to the manufacture of a royally accoutred Gospel-book. It would be the king's credit, his pass to salvation, as opposed to the status symbols that had formerly accompanied him to the pagan otherworld – a new, more efficacious version of ship and rowers.[82] The wealthy ealdorman Eanmund who in the early 700s endowed a cell of Lindisfarne – the exact site in the north of England is uncertain – himself retired to the monastery, and seems to have surrounded himself there with luxurious works of religious art, to judge from the poem *De Abbatibus* written a century later.[83]

The Gospels were read from in the ritual of the Mass, at the end of the instruction section and before the offertory act itself began. With a very small church, lacking room to contain the whole congregation, this reading might take place outside. The Gospels might then be physically showy, as a central piece of liturgical gear.[84] Another function of the Gospels is vouched for by Bede's account of the Synod of Hatfield, convened by Archbishop Theodore in 679. He quotes the synodal book recording the acts of the council 'having the most holy Gospels before us' – evidently as a sign of authority and authenticity.[85] Bishop Wilfrid had a great Gospel-book made, which was preserved at Ripon, where he himself was buried. Presumably the Anglo-Saxon diocesan organization, with the multiplication of bishops, especially in Theodore's time, would differentiate the English portion of the Columban confederation from the rest of it. Finan built his church at Lindisfarne as suitable for the centre of a see, says Bede.[86] Of course Christianity was not first introduced to Northumbria as a whole by the Irish mission. As we have seen, Paulinus had established himself in York in King Edwin's time, and the stone church begun by Edwin was completed by Oswald, says Bede.[87] The authority of bishops as exercised in Northumbria, before and after the coming of the Irish mission, may have been a stimulus to the manufacture of Gospel-books in that province.

The appearance of the Durrow Gospels may represent not only what was regarded as fitting for a royally endowed establishment, but also what a bishop's church should have. The entire spiritual career of Cuthbert – trained by Boisil and Eata, belonging to Melrose and to Ripon as constituted before the Synod of Whitby – exemplifies the self-abnegation of the Irish, praised by Bede; but Cuthbert as Bishop of Lindisfarne in the 680s *174* owned a precious pectoral cross, made of gold and garnets and with splayed arms, part of its central structure perhaps a Kentish disc-brooch. It has long sections of very plain *cloisons* or cells, like those round the boars on the Sutton Hoo shoulder-*29* clasps. This object, standing for the lost luxury-

metalwork of the north of England, straddles the royal and the ecclesiastical worlds.[88] In its manufacturing techniques and patterns it is certainly reconcilable with the tastes of Oswy's and Ecgfrith's court.

To a large extent the Northumbrian Church was frankly 'Erastian', king-controlled. Oswy directed Cedd to go to preach to the East Saxons. Oswy decided what the outcome of the Synod of Whitby would be. Ecgfrith went to compel Cuthbert to be a bishop.[89] The Book of Durrow, whatever its date, is in general principle the sort of book that we can imagine Bishop Finan of Lindisfarne having as his official Gospels, under the patronage of a powerful and opinionated king, who would want, as royal overlord[90] promoting the conversion of client kingdoms, to display the force and validity of Christianity by physical signs. It is less easy to see the Book of Durrow being produced where no Erastian situation existed, no matter how widely available in the British Isles were the right kind of secular-art models, due to the forced or voluntary exile in the seventh century of many Anglo-Saxon nobles and royal claimants.[91]

The Book of Durrow is, of course, more than an Erastian work, for its noble art clearly preoccupied its maker, the scribe and illuminator. There is no possibility of dividing the writing from the art, any more than they can be divided in the Lindisfarne Gospels.[92] One man, Bishop Eadfrith, is generally agreed to have written and decorated the Lindisfarne Gospels. Ultán, the Irish-born, Irish-trained scribe celebrated in the *De Abbatibus* poem (and in the poem circumstantially linked to Eadfrith of Lindisfarne), was revered by the subsequent inmates of his house because he wrote the mystical words of God, and his hands were thereby sanctified and themselves became miracle-working relics.[93] The good service and painstaking zeal of the Sutton Hoo goldsmith, for whatever rewards he enjoyed or anticipated, has become, in the Christian context, not much later, an act of meditation, prayer and worship, a combination of the active and the contemplative ways of life. Though rooted in professional craftsmanship of the sort absorbed and learned in a smith's or jeweller's workshop, the effort to excel is a spiritual exercise: art as devotion.

We are at the stage when Northumbrian Christianity was essentially founded on Irish experience. The Irish had long been devoted to reading the Scriptures and learning the Psalms.

They insisted on this being done even by laymen in attendance on clerics. They were always active, would tolerate no sloth.[94] Memorizing the Scriptures is an act of patient endeavour. The Irish may have inherited from the Egyptian hermits their passion for rote-memorizing. There was also, as already mentioned, a preoccupation with penance in the Irish Church. Columba harshly commanded one sinner to 'Do penance among the Britons with weeping and wailing for twelve years'.[95] A tendency to litanize and categorize and enumerate is noted by Mayr-Harting.[96] In the late eighth-century Stowe Missal (Dublin, Royal Irish Academy MS D.II.3) which represents Irish liturgical practice in our period, the expulsion of evil forces from the human soul in the baptismal rite is expressed, not merely as from the mind, but as from every physical part and orifice, in a long catalogue.[97] A similar catalogue, incidentally, occurs in the East Anglian Felix's *Life of St Guthlac*. When he describes St Guthlac's enemies, the devils which haunt Crowland, he finds an ugliness for every part of the body.[98] The tendency to elaborate, to spin out, to categorize, in one sort of spiritual exercise or devotion, may have been transferred to another – the sacred duty of copying and decorating the Scriptures. The physical make-up of the holy Gospels could easily tend to number-symbolism. According to Bede's prose *Life of St Cuthbert*, his spiritual mentor Boisil of Melrose possessed a copy of St John's Gospel written in seven quires, one for each day of the week.[99] If St Matthew's Gospel in the Book of Durrow had a carpet-page, now lost, there were originally seven carpet-pages in the book. The geometrical basis of the designs in Durrow is severe, and enumerable. Is it a coincidence, we may ask, that there are *3* forty-two spirals in the carpet-page *f.* 3v, and *41* forty-two animals on the carpet-page *f.* 192v? Forty-two is the number of the generations of Christ in Matthew, Chapter 1, verses 1–17.[100]

Iconography

Overt iconography is not lavishly displayed in the Book of Durrow, as it is in its successor, the Book of Kells. Assuming the loss of one carpet-page, the *41* originally sixth carpet-page, that on *f.* 192v, is perhaps appropriate as a recollection of the work of the sixth day, when God created all the animals on the earth, and 'everything that creepeth upon the

41 Carpet-page, the Book of Durrow, *f.* 192v

earth after his kind';[101] or as an introduction to St John's Gospel starting *In Principio*, with its implied repetition of the *In Principio* of the Creation text, Genesis I. Similar creatures are made to inhabit the *In Principio* initial of the later Gospel-book, *78, 85* Durham MS A.II.17, so some such intention may lie behind this animal-design. On the other hand, the animals are found in fairly similar form on secular metalwork, so their meaning is not perhaps to be inferred from their Scriptural context. When I

42 Four Evangelist symbols cross-page, the Book of Durrow, *f.* 2

come to discuss the Durham Gospels I shall refer to an alternative literary source for these initial-creatures.[102]

42 The really weighty iconographic display in the Book of Durrow lies in the four Evangelist symbols cross-page on *f.* 2, and to a lesser extent in the separate symbol-pages.[103] The cross on *f.* 2 is slim and straight-sided but is filled with interlace, and swells into short, broad, basin-shaped extensions at the ends of the arms and stem. A square is set over the transection. These additions to the cross make interesting shapes in the quadrants, where the four symbols stand. Crosses made up of strands and cords appear in fairly simple form at,

43 for example, Fahan, on the very northern most coast of Ireland – the coast to which one would sail directly from Iona.[104]

44 By comparison with the four Evangelist symbols cross-page in the Lichfield Gospels,[105] which shows the man symbol at the top left, the lion top right, the calf bottom left, the eagle bottom right, the Durrow system suggests the Irenaean order of man, eagle, calf, lion, as in the separate Evangelist symbol pages. The four symbols with the cross make a good prefatory page to a Gospels, symbolizing their common witness to the saving grace of Christ. In the Book of Revelation 5, the four beasts are described as standing round the sacrificed, immortal Lamb. So obvious and fundamental a pictorial synopsis and synthesis of contents of the Gospels, via Revelation, does not necessarily require an earlier pictorial model. Indeed, the strange and incongruous forms of the Evangelist symbols in Durrow do not suggest that a coherent model was available.

The man is bust-length, frontal, with an abstract depiction of the body like a balance-weight or horse-trapping. The man's arm is loosely drawn as if he were a profile figure, like the soldiers in the

46 eighth-century Pictish relief-sculpture from Birsay, Orkney.[106] That he was concocted from some such image is reasonable to suppose, since the full-length

53 symbol of the man on *f.* 21v has profile feet just like the Birsay soldiers. The man or angel in the Lichfield cross-page has a similarly positioned arm and sideways-seen feet. The *f.* 2 eagle is very like the eagle symbol on *f.* 84v but has the addition, on the cross-page, of a nimbus. The bull and lion are frontal. The lion is conceived of in terms of the man, with a pair of humped shoulders; however, the head does not project upwards, but is slumped into the shoulders, to show the beast-character of

43 Cross-slab, Fahan, Donegal. (?) Eighth century

the image. The fur is differentiated in a series of diamond-patterns, repeated in the large profile symbol on *f.* 191v – flame-like patterns which we shall see continue into a later Gospel-book, the *112* fragmentary Cotton MS Otho C.V.[107] The lion on the four Evangelist symbols page is given profile feet, with claws turned to the left, but essentially is meant to be seen frontally. A sixth-century Persian silk in Sens Cathedral Treasury, the 'Shroud of St *45* Victor', shows frontal beasts under the champion's

44 Four Evangelist symbols cross-page, the Lichfield Gospels, p. 219

45 Detail of a Persian textile called the 'Shroud of St Victor'. Treasury, Sens Cathedral. After O. von Falke, *Kunstgeschichte der Seidenweberei*. Sixth century

46 Three soldiers, detail of a relief-sculptured slab from the Brough of Birsay, Orkney. Eighth century

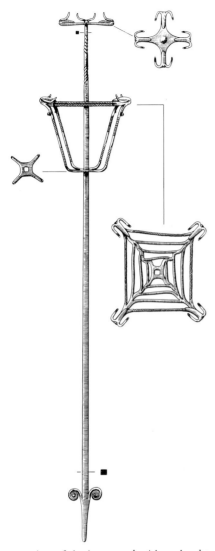

47 Reconstruction of the iron stand with ox-head terminals, Sutton Hoo Ship-burial

48 Beast's-head, detail of an incised slab at Rhynie, Aberdeenshire. First half of seventh century

feet.[108] The pose of the beast in Durrow is a difficult one, and ultimately classical-type models such as the Sens silk could have engendered it. The bull on the four Evangelist symbols page is particularly stylized, truncated like the man symbol. This abbreviation may be compared to that of the strange Pictish symbol of the beast's head, at 48 Rhynie, Aberdeenshire, and elsewhere.[109] The Durrow bull may imitate a beast-headed cap of a pole or standard. Animals' horns project from the 47 iron stand from Sutton Hoo, in a further reduction of the animal-image.[110]

Martin Werner[111] has postulated a complete model for Durrow, *f.* 2, the cross and the symbols

all in place. The principal feature of the symbols for 42 Werner is that they are zooanthropomorphic – that is, though beast-headed where relevant, they have the upright stance of men. Werner's argument that the lion stands reared up on its hind legs and that the bull is 'dressed in a garment which covers its body', and is therefore anthropomorphic, does not really tally with what is shown on *f.* 2. Werner is correct, however, in pointing out that the upright pose does occur in a number of Insular Evangelist symbols – first, those on the *soiscél Molaise*, in 49 Dublin, an early Insular bronze box with enamel inlays, elaborated upon in the early eleventh century.[112] This displays the four creatures

45

49 *Soiscél Molaise* book-shrine, from Devenish Island, Co. Fermanagh. Bronze, silver, silver-gilt and enamel. Eighth century with later additions

50 Four Evangelist symbols cross-page, the Macdurnan Gospels, *f.* 1v. Ninth century

51 Four Evangelist symbols cross-page, the Book of Kells, *f.* 27v

standing up tall on their hind legs. The details, however, are very remote from Durrow, and the symbols are markedly uniform in treatment. Second, the four symbols page (*f.* 1v) of the Macdurnan Gospels in Lambeth Palace, London, probably of the late ninth century, parallels Durrow in showing man and eagle at the top, and again an upright pose is achieved in tall multi-winged figures, strictly symmetrical and uniform.[113] Here, too, the forms are distinct from those of Durrow, but a tendency to seek an upright pose is suggested by these later depictions. The Book of Kells, like the Lichfield Gospels, turns the lion into profile and rears him into the feasible rampant pose, and in the case of the calf, turns a walking profile-beast at right-angles. Kells, on the other hand, knows zooanthropomorphic symbols, employing them on *f.* 1 and *f.* 5.[114] Again, the tendency to uprightness may represent a historical link, but the specific forms employed are not at all like those of Durrow.

Sensitive to the space at his disposal, the Durrow artist modifies his own man symbol by truncating

it, bases his lion perhaps on a three-dimensional model (such as the British bronze stag mounted on the Sutton Hoo whetstone sceptre),[115] or otherwise imitates a frontally posed model; and in the case of the bull symbol employs a formula common, no doubt, among metalworkers and smiths in devising a beast-headed terminal. The design on *f.* 2 as a whole is original, primitive as Insular manuscripts

52 Bronze statuette of a bull, from Carnwath, Lanarkshire. First century BC to first century AD

50

51

188, 202

42

52

53 Symbol of St Matthew, the Book of Durrow, *f.* 21v

go, and in the specific symbol-types employed, uninfluential.

53   The man symbol on *f.* 21v looks, in the rigid formal outline of his body and his chequered cape, like a plaque, buckle or shoulder-clasp which might have repeated the man's-head motif at the base, reversed, much as the Sutton Hoo boars are 29 repeated when the shoulder-clasps are linked in

48

symmetrical epaulettes. In the Markyate Plaque in 54 the British Museum, a man's head terminates the tray-shaped body at either end.[116] For the Durrow man's armless look, we can compare the stocky, block-like images of the twelve Apostles, and of Daniel, carved in high relief in the eighth-century Moone Cross, Co. Kildare.[117] Such figures may 55 perhaps record some older sort of human totem. The type appears again in the Myklebostad plaque-escutcheon, Viking loot of uncertain original 56 provenance.[118] We may, however, also compare cloaked figures in Roman art; for example, the relief of three figures at Housesteads on the Roman 57 Wall, where the outline of the body is broad and solid, with the join of the cloak down the front and no arms showing.[119] The profile feet of the Durrow man, projecting beyond his long robe or mantle, can be paralleled, as noted above, in the Pictish 46 Birsay relief. The Durrow man's multi-coloured cape may remind us of the wonderful robe (*peblum mirae pulchritudinis*) embroidered with splendid colours, like the colours of flowers, which according to Adomnán's *Life* was shown to St Columba's mother in a vision before his birth.[120] The robe was then carried away by an angel. The woman laments the departure of the joyous mantle (*laetificum pallium*), and then it is explained that it represents her child-to-be, and she sees the robe grow bigger and bigger, so that it overhangs the whole landscape; this is the glorious robe of Columba which we heard of before, in Oswald's vision before the battle with Cadwallon.

    Invoking such an image of Irish sanctity as St Columba's mantle in respect of the *Imago hominis* of Durrow brings us to the interpretation offered by A. A. Luce (in the facsimile edition of the *Codex Durmachensis*) of the hair-style of the Durrow man: on *f.* 21v this is heavy hair, parted in the middle and shorn off straight at the nape of the neck, but on *f.* 2, the four symbols page, it is worn longer, not shorn off straight though similarly parted in the middle. Luce suggests that this represents the Irish tonsure.[121] The Roman tonsure in the form of a crown, worn by St Peter in representations of the Prince of the Apostles, is recognizable in the *Imago hominis* in the Echternach Gospels.[122] There may be a polemical reason for this depiction, to which we shall return shortly, but it does not follow that the Durrow coiffure means anything in particular, or that it is specifically the Irish tonsure.

    The Irish tonsure, a point of dispute between the Irish and Roman clergy, is referred to in Ceolfrid's

54 The Markyate Plaque. Gilt-bronze. Early eighth century

55 Daniel in the Lions' Den, detail of the Moone Cross, Co. Kildare. Eighth century

56 Bronze and enamel escutcheon in human form, on a hanging-bowl from a Viking grave at Myklebostad, Norway. (?) Seventh century

57 Three cloaked and hooded figures, a stone relief at Housesteads, Northumberland. Third century

49

58 Figure of a man incised on a boulder, from Rhynie, Aberdeenshire. First half of seventh century

letter about the calculation of Easter sent *c.* 710 to Nechtan, King of the Picts, and quoted by Bede in the *Ecclesiastical History*. It was the tonsure worn by Adomnán, Abbot of Iona, and discarded by him under Ceolfrid's influence during the years 686 to 688.[123] The Irish tonsure might appear in the image of the man (paralleling the appearance of a Roman tonsure in the Echternach Gospels) probably only before 664 in the Northumbrian context – that is, before the Synod of Whitby – but on Iona any time before 718, the date when the Columban Church accepted the Roman tonsure.[124] However, Felix's remark in his *Life of Saint Guthlac* that his hero

received the Petrine tonsure at Repton *c.* 699 suggests that the issue was not altogether forgotten when he was writing in the 740s in East Anglia.[125]

It is not clear, however, that the Durrow figure shows any tonsure at all. Its full growth of hair is parted but not shaved to any shape or device. From Ceolfrid's criticism of Adomnán's Irish tonsure we can guess its appearance: 'In the front of the forehead it does seem to bear a resemblance to a crown (*Quae in frontis quidem superficie coronae videtur speciem praeferre*), but when you come to look at the neck, you find that the crown which you expect to see is cut short' (*coronam . . . decurtatam*). The doubtful nature of the crown at the front could mean that it is incomplete, open on the brow but then proceeding like a crown round the sides of the head as if to circle the head. At the back the crown-effect is evidently destroyed in some way, 'cut short' perhaps not by the shaving or cutting-short of the hair, but by the abandonment of the crown-effect, by the growing of the hair long. Colgrave and Mynors' view is that the Irish tonsure 'seems to have left the hair long at the back while the front was shaved bare'.[126] This is the view of Bede's principal editor, Plummer: the Irish tonsure 'consisted of shaving the whole of the front of the head from ear to ear, the hair being allowed to hang down behind'.[127] And Reeves, in the still-indispensable edition of Adomnán's *Life of St Columba*, writes '*Ab aure ad aurem* – that is, the anterior half of the head was made bare but the occiput was untouched.'[128] Ceolfrid's remarks on Adomnán's tonsure, however, imply that a bar of hair was visible at the sides, to suggest a *corona*, so that the brow rather than the sides of the head should be shaved. The Irish tonsure was mysteriously ascribed by the Roman party to Simon Magus, St Peter's adversary in Acts of the Apostles, 8, and Adomnán consented to this interpretation, according to Bede's report: 'though I wear the tonsure of Simon after the custom of my country'. Colgrave and Mynors' explanation of this is that pagan Druids wore a tonsure, of which descriptions, they say, have survived and indicate that it was not unlike the Irish tonsure. 'Hence it was easy for its opponents to associate it with Simon the arch-magician and druid.' I have not been able to trace any authentic description of a druidical tonsure.[129]

The Durrow man's hair-style seems more to agree with a hero's hair-style; compare the Latin writer Strabo on Celtic men: 'Their hair is not only naturally blond but they also use artificial means to increase this natural quality of colour. For they continually wash their hair with lime-wash and draw it back from the forehead to the crown and to the nape of the neck, with the result that their appearance resembles that of Satyrs or of Pans, for the hair is so thickened by this treatment that it differs in no way from a horse's mane.'[130] What does, on the other hand, look like a tonsure of an elaborate kind, perhaps deliberately exaggerated as the focus of the image, appears on one of the most recently found examples of Pictish incised sculpture, the figure of a profile man from Rhynie, Aberdeenshire. The hair forms a kind of crown in the region of the ear but on the nape of the neck is worn long. The vigorous delineation of the hairstyle has misled one writer to call it 'a form of head-dress'.[131] The features – nose, lips, eyebrows and beard – are strongly marked, exaggerating the 'Hittite' profile often apparent in Pictish sculpture. In world art such strong features are frequently reserved for depictions of foreigners.[132] In Ceolfrid's conversation with Adomnán on the tonsure he counselled Adomnán to discard 'the tonsure of Simon Magus, a man whose horrible face (*horrendam faciem*) you would shun to look upon'. The Rhynie man could well illustrate both the tonsure and the *horrendam faciem* of Simon Magus, though in the context of a field monument otherwise uninscribed such an identification is fraught with difficulty.

The Durrow man's shoes with the tongues at the front and heel are found in the page with St Matthew writing in the Irish manuscript, St Gall Stiftsbibliothek Cod. 1395, of the eighth to ninth centuries, and also in the St Matthew portrait in the Book of Dimma, from Roscrea, Co. Tipperary, Dublin (Trinity College MS A.4.23), of the second half of the eighth century. Shoes in the Canterbury Vespasian Psalter are not dissimilar.[133] As we have noted, free-standing tongues at heel or opening, and openings with scalloped edges have been found in shoes preserved from a leather manufactory at Iona.

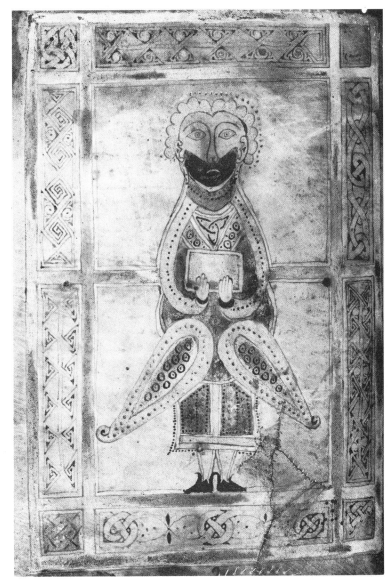

59 St Matthew, the Book of Dimma. Dublin, Trinity College MS A.4.23 (59), p. 2. Second half of eighth century

60 Drawing and reconstruction of a leather shoe from the 1979 excavation at Iona. Seventh century

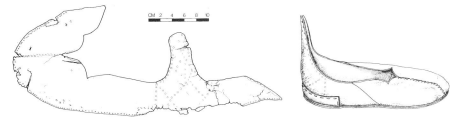

61 Eagle symbol, the Book of Durrow, *f.* 84v

62 Pair of Visigothic eagle-shaped fibulae of gilt-bronze, rock crystal and coloured stones. Sixth century

61   The eagle symbol on *f.* 84v has a round bead eye and a round framed head, very like the eagle- and

28 duck-appliqués on the Sutton Hoo purse-cover, where the (reconstructed) bare white bone or ivory background is similar. The upper beak of the Sutton Hoo eagle overhangs the lower beak in a way similar though not identical to the Durrow eagle's. There is much more naturalism in the Durrow bird's feathers, legs, rump and feet than, for example, in the great Swedish-type eagle on the Sutton Hoo shield.[134] However, the disposition of the Durrow bird with wings partly extended on either side of the upright body is artificial and heraldic; it looks like one of the familiar droop-

62 winged Visigothic eagle brooches.[135]

64   The lion of Durrow (*f.* 191v), with its aggressive chunkiness and abstract diagonal-chequered pattern of skin, is similar to the eagle, giving the

appearance of jewellery; but the curvilinear lines that articulate the joints are stylistically different, more flowing and free. The calf symbol of St Luke on *f.* 124v is more naturalistic, small and neat, not *63* stylized like the Sutton Hoo shoulder-clasp boars in spite of the similar break of the leg with a transverse bar at the joint. The scroll on the thigh and shoulder of the calf uses the spiral and trumpet motif; the upper of each of the trumpet-shaped members, differently coloured from the lower one, forms, as it were, the dark recessed trench which sets off the spiral. Normally in metalwork, for example in the Winchester hanging-bowl escut- *67* cheon,[136] the trumpet-member grades into the spiral, and is continuous with it, in the same plane. The trumpet does not become the background. The same effect as that on the calf is seen in the green trumpet which becomes the trench in the *Quoniam quidem* initial in Durrow. This kind of *66* ambiguity of plane is a painter's trick, interpreting in a free way metalwork techniques such as those displayed on the Lullingstone Bowl from Kent, *65* whose appliqué stags, with spiral haunches, are close contemporary parallels to the Durrow symbols.[137]

    The long flat scrolls that mark the haunches of the Durrow lion symbol follow the formula of the scrolls incised on Pictish symbol-stones of the *68, 111* Rhynie ugly man and Rhynie beast-head period, but in Durrow these scrolls are interpreted as if obeying the technical requirements of inlaid metalwork, adapted to a recognizably Germanic animal of the Sutton Hoo purse-lid type. The expressively naturalistic linear Pictish idiom itself is not accepted throughout the design of the squat

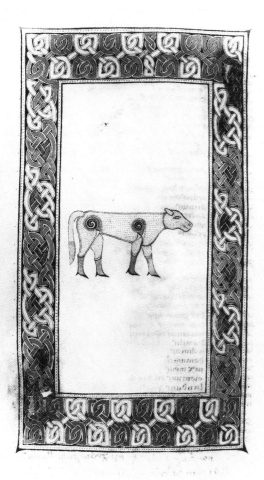

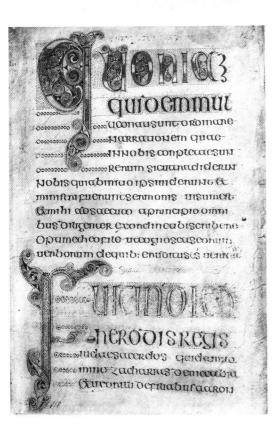

63 (*top left*) Calf symbol of St Luke, the Book of Durrow, *f.* 124v

64 (*top*) Lion symbol, the Book of Durrow, *f.* 191v

65 (*above*) Hanging-bowl with zoomorphic applied ornaments and spiral escutcheons, from Lullingstone, Kent. Seventh century

66 (*far left*) Beginning of St Luke's Gospel, *Quoniam quidem*, the Book of Durrow, *f.* 126

67 (*left*) Bronze and enamel escutcheon of hanging-bowl from Winchester. Seventh century

68 (*below*) Bull, incised slab from Burghead, Moray. First half of seventh century

lion, though it comes very near to being accepted in the long silhouette of the calf. This is a point of interest in the chronology of Insular manuscripts, since, as we shall see, there are two other Gospel-books, usually associated with Northumbria, which accept the Pictish idiom more wholeheartedly, as if from greater exposure or closer proximity to Pictish influence.[138]

Provenance and date

The Book of Durrow marks an early experimental phase in the development of the Insular Gospel-book. The survey of its contents in the previous section enabled us to define the kinds of visual resource on which its designer could draw, and to offer some historical explanations of his particular mode of symbolic representation. Taking the implications of his choice of decoration and imagery into account, how far can we go, at this stage in our enquiry, towards determining the origin-centre and the date of the Book of Durrow?

According to Bede, King Oswald held under his sway peoples of four different languages: British, Pictish, Irish and English.[139] This 'union' of peoples suffered all kinds of upsets and imbalances in our period; for example, war was waged between Ecgfrith of Northumbria and the Irish and the Picts in the 680s. But in the seventh century these peoples were constantly interacting, and, with the exception of the Britons, their cultural relations were promoted and cemented by the Church. Iona, an Irish foundation, was the head of monasteries among the Picts. Aidan could well have worked in Pictland before coming to Lindisfarne. Their common allegiance to Iona formed a link between the churches of Pictland and Northumbria. Northumbria, of course, had its own direct interest in Pictland: for about thirty years, up to 685, Northumbria controlled part of southern Pictland;[140] Wilfrid was for a time Bishop of the Picts, a responsibility which Trumwine took over from him. Trumwine was a friend of Cuthbert, and was involved in persuading him to accept episcopal office in the 680s.[141] Earlier, as Prior of Melrose, Cuthbert himself had worked among the Picts: he went on expeditions across the River Forth, the Northumbrian border, to the nearest region of Pictland, Fife.[142]

Until 664 the island monastery of Iona must have derived many advantages from its contacts with the vigorous new Columban province of Northumbria – gifts to its altars from Oswald perhaps? Even after the Synod of Whitby, when the Irish computation of Easter and the Irish form of tonsure were repudiated in Northumbria, spiritual and practical links with Ireland remained. The Irish-trained Eata of Melrose was put in charge of Lindisfarne monastery at the retiring Colman's own request. The quarrel between King Oswy and his son Alchfrith, to which Bede alludes, entailed the loss of the bishopric of York by the Roman champion Wilfrid, who was Alchfrith's protegé. Significantly, Wilfrid was replaced by Chad, trained in Ireland, disciple of Aidan. The appointment as Bishop of Lindisfarne of Tuda, an Irishman whose tonsure was Roman, may also have improved relations.[143]

Bishop Colman's retiral to Iona in 664 may have stimulated the first *Life* of Columba (that written by Cummené, which underlies Adomnán's later official *Life*), to show what Columba, denigrated by the Roman party, really stood for.[144] Colman felt reverence also for the much more recent saints of his own Northumbrian Church. When he left Lindisfarne he took some of Aidan's bones away with him, leaving some others to be interred in the sanctuary of Lindisfarne church.[145] Willibrord, who began to follow the religious life at Wilfrid's Ripon, went as a young man – he was twenty in 678 – to Ireland, and there he is reported by Bede to have owned part of the stake on which King Oswald's head had been impaled.[146] Oswald's head, after it was rescued from the battlefield, was buried by King Oswy *in cymiterio Lindisfarnensis ecclesiae*.[147] The miracle-working relic owned by Willibrord may have left Lindisfarne on the removal of cult objects when the Columban party withdrew.

The Durrow Gospels claims to have a historical link with Columba. On *f.* 247v, the second last leaf *162* of the manuscript before the last carpet-pattern, *f.* 248, and after not merely the end of St John's Gospel but also the oddly displaced *capitula* of Luke and John, there are two formal inscriptions.[148] One, obviously in the same handwriting as the *capitula* entries opposite, reads: 'Pray for me, my brother (*Ora pro me, frater mi*). The Lord be with you (*Dominus tecum sit*)', while above it there is a longer inscription beginning: '*Rogo beatitudinem tuam . . .*'. Part of this inscription has been scraped, rewritten or expanded, and it is blurred also as a result of being repeatedly kissed by the faithful. This *Rogo* inscription is discussed by Luce, both as to its present form of words and a possible earlier form of words. The inscription, translated, reads: 'I ask your Beatitude, holy priest Patrick (*Patricius*), that whoever holds in his hand this little book (*hunc libellum*) may remember [me] Columba the writer, who wrote this Gospel for myself in the space of twelve days by the grace of our Lord S.S.' (*superscriptus*, 'the undersigned'). Originally the inscription may have read: 'I ask your Beatitude, holy priest Patrick, that whenever you hold in your hand this little book you would remember me who wrote this Gospel for myself in the space of twelve days by the grace of our Lord. Undersigned.' The original signature has been replaced with the name Columba and the book's use generalized from Patrick's own to that of whoever holds it.

This, however, is not a colophon to Durrow. It is presumably a colophon copied from Durrow's textual exemplar, evidently a small private copy of the Gospels, or of a single Gospel, written in twelve days for his own use by Columba but subsequently given by him to a priest Patrick. The *libellus* mentioned is not, of course, Durrow itself, since palaeographically the Durrow manuscript is *16, 17,* in advance of the Cathach (palaeographers *258* generally regard the Cathach as post-Columban, although the attribution to Columba is defensible), and the work of writing the Durrow Gospels, and all that is entailed in the ornamental letters, could not possibly have been accomplished in twelve days. Either the Durrow Gospels reflects a Columban textual exemplar, in whole or in part, or quite early in its history it was in the hands of a community which wished it to represent a direct link with St Columba.

In Adomnán's *Life* various books – a hymn book, a partially completed Psalter, and other manuscripts (unspecified) – are attributed to Columba. These books are reported possessed of miraculous powers, and were in some cases revered relics of the community on Iona.[149] On Adomnán's evidence, a single leaf written by Columba had power to resist the destruction that accidentally overtook the rest of the volume.[150] It is perfectly possible that a Columban book or part of a book would have been brought by Aidan to Northumbria, especially in view of the esteem in which King Oswald is reputed to have held St Columba.

Oswald himself might have owned such a book. The Columban connection of the Book of Durrow, asserted by the colophon, has some basis in fact. We can account for the artistic style of the Book of Durrow most easily if we think of it as a product of the Columban Church in England, but we then have to account for the book's removal to Durrow, probably via Iona.

Ceollach, Finan's nominee as Bishop of the Middle Angles, could have taken such a book away from Mercia when he returned in 659 to Iona.[151] A Gospels of Bishop Finan of Lindisfarne would date between 651 and 661. Bishop Colman's own Gospels would date between 661 and 664. The Durrow Gospels is conventionally dated to 675, and the Durham MS A.II.10 conventionally dated *20* around 650.[152] Why should Durrow be twenty-five years later than Durham MS A.II.10, and not, say, ten years later? These dates are all relative, and depend on function, patron – on all sorts of differentiating factors.

We probably need the presence of a Book of Durrow-like manuscript in Northumbria to account fully for the recollections of Durrow's ornamental layout and emphasis which are apparent in the Lindisfarne Gospels; yet Durrow itself probably has to be taken to Iona, because there are close connections between it and the Book of Kells (discussed in a later chapter), and Kells by and large makes best sense as an Iona production.[153] The weight of English experience and taste at Iona after 664 should, however, not be forgotten. Colman withdrew from Lindisfarne and took with him not only the Irish community but also thirty English monks. We shall continue to see this Anglo-Saxon presence in Ireland as a factor in the next generation of manuscripts, but we might conclude that the Northumbrian elements, royal and 'Erastian', in Durrow, could have been conveyed to Iona after the debacle of the Synod of Whitby in 664 along with important relics from Lindisfarne. If the conventional date of Durrow, *c.* 675, has, however, to be accepted, then we could reasonably see the Gospel-book as undertaken on Iona as a boost to Columban confidence at that time, rather than as a product of the uncertain and shifting cultural conditions existing, say, at Lindisfarne in the same period.

&hierusalem ⁊ maritima ⁊ turi ⁊ sidoonis qui
uenerant ut audirent eum. ⁊ sanarentur a lan
guorib; suis ⁊ qui uexabantur · a spiritib; in
mundis curabantur ·⁊ omnis turba querebat
eum tangere · quia uirtus de illo exiebat ⁊ sana
bat omnes ·⁊ ipse eleuatis oculis in discip
los suos dicebat ·⁊ beati pauperes quia ues
trum est regnum di ·⁊ beati qui nunc esuritis quia
saturabimini ·⁊ beati qui nunc fletis quia ride
bitis ·⁊ beati eritis cum uos oderint homines
⁊ cum separauerint uos ⁊ exprobrauerint
⁊ eiecerint nomen uestrum tamquam malum
propter filium hominis gaudete in illa die ⁊ ex
ultate ecce enim merces uestra multa est in cae
lo secundum haec enim faciebant prophetas
patres eorum Uerumtamen uae uobis diuitab;
qui habetis consulationem uestram ·· Uae uobis
qui saturati estis quia esurietis Uae uobis qui
ridetis nunc quia lugebitis ⁊ flebitis ·· Uae
ben uobis dixerint omnes homines secundum
haec faciebant pseudo prophetas patres eor.
sed uobis dico qui auditis Diligite inimicos ues

69 'Beatitudes' text, St Luke's Gospel, Chapter 6, the Durham Gospels, *f.* 79v

3 The Durham, Corpus and Echternach Gospels, with minor fragments

Design

The Durham Gospels (MS A.II.17)[1] is a copy of the Vulgate Gospels measuring 34.4 cm by 26.5 cm. It survives in a damaged and vandalized condition, and consists of only 108 folios, in contrast to Durrow's 248 folios or Lindisfarne's 258. It lacks St Jerome's letter to Pope Damasus, and the canon-tables; St Matthew's Gospel has no *capitula, argumentum*, or great prefatory initials. Losses at the beginning of the Gospels of Mark and Luke have likewise deprived us of their great initials. Only St *78* John's Gospel preserves its decorated *In Principio*. The Durham Gospels must once have contained Evangelist portraits, carpet-pages and full-page miniatures illustrating the text, but all that remains is one illustration at the end of St Matthew's Gospel. Durham's text is arranged on the page like that of Durrow, written in long lines, but the text itself is distinct in its variant readings from that of Durrow, and equally from that of Lindisfarne. The *69* ordinary text-pages of the Durham Gospels have small decorative initials throughout, in this respect resembling the Book of Kells. Durham also anticipates Kells in being planned as an illustrated Gospels.

The single surviving illustration is very remarkable, and is carefully prepared for by the scribe in laying out his text. To appreciate the illustration, we have to be aware of the contents of St Matthew's Gospel written on the folios immediately preceding it. Chapters 24 and 25 describe what is called in the synoptic Gospels the 'Little Apocalypse' – Christ's prophecy of the final tribulations and the end of the world, which will ensue when Christ's Gospel has been preached in all regions of the earth. Then the stars will fall and the sun will be darkened. Then the

sign of the Son of man will be seen in heaven. 'He will send his angels with a great sound of a trumpet. The Son of man shall come in his glory and all the holy angels with him.' Then, says the Gospel, the division of souls will be made, eternal fire for sinners, and for the virtuous and charitable, eternal life. In Chapter 26 Matthew begins the account of the Passion, with the assembling of the chief priests to plot Christ's death, the incident of the woman with the alabaster vase of precious ointment, the institution of the Eucharist, and next the betrayal and the trial before Caiaphas. Verse 1, *et factum est*, is emphasized with a larger initial, and the chapter has a second emphatic initial at the end of the account of the Last Supper at verse 31, when the disciples go out to the Mount of Olives: *Tunc Iesus dicit illis*. The text of Chapters 27 and 28 has long been missing, and the writing of that word *tunc* is offset, in reverse, on the last page of St Matthew's Gospel; this last page has the text of Matthew Chapter 28, from verse 17 onwards, the closing sentences of the Gospel: 'And they seeing him, worshipped him, but some doubted. And Jesus came to them and said: "All power is given unto me in heaven and on earth. Go therefore and teach all nations, baptising them in the name of the Father and the Son and the Holy Ghost, teaching them to observe all things I have commanded you, and lo, I am with you always to the end of the world."' The amount of text displayed on the last page of St Matthew's Gospel is carefully calculated to allow decorative treatment. The text is framed by fine *70* interlace (strings, not cords or ribbons) which moves in on all four sides, the text withdrawing to make room for the side frame. So the liaison of text

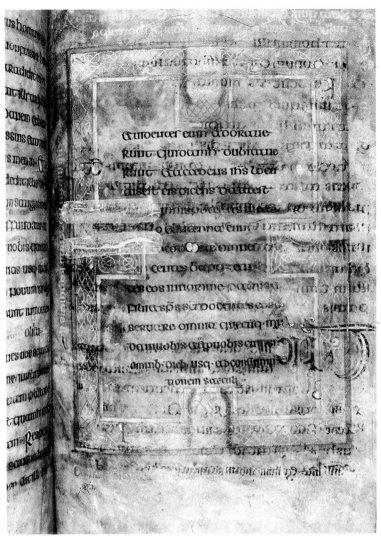

College MS A.4.15 tentatively anticipates the cross of Christ Crucified in the Durham Gospels. Durham MS A.II.10 has a framed text at the end of Matthew, the *explicit* of Matthew and the *incipit* of Mark, to which was added the Greek *Pater Noster*; thus the idea of marking a break for meditation at this point in the Durham Gospels may be based on the tentative precedent of A.II.10, textually a close relative of the Ussher Codex. MS A.II.10 was in Durham Library in the fourteenth century.

On the other hand, the Durham Gospels phenomenon is very much more complex, because it isolates and makes a visual pattern out of a portion of the Gospel-text itself, namely the commission given by the Risen Saviour to the Apostle-missionaries. The framing of texts in a Gospel-book has at least one Late Antique/Early Byzantine parallel, the framing of one of the Gospel prefaces in a sixth-century Greek Gospels at Rossano in southern Italy.[3] Framed portions of text occur in other Insular manuscripts, in books significantly with Echternach connections. In the Gospels formerly at Schloss Harburg,[4] now in Augsburg, before the canons on *ff.* 7–12 the words *Evangelia veritas* are written again and again, and framed to make a decorative block. The frame here is very similar to the Rossano Gospels preface frame. In a fragment of a Gospels in Freiburg University Library,[5] which comes from the rent-roll of a Benedictine monastery near Trier (that is, close to Echternach), the *argumentum* to Luke is framed, written in a cross-shaped block of text, with the four corners separated and filled with *Incipit argumentum secundum lucam*. These cross-shaped texts may perhaps reflect the influence of Jarrow-Wearmouth, and Late Antique models likely to have been available in its library, since the Hilary page (the list of books of the Bible as arranged by St Hilary), on *f.* VII of the *Codex Amiatinus*,[6] the great Vulgate Bible written at Jarrow before 716, contains texts in cross-shaped blocks, with cruciform frames. Framed texts occur also in the Lichfield Gospels, namely the Matthew Genealogy, a focal point of text before the *Christi autem* second opening of Matthew 1, 18, and interestingly enough, the last page of St Matthew's Gospel, p. 141, as in the Durham Gospels.[7] Lichfield recalls Durham MS A.II.10 by inserting the text of the *Pater Noster* between two Gospels, not at the end of Matthew, as in Durham MS A.II.10, but at the end of Mark. The Lichfield *Pater Noster* text is not, however, framed. Texts in the Book of Kells

70 The framed end of St Matthew's Gospel, the Durham Gospels, *f.* 38

and frame is consciously planned. On the reverse of this leaf is a full-page picture of Christ hanging on the cross, with two seraphs above the cross and the spear- and sponge-bearers on either side.

The framing of a passage of text at the end of a Gospel has a rough parallel in the 'Old Latin' Gospels, the Ussher Codex I, in Trinity College, Dublin (MS A.4.15), of early seventh-century date,[2] where it is merely the *explicit/incipit* of Luke to Mark that is given a square dotted surround, with a cross or Chi-Rho with Alpha and Omega attached – quite a neat way of expressing a beginning and an end. Christ is present in the Gospel witness, and the end and the beginning are dedicated to him. The cross-design in Trinity

71 Framed *Evangelia veritatis* inscription, Gospel-book formerly at Schloss Harburg, *f*. 2. Early eighth century

72 Framed *argumentum* to St Luke's Gospel, fragmentary Gospel-book at Freiburg, *f*. 1v. Early eighth century

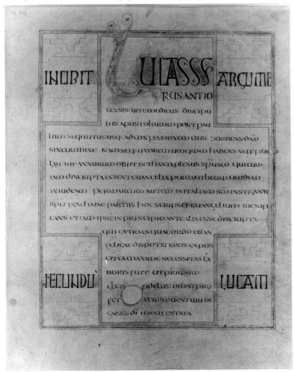

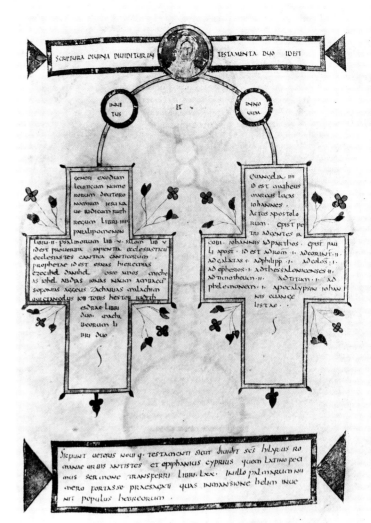

73 Framed lists of the books of the Bible, arranged according to St Hilary, the *Codex Amiatinus*, *f*. VII. *c*. 700

are also framed, for example the elaborate indented and diagonally written text of Matthew 27, 38.

The *Initium* initial to St Mark's Gospel, such as survives in Durham MS A.II.10 and the Durrow Gospels, is not extant in the Durham Gospels, but there is prefatory matter to Mark at this point in the manuscript, showing therefore a different system from Durrow, since the prefaces in Durham come at the start of the individual Gospel, not gathered in a bunch before all the four Gospels. The *capitula* to Mark, starting *De Iohanne Baptista* (these inflated words followed by text containing filled-in coloured lesser initials), are followed in their turn by the initial to the glossary of Hebrew names in Mark – possession of the Hebrew names glossary is

59

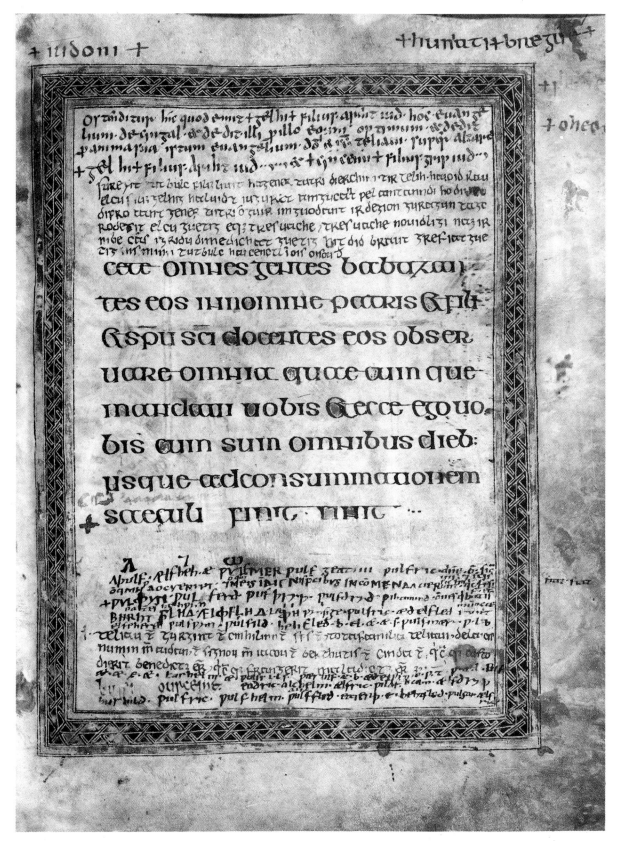

74 Framed end of St Matthew's Gospel, the Lichfield Gospels, p. 141

75 Glossary of Hebrew names and beginning of the *argumentum* to St Mark, the Durham Gospels, *f.* 39

a link with Durrow – and then the *argumentum* to Mark, with *Marcus* written large. A large initial emphasizes Mark 14, 27, *Et ait illis Iesus*, which is the equivalent passage after the account of the Eucharist to Matthew 26, 31. The account of the Resurrection which is missing from the Durham Gospels' Matthew text is extant in Mark's version, 90 Chapter 16. The initial *Et valde*, 'and very early in the morning', is emphasized at verse 2.

There is no Luke text until Chapter 1, verse 26 – that is, the *Quoniam quidem* initial has been cut out – and verse 5, *Fuit in diebus Herodis*, the second beginning of St Luke's Gospel, which is em-

phasized in Durrow, is also missing; but verse 26 of Chapter 1 is emphasized, *In mense*, the sending of 76 the angel of the Annunciation, so that we have here a decorative flourish to signal the role of the Virgin Mary and the beginning of the Nativity story. Again, after the narrative of the Visitation and the *Magnificat*, at verse 68 of Chapter 1, Zacharias's prophecy of the coming redemption of Israel is given a large initial, and also verse 1 of Chapter 2, *Factum est*, the beginning of the Nativity text proper, starting with Caesar Augustus's tax. The naming of Christ and the Circumcision in Chapter 2, verse 21, '*Et postquam*', is similarly signalled. Thus we see the text of the Nativity is very much elaborated.

The beginning of the Passion narrative in St Luke's Gospel, Chapter 22, after St Luke's version of the Little Apocalypse and before the plot against Christ, and the Last Supper, has a large initial, *Adpropinquabat autem*.

St John's Gospel fortunately preserves its great *In Principio* initial, alone of the four Gospel- 78 openings, and at verse 6 of Chapter 1, emphasizes with very angular fancy capitals *Fuit homo missus a* 77 *deo*, the St John the Baptist account in St John's Gospel; and again, verse 1 of Chapter 2, the story of the marriage at Cana, *Et die tertie*, has a large initial in flowing script.

The narrative of the miracle at Cana was often imitated by hagiographers. It is, for example, one of the universal and challenging claims made by

76 (*above*) Initial of St Luke's Gospel, Chapter 1, verse 26, the Durham Gospels, *f.* 74

77 (*right*) Initial letters of St John's Gospel, Chapter I, verse 6, the Durham Gospels, *f.* 2v

78 The beginning of St John's Gospel, *In Principio*, the Durham Gospels, *f.* 2

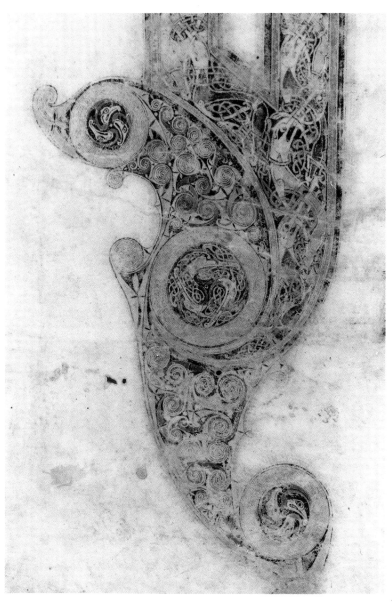

79 Detail of bottom of IN of *In Principio*, the Durham Gospels, *f.* 2

Adomnán for St Columba that he changed water into wine; Adomnán writes: 'So Christ the Lord manifested through his disciple, as a first evidence of power, this that he performed through himself in Canaan of Galilee, when he made the same thing the beginning of his signs. Let this miracle of God illumine like a lantern the opening of this book.'[8] These words written in the 690s suggest a way of looking at the great initials of Insular Gospel-books – that they were intended as spiritual highlights and points of devotion as well as 'embellishment'.

The artist of the Durham Gospels offers the viewer a quite particular selection and co-ordination of decorated motifs. In the first place, he appears to have little feeling for trumpet-spirals as we have seen them on hanging-bowl escutcheons, 67 and painted on *f.* 3v of the Book of Durrow. He 3 queues up his small spirals, and confines them in two curved segments at the base of his initial letter, 79 reserving the large discs for a spinning motif, a wide frame filled with fine concentric lines, which encloses and slides imperceptibly into groups of heads – at the top and bottom heads of birds, and in the middle more dragonish heads with longer bills, but still probably of birds. As we shall see, the artist of Corpus Christi College MS 197B gives his equivalent creatures teeth. Wide-bordered sworls

and discs completely filled with a concentric, thin
66 strand are a feature of the *Quoniam quidem* initial of
Durrow, but Durrow makes much more use of
spiral forms as construction-units and space-fillers.
No bird-heads appear in Durrow's spirals. The
proportions of the circles one to another in Durrow
are richer in variety and more symmetrical, whereas
Durham shows much less interest in the crowds of
little circles. In Durrow's very small *Christi autem*
80 initial there is more genuine feeling for spiral- and
trumpet-ornament as learned from earlier and
contemporary metalwork. Perhaps only Kells,
however, really develops and makes effective use of
spirals in illumination, and that is part of Kells'
artistic brilliance which sees the potentialities of
everything, paralleling the zest for large complex
schemes of spirals and other Insular patterns which
we find in mature Pictish sculpture such as the
81, 82 cross-slabs at Shandwick and Nigg in Easter Ross.[9]

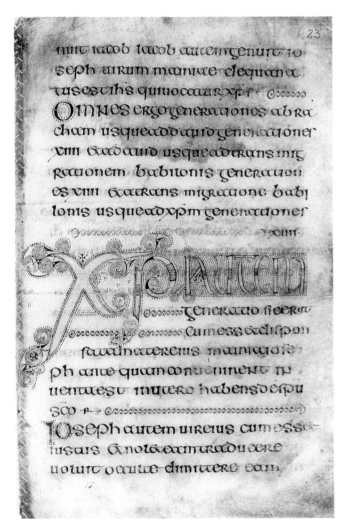

80 (*left*) *Christi autem* initials and surrounding text, the Book of
Durrow, *f.* 23

81 (*above*) Spiral ornament at the bottom of the west face of the
cross-slab at Shandwick, Easter Ross. Eighth century

82 (*below*) Detail of spiral ornament at bottom right of the east
face of the cross-slab at Nigg, Easter Ross. Eighth century

83 Detail of IN of *In Principio*, the Durham Gospels, *f.* 2

84 Bronze and enamel mount on the base of a hanging-bowl, Sutton Hoo Ship-burial. Early seventh century

At the top of the great letters on the Durham *In* 83 *Principio* page, the groups of three discs are filled with brown and buff interlaces, negating their spiral origin, and the cords extending below form an angular pointed motif; at the sides they form extra maze- or fret-patterns, each of which have leaning on them, guarding them, chin to chin, two dragons, with crests or lappets of fine hair. These dragons are descended from the kind of creatures that rest their chins on the boss at the end of the Sutton Hoo buckle, and the fluent relation of the 31 creatures on the buckle, one fitting into the next, is not too far from the infilling beasts in Durham. The three heads in the medallion at the base of the same 79 great initial are paralleled in Sutton Hoo by the second hanging-bowl base-disc, with its dragon- 84 faces forming a triple design. The great uprights of 86 the IN of *In Principio* are filled with repeat dragon- 85 monsters, alternatively buff and rose, like the Durrow St John's-page creatures but with longer 41 jaws, teeth, and horns or lappets, mostly going back across the skull but sometimes coming forward. Each bites the body and forelegs of the

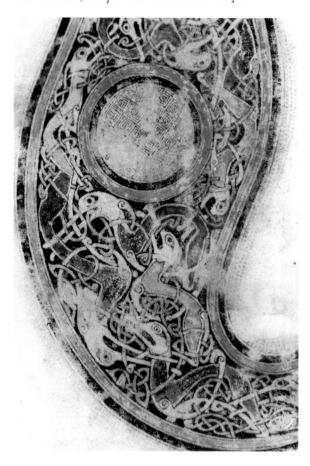

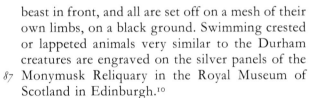

beast in front, and all are set off on a mesh of their own limbs, on a black ground. Swimming crested or lappeted animals very similar to the Durham creatures are engraved on the silver panels of the *87* Monymusk Reliquary in the Royal Museum of Scotland in Edinburgh.[10]

Smaller letters of the *In Principio*, P and R and I, have interlaces only, and a zig-zag or tightly *10* packed-in cord such as we see in the I of *Initium* in

85 (*above left*) Detail of curved bar of N from *In Principio*, the Durham Gospels, *f.* 2

86 (*above*) N from *In Principio*, the Durham Gospels, *f.* 2

87 (*below left*) Front view of the Monymusk Reliquary, *c.* 700, after J. Anderson, *The Early Christian Monuments of Scotland*, Part I

88 (*below*) Snake symbol, incised slab at Newton, Aberdeenshire. First half of seventh century

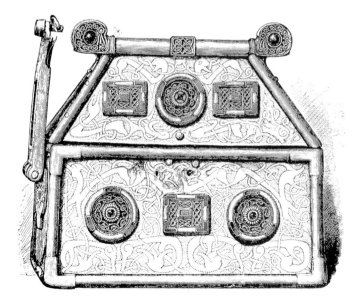

89 *Capitula* to St Mark's Gospel, the Durham Gospels, *f.* 38

90 Initials *Et valde*, St Mark's Gospel, Chapter 16, verse 2, the Durham Gospels, *f.* 69

the Durrow Gospels and on its close relative, the
65 Lullingstone Bowl. The twist of the linking bar between the uprights of the N in the Durham initial is very fluent, like the Pictish snake-design at
88 Newton in Aberdeenshire.[11] The creatures in the initial wriggle and bite with great ferocity. By means of these creatures we can perhaps visualize the disturbing experience of St Columba's disciple, Cormac, on his sea voyage described in Adomnán's *Life*, when his boat collided with a swarm, all over the surface of the sea, of 'small things like frogs, with beaks of birds, that do not fly, but swim'.[12] At the top of the curve of the initial, the creatures cross

68

jaws, whereas elsewhere they bite across the body of their neighbour. The same biting-across of jaws or bills occurs in the initial to the Annunciation, in 76 Luke 1, 26.

The most impressive of the other initials in the Durham Gospels is the *De Iohanne Baptista* of the 89 *capitula* to Mark, where there is a green dragon-head, with a body containing slender yellow featherless birds with necks reduced to mere ribbons, and three toes on the one leg, and containing two discs, and a simple pair of trumpet-motifs, the discs with no infill but a thin-lined frame or edge. There are coloured infills to the other, very angular letters. Mark's *argumentum* has birds' heads, 75 very like the dragons', again with lappets and tongues that become a disc. In the *Fuit homo* initial 77 in St John's Gospel, Chapter 1, there are fine-line interlaces, which sometimes solidify to form a point. There are very few conventional hanging-bowl-type centres to the scrolls: Mark 14, 27, *Et ait*, has one, but all the others are tight continuous spirals or isolated scrolls. The initial to *Et valde* in 90 Mark's Passion-account places panels of interlace within the letters, and weaves together two long slim dragons enclosed in the letter, not tail-to-tail as in the *In Principio* initial, but facing in different directions. These are extremely like the pair of opposed dragons which fill up the left and right uprights of the *In Principio* initial in the fragmentary 92 Gospels in Cambridge, Corpus MS 197B.[13]

Corpus MS 197B, which consists of only 36 folios, measuring 28.5 cm by 21.2 cm, contains parts of the Gospel of St Luke and St John, with no prefaces surviving. St Luke's Gospel has no illumination, but St John's has its *In Principio* (*f.* 2) painted in black, orange, yellow and green. The eagle symbol of St John also survives (*f.* 1) – a 109 change of symbol from that used for John in Durrow. The eagle has a frame with an outer band of orange and inner band of green, with crosses entering the space containing the bird.

On *f.* 2 the top terminations of the uprights and the bottom of NP have excellent authentic spreading trumpet-spirals, very like those in the *Quoniam* initial of Durrow. Pairs or triplets of loops 66 meet in the centre, and there are large trumpet-motifs with conspicuous vents across them. Spirals sometimes contain symmetrically placed and other fillers, playful but authentic within the vocabulary of spirals, such as we see in the creatively-inventive spirals on one of the puzzling dome-shaped objects 93 in the Pictish St Ninian's Isle treasure.[14] The

91 (*above*) Detail of P of *In Principio*, Corpus MS 197B, *f.* 2

92 (*right*) Beginning of St John's Gospel, *In Principio*, Corpus MS 197B, *f.* 2

93 (*below*) Three silver-gilt dome-shaped mounts, St Ninian's Isle, Shetland. Eighth century

94 Fragment of the beginning of St Mark's Gospel, *Initium*, Cotton MS Otho C.V, *f.* 28

Corpus MS 197B artist does indeed fill one pair of major discs with gaping-jawed dragon-heads, showing his affinity with the Durham illuminator, but his other discs keep within the spirals canon.

To Corpus MS 197B can be attached the portions of the Gospels of St Matthew and St Mark, Cotton MS Otho C.V in the British Library, partly burnt in the Cotton Library fire at Ashburnham House in 1731.[15] It consists now of 64 mounted fragments of originally 110 folios. According to Smith's late seventeenth-century Cotton Library Catalogue, it then contained before Matthew an image inscribed *Imago hominis*, and before Mark an image inscribed *Imago leonis*.[16] This lion, and the *Initium* initial of Mark, survive in part, shrunken and discoloured. There also survives in a copy published by Thomas Astle in 1784[17] the initial to the preface of Mark before the glossary of Hebrew names. The words are Greek: *Cata Marcum* (that is, *Secundum Marcum*), and have a more rigid, rectilinear set of capitals than those in the Mark *argumentum* text in the Durham Gospels, but are nonetheless recognizably close to Durham. The Cotton MS Otho C.V letters have hair-fine scrolls at the corners, a feature which occurs also in both the *De Iohanne Baptista* initial in the Durham Gospels and the *In Principio* initial in Corpus MS 197B. The contrast of the rather less curvilinear Mark *argumentum* of Cotton MS Otho C.V with the rounded M in Durham is quite instructive, since this is the same contrast as between the Corpus MS 197B *In Principio*, with a stiff, broken-backed central bar in the N, and the curvaceous Durham version. The birds in Durham are featherless, as we noted, but the bird-head terminal in Cotton MS Otho C.V has small-scale feathers on its breast. The feathering in the great

112, 94

95

75

89

95 Glossary of Hebrew names, St Mark's Gospel, Cotton MS Otho C.V, from T. Astle, *The Origin and Progress of Writing*, 1784

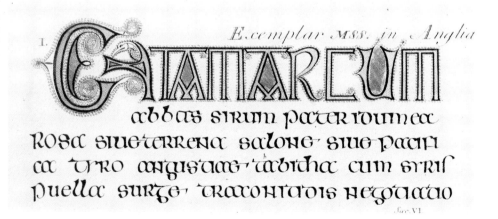

109 symbolic eagle in Corpus 197B is of course a marked feature.

Another element in the former construction and design of the partitioned book Corpus MS 197B/Cotton MS Otho C.V probably survives, as Lowe first suggested,[18] in the fragmentary canon-*96* tables in British Library Royal MS 7.C.XII, *f.* 3. They are Canons IX and X, comprised of five or six panels of numbers without arches or frames. Offset on *f.* 3, however, is the evidence of what went before this section: smudged colour reveals four panels framed by five columns, filled with fret or interlace patterns, with square capitals and two arches up above. The arched, framed, canon-system therefore broke down after Canon VIII. Since the canon-tables of the Book of Kells are *202-3* similarly defective after Canon VIII, Kells was either copied from Corpus MS 197B/Cotton MS Otho C.V, or it shared the defective model employed to draw up the latter's canon-tables.[19] This is very important evidence bearing on the provenance of several Insular Gospel-books.

The Echternach Gospels in the Bibliothèque Nationale in Paris, latin MS 9389,[20] survives in good condition, comprising 223 folios, measuring 33.5 cm by 25.5 cm. In its principal initials the *97* Echternach Gospels tends to use the large disc with fine concentric lines forming a broad frame, as does the Durham Gospels, but the centres are elegant formal trumpets, spirals and lobes, more strictly conventional, in the hanging-bowl tradition of Durrow, with, like Durrow, no animal-head centres, and no half-discs or any fancy infills. Echternach forms the natural third member of this group of manuscripts, which might all spring from the mind of a single man, consciously varying his handling of the trumpet-spiral motif, so that while all the books show the same metallic elegance of ornament there is a distinctive visual flavour to *92* each. The fine cord interlace in Corpus MS 197B varies in thickness (in this following Durrow, as, for example, in Durrow's *Initium* initial). At the base, it is wiry, loose, with long antennae-like terminals, the end of the long thin wire suddenly rolled up tight. The interlace infill of the Echternach letters is more delicate again. The *97* *Quoniam quidem* initial is indebted to Durrow's *66* version, and uses Durrow's trick of differently coloured cords. Here they are tightly packed, with step-patterns in between. The *Fuit* initials are very similar in Echternach's St Luke text and Durham's *77* St John text. As with Durham's great St John

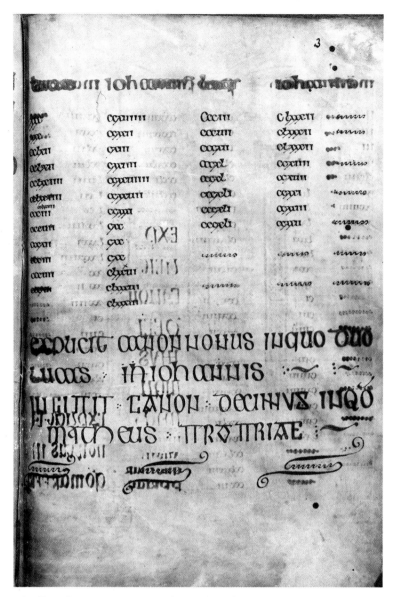

96 Offset of architectural canon-table, Royal MS 7.C.XII, *f.* 3

initial, Echternach relies on interlaced cords to fill *83* the basin-shaped terminals of the Mark *Initium* *98* initial. Corpus MS 197B has birds with layered multi-coloured feathers and slim necks in its P of *91* *Principio*, and Durham has, as we saw, birds in the *De Iohanne* initial, but there no feathers were shown. Again, deliberate variation within a common motif can be postulated.

The Echternach Gospels contains, first, St Jerome's letter, *Novum opus* (*f.* 1), looking *99* extremely like the lesser initials in the Durham Gospels, followed by the canons (*ff.* 2v–13v), *204, 205*

97 Beginning of St Luke's Gospel, *Quoniam quidem*, and in column 2, *Fuit in diebus*, the Echternach Gospels, *f.* 116

98 Beginning of St Mark's Gospel, *Initium evangelii*, the Echternach Gospels, *f.* 76

written in columns with regular frames in yellow or orange, similar to those in Durrow. Each Gospel has its *capitula* and *argumentum*, with the glossary of Hebrew names, as in Durham. St Matthew's symbol, inscribed *Imago hominis*, appears on *f.* 18v. *102* Before *f.* 18 a leaf is missing which may have had a four Evangelist symbols design, or a carpet-pattern; it has left no rubbed-off traces, so its contents are uncertain. The *Imago hominis* should be opposite *Liber*, which is now *f.* 20, with *Christi* *100* *autem* misplaced as *f.* 19. In later Gospel-books *101* symbolic figures intrude between *Liber* and *Christi autem*, but that is not likely to have been the designer's intention at the stage of evolution marked by Echternach, especially as the text displayed by the man is *Liber Generationis*.

In the Echternach Gospels the layout of the text is different from that of Durrow and Durham. Instead of being written in lines as wide as the page allows, the text is arranged in two columns of short 'sense' lines, and is punctuated and broken into clauses. This layout accords with a system advocated by St Jerome, known as writing *per cola et commata*, and was originally conceived to facilitate reading;[21] when employed in the Echternach Gospels it evidently reproduces the layout of an admired textual exemplar.

The imagery of the Evangelist symbols

102 The Echternach man is formal in shape, with a segmented body with heart-shaped upper part and two horse-shoe-shaped flaps with running spirals, then two wing-shaped panels enclosing the feet. He holds a codex open before him. If we cover the head it is difficult to recognize a man-shape at all. The

99 (*right*) Initial to the preface *Novum opus*, the Echternach Gospels, *f.* 1

100 Beginning of St Matthew's Gospel, *Liber Generationis*, the Echternach Gospels, *f.* 20

101 *Christi autem* initials and following text, the Echternach Gospels, *f.* 19

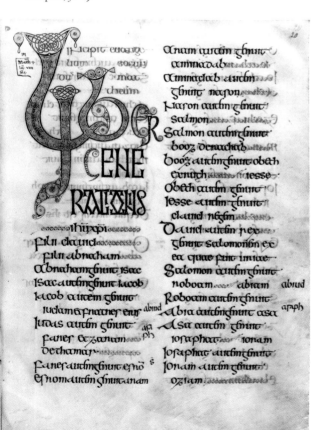

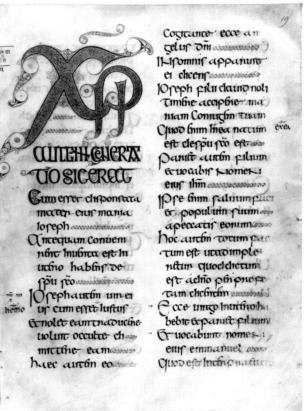

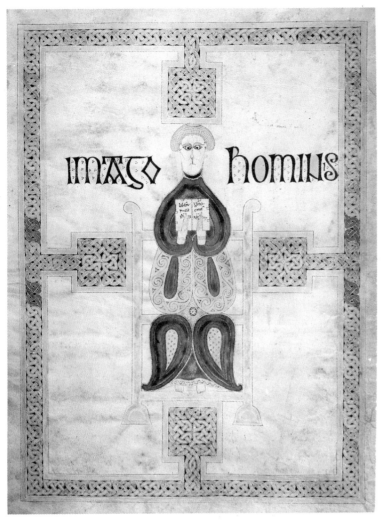

102 Symbol of St Matthew, the Echternach Gospels, *f.* 18v

103 Statue of Juno Regina, Chesters. Early third century

intention may be to emphasize the Evangelist symbol's seraphic nature, with the sense of layers of differently shaped wings. The three sets of shapes which compose him can be likened to footprints or to hoofprints – to horses' hoofprints shod and unshod, or to two sections of a deer's or a boar's hoofprint. Ezekiel's vision of Almighty God and his attendant spirits, which parallels St John's vision in the Apocalypse, involves the description of four flying creatures whose 'feet were straight feet, and the sole of their feet was like the sole of a calf's foot' (*pedes eorum pedes recti, et planta pedes eorum quasi planta pedis vituli*).[22] The picture in the Echternach Gospels may be an experimental visualization of that mysterious theme.

The lobes and curved panels of the Echternach man could be put together out of such decorative

104 Tetramorph page, the Trier Gospels, *f.* 5v. Early eighth century

105 Lion symbol of St Mark, the Echternach Gospels, *f.* 75v

A prefatory image in the Trier Gospels,[25] a book *104* modelled, perhaps, on the Echternach Gospels, shows a bust-length man with feet at the very base of the figure, whose lower half consists of the legs of other creatures, eagle, calf and lion, in layers. This image again suggests an experiment in visualizing the Evangelists in terms of tetramorphs, with bizarre results.

The Echternach man has a tonsure, like St Peter *102* on the wooden coffin of St Cuthbert, probably *166* dated 698.[26] The man has priestly dignity, as he holds up the book, like a formal figure in a sixth-century mosaic. The Roman tonsure is very unusual in Evangelist portraits, and we shall return to its significance shortly.

The rosette placed between the middle and lower lobes of the Echternach man is the same as marks

106 David rending the lion's jaws, from the front panel of the St Andrews Sarcophagus. Eighth century

10 elements as we find in the *Initium* initial of Durrow.
53 In Durrow we thought of the *Imago hominis* as derived from a functioning object such as a man-headed shoulder-clasp. The analogy of the
54 Markyate Plaque, with a head at either end, was cited then. The spreading of the skirt of the Echternach man may simply reflect the modification of a heart-shaped member (as occurs at the upper end) to accommodate the feet. Were it heart-shaped, with a head also at the base, we could again imagine a reference to a piece of equipment, a trapping of some sort, with human attributes. The representation is essentially non-naturalistic, non-classical. Yet the loop with the running pattern of scrolls appears on the naturalistic Romano-British
103 statue of Juno Regina from Chesters on the Roman Wall:[23] her great aprons are decorated along the edge in just this way. Romano-British sculptures were certainly scrutinized by St Cuthbert of Lindisfarne, as Bede records, during his visit to Carlisle,[24] and anyone being baptised *Ad Murum* in the seventh century would have been able to see such things.

the mid-point in the *In Principio* initial. The pattern of dots that appears on the knees of the figure (so to say) also appears within his identifying inscription, and is also on the cheek of the lion in the *Imago leonis*

105 (*f.* 75 v). These triple dots appear around the *Initium*

10 initial in Durrow. The body of the lion (the Echternach *Initium* initial is on the opposite recto, *f.* 76) is covered with lobed scrolls, like a bird's beak, similar to the terminal hook made of two trumpet-shapes at the top of the *Quoniam* initial. The marvellous sinuous curve of the lion's body, with its full shoulders, slim waist and long thrashing tail, belongs to the same school of design as the *In*

86 *Principio* initial in the Durham Gospels. The lion misses ferocity in its decorative flow and animated expression, but it must surely have a relationship on the one hand with the scroll-eared, open-

64 mouthed, tongue-projecting, scrolled-tailed lion of Durrow, and on the other hand with the more fierce naturalistic leaping type of lion which we meet later in Pictland in the St Andrews

106 Sarcophagus.²⁷ Such ultimately Roman or Eastern lions may have been conveyed to the British Isles by textiles, of the sort represented by the Persian sixth-century 'Shroud of St Victor', which I have already invoked in respect of the frontal lion on the four Evangelist symbols page of Durrow. The St

45 Victor textile also contains an upright pair of fiery lions, clearly the sort of lion the Echternach lion seeks to imitate.

107 Eagle, incised slab at Knowe of Burrian, Birsay, Orkney. First half of seventh century

108 Eagle symbol of St John, the Echternach Gospels, *f.* 176v

The quiet *Imago vituli* on *f.* 115v, opposite *110* *Quoniam* on *f.* 116 (the Echternach Gospels lacks any carpet-pages such as appear in Durrow), is very like the Durrow St Luke symbol, but the scrolls on *63* its shoulders and haunch are continuous framing scrolls, not grooved and coloured metalwork-type trumpet-spirals. The *Imago aquile* on *f.* 176v, *108* opposite *In Principio* on *f.* 177, is, as compared with Durrow, in naturalist profile. It is in a perching position, with closed wings. Compared with the tremendous eagle in Corpus MS 197B it has a mild *109* pigeon-like appearance despite its talloned feet, which are quite like the Durrow eagle's feet. *61*

There are divided between the three Gospel-books, Durham, Corpus MS 197B/Cotton MS Otho C.V, and Echternach, seven extant or partly extant full-page miniatures, with subject matter as opposed to patterns and ornament. Six out of these seven are Evangelist symbols – two eagles, two lions, one calf, and one man. The one man (of Echternach) is intruded upon by the cross-layout of the frame, as is the figure of Christ on the Cross in the Durham Gospels. The extraordinary faces and features and tiny feet of the *Imago hominis* of Echternach and the Christ on the Cross in Durham

109 Eagle symbol of St John, Corpus MS 197B, *f.* 1

are the same; and so, too, is the abstract treatment of dress. There is in these two images, Matthew's man, and Christ Crucified, the same intensely *102, 114* spiritual quality of illustration.

In Corpus MS 197B we see more or less the *109* authentic Pictish formula, derived from the Knowe of Burrian eagle, or some such Pictish design *107* familiar to Columban clergy stationed in, or moving through, Pictland. That being so, the pigeon-like eagle in Echternach may have been designed as a deliberate variant. In Echternach we see the pure Pictish formula of the calf, following *110* precisely the conventions of the Ardross wolf and *111* the Grantown stag;[28] so in Corpus MS 197B the artist could perhaps have used, as an alternative visualization, a heavy bull designed like the bull symbol on St Cuthbert's coffin. The two extant *168* lions, in Echternach and Cotton MS Otho C.V, are *105, 112* admittedly close, but they are not identical; one has flame-like hanks of hair, the other a paired trumpet-shaped lobe-motif for its locks of hair. The *Imago hominis* in Echternach suggests that as a variant, the equivalent man in MS Otho C.V, which existed up to the Cotton Library fire, might have looked more Durrowish, or might have been a profile angel with an authentic Pictish scroll on his wing, the design found on the Matthew portrait-page of Lindis- *170* farne, *f.* 25v. What the lost Evangelist symbols in the Durham Gospels may have looked like is a fascinating topic for speculation. Perhaps the artist behaved like his contemporary, or junior, Bishop Eadfrith, and designed for once a naturalistic *Imago hominis*. Nothing is beyond the capability of this

110 Calf symbol of St Luke, the Echternach Gospels, *f.* 115v

111 Wolf, incised slab from Ardross. First half of seventh century

78

112 Remains of Lion symbol of St Mark, Cotton MS Otho C.V, *f*. 27

artist; his books are marked by deliberate variations on common themes. Pictish symbol stones featuring human figures are essentially naturalistic.[29] I am tempted to support the possibility of an Eadfrith classicizing type of figure appearing somewhere in this Gospel-series because in the Trier Gospels, an Echternach production stemming from the same artistic tradition of Durham, *130* Corpus MS 197B and Echternach, the *Imago hominis 113* and *Imago Sancti Mathei* are naturalistic, classicizing, and, in the latter, retain the intruding cross-shaped frame.

113 Portrait of St Matthew, the Trier Gospels, *f.* 18v. Early eighth century

The iconography of the Last Judgment-Crucifixion

The Apocalyptic passage just before the Passion narrative in the three synoptic Gospels emphasizes the spread of the Gospel throughout the world leading on to the Last Things: when the ends of the earth had heard Christ's Gospel, Judgment Day would come. This view of history was inculcated in the Anglo-Saxon Church. Pope Gregory's letter to King Aethelbert of Kent, quoted by Bede, states that the end of the world is at hand. Gregory points to symptoms of the end of the world, 'warning us to prepare for the Last Judgment'.[30] In Ireland, or Iona, rather, the same view is expressed in Adomnán's account of a prophecy foretelling the birth of St Columba in 'the last years of the world'.[31] Zeal to hasten on the divine plan, and Judgment Day, when all the ends of the earth are converted to faith in Christ, may account in part for the missionary activities of Irish and Anglo-Saxon clerics. Irish and Irish-trained clerics were much exercised with visions of the Judgment. Bede quotes from the Irish monk-missionary Fursey's visionary visit to a dark valley where devils and angels contended for human souls and where he saw the four fires of the cardinal vices that will finally kindle the whole world.[32] Bede also reports at length the vision of purgatorial torments and rewards recounted by Dryhthelm at Melrose. Bede cites as his authority for Dryhthelm's story an eminent priest and monk, Haemgisl. Haemgisl belonged for a time to the community at Melrose, but later lived as a hermit in Ireland.[33] Bede's *Ecclesiastical History* records many such examples of the movement of monks from one province to another. Dryhthelm himself was enrolled as a monk at Melrose on the recommendation of the King of Northumbria, Aldfrith.[34] As we have seen, Aldfrith was educated at Iona. Abbot Adomnán was his intimate friend and mentor. Cuthbert, of Melrose and Lindisfarne, is represented in Bede's prose *Life* as prophesying Aldfrith's accession to the throne while he was still living at Iona. The Irish-Ionan links with Northumbria were strong, and Irish spirituality provides the natural context for Dryhthelm's concern with the Last Things and the fate of the redeemed and the damned.

The visions of Judgment of Fursey and Dryhthelm are independent literary excursions. But Bede represents the Irish-trained Chad as directly concerned with the Judgment as defined by

the Gospels. Chad is reported as anxiously awaiting the coming of the Lord. Trumberht, a monk educated at Chad's monastery at Lastingham, was 'one of those who taught me the scriptures', says Bede. Trumberht was Bede's authority for Chad's reactions to storms and gales.[35] When a storm was imminent or had broken out he went into the church and prayed and recited the Psalter until the sky cleared. 'Have you not read, the Lord also thundered in the heavens, and shot out lightnings to rouse the inhabitants of the world to fear him, to remember the dread time when he will come in clouds with great power and majesty, to judge the living and the dead, when the heavens and the earth are aflame?' Chad's reputation and holy death were a matter of interest and topic of conversation for Egbert, the influential English monk living in religious exile in Ireland.[36]

In respect of Judgment imagery, it is worth remembering that Benedict Biscop's Wearmouth had painted decorations, probably on panels, including some form of Judgment scene, if we take literally Bede's comment that everyone who entered the church, 'wherever they turned their eyes might see before them the amiable countenance of Christ and his saints', and also 'having before their eyes the perils of the Last Judgment, they might examine their hearts the more strictly on that account'.[37] Here Bede echoes Chad's sentiments. The link between Chad and Bede's exegesis, via Trumberht, is interesting. Bede can contribute, I believe, to our understanding of the last framed words in St Matthew's Gospel in the Durham Gospels: 'I am with you always, even unto the end of the world' (*ad consummationem saeculi*). According to Bede, Christ is present with his people in the sacraments which he ordained, until the end of the world. Thus Christ's Passion and the Judgment at the Second Coming are encapsulated in the final phrase of St Matthew's Gospel. The cruciform frame around the end of St Matthew's Gospel in the Durham Gospels, as already noted, prepares us for the miniature of Christ on the cross.

We have seen that the small cross-diagram at the end of St Luke's Gospel in the Ussher Codex I foreshadows the larger and more explicit image of the cross in the Durham Gospels. But the text of the 'Little Apocalypse' in St Matthew's Gospel, Chapters 24 and 25, which I quoted earlier, connects the cross with the theme of Judgment, Christ's Second Coming. The Son of man will come in his glory in the clouds of heaven, with all

114

22

114 Crucifixion page, the Durham Gospels, *f.* 38v

the holy angels. 'And then shall appear the sign of the Son of man in heaven.' This 'sign' is the cross. The same theme is taken up in the Book of Revelation 1, 7: 'Behold, he cometh with clouds; and every eye shall see him, and they also which pierced him . . .', an allusion to those who killed Christ. In the Durham Gospels miniature Christ is shown being pierced by Longinus, the spear-bearer. The spear-wound in Christ's side was traditionally viewed, for example by Pope St Leo the Great in the fifth century, as the source both of the blood of redemption and the water of baptism.[38] The command to the Apostles to

'Baptise all nations' is implied by the picture of the death of Christ on the cross. Christian baptism involved a sharing of Christ's death, as St Paul teaches in his Epistle to the Romans 6, 3–4: 'Know ye not, that so many of us as were baptised into Jesus Christ were baptised into his death. Therefore we are buried with him by baptism into death, that like as Christ was raised up from the dead by the glory of the Father, even so we also should walk in newness of life . . .'

At the right of the Durham miniature is an inscription, beginning *Auctorem mortis*, which reads in translation: 'Christ, casting down the

115 Right cross-arm, and cast of reconstructed cross-head, west face of St John's Cross, Iona. Eighth century

116 The Athlone Plaque. Bronze. Eighth century

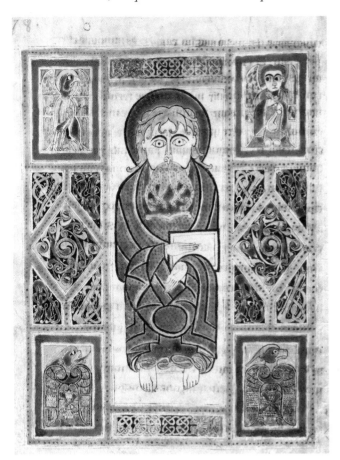

117 Portrait of St Mark, St Gall Codex 51, p. 78. Eighth century

118 Crucifixion page, St Gall Codex 51, p. 266. Eighth century

author of death, renews our life if we suffer along with him.' At the left is another inscription, beginning *Surrexit*, which states: 'He rose from the dead and sits at the right hand of the Father, so that when we have been restored to life, we may reign with him.' The tone and vocabulary of these inscriptions are derived from the Book of Revelation. In Revelation 20, Christ, seated on the throne of judgment, casts down hell and death 237 (*infernus et mors*) into the lake of fire, and in Revelation 21 we read: 'There will be no more death' (*Mors ultra non erit*). In Revelation 1, 6, Christ is called 'the first-born of the dead, who made us kings' (*fecit nos regnum*); verse 7 describes the Second Coming, in the clouds; verse 8 states: 'I am Alpha and Omega' (*Initium et Finis*). The letters Alpha and Omega and the words *Initium* and *Finis* are written on either side of Christ's head in the Durham miniature. All these sacred inscriptions and the seraphs over the cross-arms[39] raise the image above any mere narrative historical repre-

sentation to an hieratic symbolic status, reflecting and expounding Christian doctrine.

The shape of the cross is extremely elegant, with very long outstretched transverse bar, thickening at the terminals of cross-bar and stem, but still straight, not curved. Although the terminals are more curved in the eighth-century Iona crosses, St Oran's Cross and St John's Cross (originally not designed with a ring linking the cross-arms) show the same elegant slim silhouette.[40] A straight-sided 115 swelling of the cross-terminals similar to that in the Durham Gospels occurs in the gilt-bronze crucifixion plaque from a site on a promontory on 116 Lough Ree on the Shannon river, near Althone in Ireland. Christ's nimbus is also similar, an inverted pear-shape, kept close around the head. The Athlone figure is robed, accompanied by Longinus with the spear and Stephaton with the sponge, their positions reversed from the Durham version; multi-winged seraphs crouch over the cross-arms. In the plainness of its ornaments – large motifs,

83

119 The Last Judgment, St Gall Codex 51, p. 267. Eighth century

120 The Ascension, the Turin Gospels, *f.* 1v. Eighth or ninth century

kept separate – the style of the Athlone Plaque is not unlike that of the Book of Durrow.[41] The breast-plate appearance of the spiral ornaments in the upper part of the Athlone Christ's body, however, is best paralleled in the upright lion and *117* bull Evangelist symbols on p. 78 of St Gall Codex 51,[42] an Irish eighth-century Gospels. Like the *118* Durham Gospels this book contains a miniature of the crucifixion. The cross itself has straight stem and cross-bar; the stiff right-angled gesture of Christ's arms, common to both the Durham picture and the Athlone Plaque, is retained in the St Gall Gospels; also the robe, and the two attendant figures, reversed from their position in Durham as in the Athlone Plaque, the spearman being at the right. The angels are changed from seraphs to the kind of book-holding angels that throng the pages of the Book of Kells. The narrative content is enlarged by the demotion of the angels, and the healing of the blindness of Longinus represented by a zig-zag ink-line joining Longinus's eyes to the

84

wound in Christ's side. The image, at its most hieratic and intellectual in the Durham Gospels, may be seen reflected, but in decline, in these two Irish versions. Interestingly St Gall 51 introduces on a subsequent page (both miniatures are placed at the end of the four Gospels, after John) a picture of a bust-length Christ blessing, with trumpeting *119* angels on either side, and the figures of the twelve Apostles looking up. Jonathan Alexander proposes that this second miniature contrasts the power of Christ as Almighty Judge with his sufferings as man in the first miniature.[43] There is here a change of interpretation of the crucified figure, who himself in Durham is the suffering and redeeming Saviour, Judge, and Almighty God, the beginning and the end.

The contents of the second St Gall miniature are suspiciously like those in another Irish Gospel-book, probably from Bobbio, the eighth- or ninth-century Codex O.IV.20[44] in the Bibliotheca Nazionale in Turin, which illustrates first the

121 The Second Coming, the Turin Gospels, *f.* 2. Eighth or ninth century

120, 121 Ascension and secondly the Second Coming. In the Second Coming Christ stands in a narrow rectangle, holding a cross, entirely framed by bust-length figures. The effect is rather like the Durrow carpet-page before St John's Gospel, but with stereotyped segmented humans instead of inter-woven animals. Pictorially and iconographically the miniature is rather abstract, reminiscent, in the repetitiveness and the frontality of the figures, of *55* the eighth-century Moone Cross. The Turin Ascension miniature declares its subject by inscriptions: 'As you see him going so you will see him come.' Christ holds a book, and blesses, bust-length in the upper half of the picture space. Twelve bust-length Apostles are placed in separate spaces, like an Advent calendar below. A common model might have served to create the Last Judgment/Second Coming in St Gall 51 and the Ascension in the Turin Gospels.

123 The Ascension, Rabbula Gospels, *f.* 13v. Sixth century

122 The Ascension, a panel from the base of the shaft of the Rothbury Cross, the Church of All Saints, Rothbury, Northumberland. (?) Second half of eighth century

The theme of Ascension is popular in hagiographical literature, for example, Adomnán's *Life* of St Columba, where many redeemed spirits are witnessed ascending to heaven accompanied by angels.[45] Arculf, Adomnán's informant about the Holy Places, mentions the site of the Ascension, the church being open to the sky.[46] A pictorial representation of the Ascension may have been formulated in some Insular centre from which the St Gall Judgment was derived. The Ascension is represented in a very similar way – Christ with angels above, closely crowded Apostles below – in the Northumbrian Rothbury Cross, probably *122* dating from the second half of the eighth century.[47] Much the same basic vocabulary of forms can be recognized in the Book of Kells' illustration of Christ's Temptation – Christ bust-length above, *242* angel attendants, and large numbers of bust-length figures (though profile, not frontal) below. One figure in the bottom centre is frontal.[48] Thus a number of adaptations may have been made from one simple formula. It is an interesting coincidence that the Ascension of Christ is one of the small *124* number of themes which are represented on holy

124 The Ascension, on a silver ampulla, Palestine. Sixth century. Monza, Cathedral Treasury

125 Crucifixion, on a silver ampulla, Palestine. Sixth century. Monza, Cathedral Treasury

126 Crucifixion page, Würzburg Epistles of St Paul, *f.* 7v. Late eighth century

oil flasks and other reliquary flasks exported in the sixth century from the Holy Land.[49] The collection of these ampullas at Monza, near Milan, was gifted to Queen Theodolinda, wife of Agilof, King of the Lombards, by Pope St Gregory the Great. As we saw (p. 12), Agilof played host in Lombardy to St Columbanus, founder of Bobbio. Monza ampulla 11 shows the Ascension very much as it appears in the sixth-century Syrian Rabbula Gospels now in *123* Florence,[50] with the Virgin among the Apostles below, and Christ raised in an aureole by angels. This kind of minute relief-sculpture could pass directly into larger stone relief-sculpture in the Rothbury Cross, although it is true that in the Rothbury version the Virgin is not represented. The obverse of ampulla 11 shows a formalized Crucifixion, the Tree of Life standing for the Cross, with Christ's head only, represented at the top. At either side the crucified thieves' arms are stretched down and outwards, roughly in the position of

87

Christ's arms in the Durham Gospels. On another *125* Monza ampulla, 13, Christ is represented as a full-length figure, robed, with his arms disposed very much as in the Durham Gospels, with the upper arms close to his sides, and his forearms (only) extended at right-angles.[51] Again we can evoke Arculf's narrative of his visit to the Holy Places, transcribed by Adomnán. It seems possible that Arculf could have possessed such a figurative moulded ampulla, and that Adomnán might have seen it. Adomnán could have conveyed some register of its appearance to Northumbria in 686 or 688. Thus the designs of both robed crucifix and Ascension could have been current in Jarrow and Lindisfarne and elsewhere in northern England, as well as on Iona. On the other hand, Adomnán certainly derived gifts, possibly including relics, from Northumbria.[52] The St Gall 51 versions will represent, as I have already suggested, a later Irish interpretation of the same material, and the Turin leaves might mark an independent parallel stage of evolution to St Gall – in the preservation of the Ascension theme more conservative, but in the fuller form of the triumphant Second Coming more distant from the original.

126　　The Crucifixion with a robed Christ with straight arms occurs also in a Würzburg Epistles of St Paul,[53] where large birds perch in the place of the angels, the thieves being represented on subsidiary, perhaps pendant crosses, below the arms of Christ's cross. Flying ascending birds below the cross give the image the effect of 'the sign in the sky'. There is the head and stem of the sponge at the right of Christ's chest, and the lance-head on the left (in the Durham position) but no trace of the wielders of these instruments. Underneath the Crucifixion is a scene with a cross-nimbed Christ in a boat, with other lesser figures, and fish in the water below. The voyages of St Paul, appropriate to the Epistles, seems to be ruled out by the cross-nimbus. This may represent Christ calming the storm, and if so is an interesting juxtaposition of a narrative Gospel-scene and a formal Crucifixion of the Durham Gospels kind. The style is strange, and might be a Continental copy of an Insular picture. At Würzburg Irish materials could accumulate after the enshrinement of the Irish missionary to Bavaria, St Kilian,[54] in 752, if not before.

Related manuscripts

Another manuscript evidently stemming from the same artistic tradition as the three great Gospels is the volume of ecclesiastical law canons in Cologne Cathedral Library, Codex 213.[55] On *f.* 1 the round *127* base and horizontal down-stroke of the initial D goes back ultimately to the Cathach and its kind, but in its bent and slotted form it derives from the indented frames of the Durham Gospels (end of *70* Matthew) and the intrusive frames of the symbol-pages in Echternach. The stepped motif in the *102* middle of the great initial is blown up to a large scale from the panels of step-pattern in the *Quoniam* *97* page in Echternach, while the surrounding interlace is as ambitious as the fine small interlace of Echternach. The running of a small interlace band in a narrow space between larger ones happens in Durrow, on a much bigger scale. Very similar to *3, 11* decorations in the Durham Gospels is the ghostly *77* bird-head appearing at the end of fine black-pointed scroll-work. The hard, square capital letters of *Domino vene-(rando)* are like the fancy capitals of Corpus MS 197B. Spiral scrolls in the top left corner look like an amalgam of the top and bottom of the *In Principio* initial in Corpus MS *92* 197B, where thin lines interlace and go into scrolls at the bottom, and where at the top, quite complex trumpet-spiral motifs and triple loops occur. Corner motifs of key- or fret-patterns with L or inverted T motifs are used as in the Book of *11, 12* Durrow, firmly framed and encased.

　　The big coarse interlaces of the side frames in the lower half of the same page are identical to Durrow's interlace, heavier than the frame round *2* the *Imago hominis* in Echternach or in Echternach's *Quoniam quidem*. But the fantastic layout of the page, *97* with the sudden blocks of letters and the floating-legged rectangle of the O, suggests that the artist was familiar with a design such as that of the Echternach lion page. The two upper side-frames *105* contain birds, one group at the right with no wing-feathers, as in the Durham Gospels, and the other, at the left, with enamelled layered wings like the Corpus MS 197B/Cotton MS Otho C.V birds. Both *91, 95* groups are fantastical, with long, distended, bent and crooked necks. The upper frame contains one intrusive bird – a novelty this – in a queue of Durham Gospels-type flowing long-jawed creatures. The other three kinds of animal in the frame – one very wormy, one more dog- or wolf-like in the head, with multiple Durrow-like ribbon-knots in

127 Opening page, *Collectio canonum*, Cologne, Dombibliothek Cod. 213, *f.* 1. Early eighth century

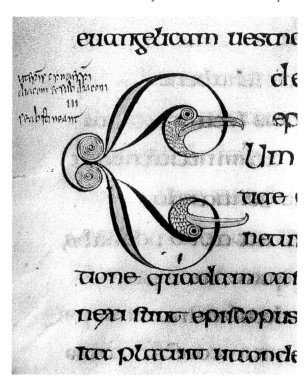

128 Initial E of *Episcopus*, *Collectio canonum*, Cologne, Dombibliothek Cod.213, *f.* 4v. Early eighth century

129 Initial C of *Cum*, *Collectio canonum*, Cologne, Dombibliothek Cod.213, *f.* 36v. Early eighth century

its body, and then the creatures at the bottom,
41 quadrupeds of the Durrow St John carpet-page type but with distended necks, inverted heads, bulging brows and jaws as thin as cords – are all playful variants of the archaic Durrow type. This type does not occur at all in Lindisfarne. Alexander refers the bird-frames to the model of the
137 Lindisfarne Gospels,[56] but the necks of the birds are far longer, agreeing in this respect better with
91, 89 the Corpus MS 197B or Durham birds. Thus the style of the Cologne canons has Durrow elements, and seems contemporary in handling to, or only a little later than, Corpus MS 197B, Echternach and
128 Durham. The letter E of *Episcopus* on another page of the canons has a trumpet-vent on the far side of the letter, developing the vent-form on the *Et valde*
90 initial in Durham, and the identical form on top of
100 the *Liber* initial in Echternach. The E of *Liber* in Echternach is very similar to the canons' E in outline. Long trailers bearing large scrolls rise from the angular corners of the letters as in the *Cata*
95 *Marcum* initial from Cotton MS Otho C.V. Two bird-heads peck at the strand that they grow from
129 in the canons' initial C of *Cum praeterito*. This initial has much in common with the Luke Annunciation
76 initial in the Durham Gospels.

The same delicate scrolls, lifting up high above the broad terminals of a letter, appear in the Freiburg Gospels, in the *argumentum* to Luke, 72 arranged, as we saw, as a cross-shaped area of text with the corners reserved for delicate step-patterns of dots. The use of background patterns resembles the Cologne canons. The framed text, and indents, and quite elaborate ornament applied to a mere *argumentum*, suggest that the Gospels from which this small portion alone survives may have been extremely splendid and ambitious in design.

The Gospels in Trier itself, Codex 61 in the Cathedral Treasury, has a four Evangelist cross- 130 page, related to the Echternach Gospel symbols but freely adapted or perhaps based on a lost Echternach preface. It would be very easy to confuse the *Liber Generationis* in the Trier Gospels with the equivalent initial in the Echternach Gospels. The other related Gospel-book, formerly at Schloss Harburg, has a carpet-page before St 131 John's Gospel containing a cross filled with diagonal fret-patterns. Diagonal fret is the favourite pattern of the artist of the Lichfield Gospels. The strong patches of ornament in the quadrants, and the angular turns of the outlines, are like the ornaments on the Echternach lion symbol page; 105

90

109 the fold-back of the outline, a key-pattern motif, is paralleled in the frame of the Corpus MS 197B eagle page.

The historical context: the role of Egbert, *Pontifex Dilectus*

The Durham Gospels provides internal evidence of its early history. Personal names inscribed at several places in it show that it belonged in the tenth century to the community of St Cuthbert at Chester-le-Street in Northumbria.[57] It was then already bound up with a portion of St Luke's Gospel, quite extra, written in the distinct uncial script practised in the combined monastery of Jarrow-Wearmouth (founded 674/681), most nota-

73 bly in the great Vulgate Bible, the *Codex Amiatinus*. The Northumbrian context of the Durham Gospels is supported by the opinion expressed by Julian Brown and Christopher Verey, that a series of corrections in the Lindisfarne Gospels (not to the

131 Cross carpet-page, Gospel-book formerly at Schloss Harburg, *f.* 126v. Early eighth century

130 Four Evangelist symbols cross-page, the Trier Gospels, *f.* 1v. Early eighth century

Gospel-texts themselves but to liturgical additions) are by the same hand as more general corrections in the Durham Gospels.[58] Evidently a contemporary scholar who worked over the text of the Durham Gospels also had access to the official Gospels of St Cuthbert's community at Lindisfarne. This may mean that a single scriptorium produced both books, or that scholars and scribes moved around a number of centres, for example within the confederation of St Columba, narrowly or broadly defined; or that books moved around for critical appraisal of their texts.[59]

Corpus MS 197B came to Corpus Christi College, Cambridge, from Matthew Parker, Queen Elizabeth's Archbishop of Canterbury.[60] It is unlikely that he obtained the book in Durham, although Sir Robert Cotton later owned the other

94 half of the partitioned Gospels, and also owned the Lindisfarne Gospels, which is recorded in the medieval library catalogue of Durham. How and when Cotton obtained the Lindisfarne Gospels is not known.[61] But the Corpus portion of the partitioned Gospels was available to Parker before the last quarter of the sixteenth century, and the

96 Royal MS into which the fragmentary canon-tables are bound is an eleventh-century copy of Aelfric's *Homilies* that formerly belonged to Cardinal Wolsey, who died in 1530.[62] So the Gospel-book was evidently already split into various parts in the early sixteenth century. Cotton obtained the eighth-century illustrated Psalter now known as

132 the Vespasian Psalter from Sir William Cecil's collection. It is recorded in an inventory drawn up at St Augustine's, Canterbury, in the late Middle Ages as a revered treasure of that house, kept on the High Altar.[63] Parker owned an illustrated sixth-

173 century Italian Gospel-book[64] which, although less certainly a treasure of St Augustine's monastery, is exactly the right kind of book to have come to St Augustine's through the good offices of Hadrian and Archbishop Theodore in the late seventh century, if not by a gift from Pope Gregory directly to St Augustine himself around 600. One of

109 Matthew Parker's clerks inscribed the eagle page of Corpus MS 197B with the words: 'This book was sent by Pope Gregory to Archbishop Augustine.'[65] Such was Matthew Parker's opinion of it, as a traditional treasure of St Augustine's Abbey. The late seventeenth-century catalogue of the Cotton Library says of MS Otho C.V: 'It is said that this was once the book of St Augustine, Apostle of the English, but I cannot confirm this. Perhaps a folio has been cut out, in which this tradition was stated.'[66] This may be independent evidence, or somehow link with Parker's opinion about his half of the book.

A Canterbury provenance/ownership for Corpus MS 197B and Cotton MS Otho C.V might be consistent with, and relate to, the time of energetic book-making in the north of England about which Bede tells us. On Bede's evidence we can conclude that in the years leading up to 716, scribes and artists at Jarrow-Wearmouth not only undertook the task of making the *Codex Amiatinus*, the great Vulgate Bible destined for presentation to Pope Constantine or Pope Gregory II, but also worked on two other Bibles on the same grand scale.[67] The fact that Jarrow-Wearmouth was able to undertake multiple production of this ambitious

kind makes it not unreasonable to suppose that around this time another scriptorium, or other cooperating scriptoria, could have tackled multiple production of Gospel-books. As for the purpose and destination of these multiple copies, we have the evidence of the foreign provenance, perhaps as the result of a deliberate gift at the time of its making, of one of our closely associated Gospel-books, namely the Echternach Gospels. Some of the decorative formulae of these Gospel-books are *77, 89,* exactly reflected in the Vespasian Psalter, a *92, 132* Canterbury product of the early eighth century. A Gospel-book of this type may therefore have been actually present at Canterbury.

The Echternach Gospels[68] has the same fifteenth-century table of contents that is found in other books brought from Echternach to Paris around 1802, with the secularization of the monastery in the French Revolution. Echternach was founded by Willibrord in 698. The Echternach Gospels contains a colophon (*f.* 222v) which states that the Gospel-text was revised in 558 from an exemplar written by the priest Eugippius (who was abbot of a monastery near Naples). This colophon was evidently reproduced by the scribe from the Gospel-text that he was copying. It proves that Insular Gospel-books were constructed on the basis of older Continental models. In the same way the Lindisfarne Gospels contains lists of rubrics for liturgical feasts, including the exotic St Januarius of Naples, which clearly derive from a Naples Gospel-book. The Echternach Gospels does not share Lindisfarne's Naples rubrics.

Lindisfarne may have owed its knowledge of the Naples feasts to Jarrow. Bede's *Homilies*, a sequence of sermons for use throughout the Christian year, follow the order of the liturgical feasts of Naples.[69] Naples influence could, of course, have spread anywhere that Archbishop Theodore and his companion Hadrian went: Hadrian was formerly an abbot in Naples.[70] Benedict Biscop, the founder of Jarrow, was for a long time a colleague of Theodore and Hadrian as abbot of St Augustine's, Canterbury. Theodore went in person to Northumbria: he dedicated the church at Lindisfarne, probably in 678. A courteous exchange of books could well have taken place on such an occasion. To revert to the question of the early provenance of Corpus MS 197B, perhaps the inscription on the eagle page should have said '. . . given' by Bishop Eata to Archbishop Theodore'.[71]

The Willibrord connection is even more

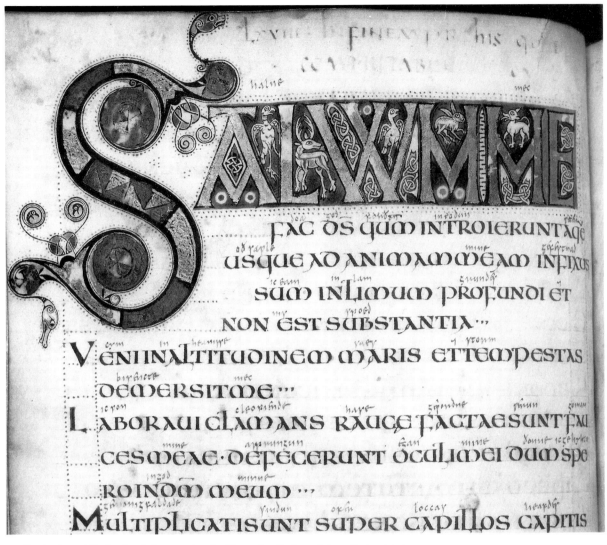

132 Beginning of Psalm 68, *Salvum me fac*, the Vespasian Psalter, *f.* 64v. Early eighth century

suggestive for the Echternach Gospels than speculation as to how Theodore/Hadrian material could have reached the north of England. Willibrord, eventual founder of Echternach, was himself interested in Northumbria, and was a keen exponent of the cult of St Oswald.[72] He went to Ireland after an initial period in Wilfrid's monastery at Ripon (showing the mobility of men and monks in the second half of the seventh century).[73] He owned a miracle-working relic of St Oswald which may have come from Lindisfarne's graveyard when Colman left, or may have come from Lindsey, the province where Oswald's body was interred, with Hygebald, an abbot there. Hygebald visited Egbert in Ireland and spoke with him about the holy death

of Egbert's former companion, Chad, Bishop of Lichfield, who died in 669.[74] Willibrord was one of Egbert's disciples. Egbert is in Bede's mind at the very start of his account of the Columban mission to Northumbria, because he knew that Egbert would in due course draw the schism to an end in 716, by bringing Iona into conformity in the calculation of Easter; and so he anticipates, and introduces Egbert's name into the *Ecclesiastical History* at an early stage,[75] marking Egbert's vital importance in the international arena of Insular Christianity.

Egbert was twenty-five in 664, the year of the Synod of Whitby. He lived among the Irish and among the Picts, a pilgrim (*peregrinus*) in self-imposed exile for the sake of spiritual gain. About the time when Theodore died, in 690, and Berthwald succeeded him as Archbishop of Canterbury, Egbert was planning[76] to go to convert pagan Germans in Frisia, or alternatively, he intended to go to Rome, to worship at the shrines of the Apostles, and presumably to interest the Pope in the proposed missionary activity. Instead of going to Frisia himself, he sent a monk, Wihtbert.[77] Judging from this man's name, Egbert had English disciples at his disposal. He could evidently draw on the personnel and successors of the strong Anglo-Saxon contingent which left Lindisfarne with Colman and settled eventually in *256* the monastery of Mayo in Ireland. Mayo was known to Bede, writing *c.* 730, as a great monastery, austere but Roman in its orders and customs, still wholly English in its personnel.[78] Letters written by Alcuin at the end of the eighth century witness to the reputation for learning of the Mayo community, and its active Continental contacts. N. K. Chadwick sees Egbert as intimately concerned with the early days of Mayo.[79]

Wihtbert was unsuccessful in his mission and returned to Ireland. Egbert then charged twelve disciples, including Willibrord and White Hewald and Black Hewald, with the task of preaching the word in Frisia. As Bede notes, this missionary-band consisted of Englishmen, priests who had long lived in Ireland for the sake of their eternal fatherland.[80] Egbert himself, however, was guided by a dream-vision – a message from the dead Boisil, Cuthbert's former master, Prior of Melrose (Lindisfarne's sister house in inland Northumbria, *133* on an island-like site on the River Tweed) – which urged him to go to instruct Columba's monasteries, for 'they were cutting a crooked furrow'.[81] This story ties in well with the activities of Adomnán, who had himself resolved to follow Roman practices as a result of his expeditions to Northumbria, but who failed to convert the community in Iona and its dependencies to the reform. It cannot be a coincidence that the Pictish King Nechtan, son of Derile, was negotiating with Jarrow for assistance in the reform of the Pictish Church to Roman practices, *c.* 710.[82] In Cuthbert's time, Melrose had contacts with the Picts.[83] Bede says that Egbert brought blessings to the Picts, among whom he lived.[84] Kirby sees Egbert as instrumental in bringing about the Romanization of the Pictish Church.[85] In 716 Egbert succeeded where Adomnán had failed, and persuaded the Iona

monks to accept the Roman Easter. The adoption of the Roman tonsure followed between 716 and 718.[86] This unification of Iona with Northumbria and Pictland in its customs and orders may have increased, not decreased, the potency of the cult of St Columba. Adomnán represents Columba as foretelling the troubles which the division in customs of the western Churches would entail.[87] Adomnán was at pains to aggrandize St Columba as a saint of universal validity, as a prophet as well as an apostle, and as one whose merits were famous in Rome. There was nothing parochial about St Columba in the first half of the eighth century. Although he modified the former rules of the Iona community, Egbert was so devoted to the cult of the saint that he remained on Iona until his death in 729.[88]

Bede's information about Egbert is impressive and explicit. Bede evidently saw him as a key figure in major changes and unifications in Insular religion, stretching out with Continental missions at the same time as making Iona truly Catholic. Egbert's international career is significant for the arts. As a worker for and among the Picts around 700, he will have been familiar with their lively visual conventions. Egbert was the most powerful man in Iona for thirteen years and more.[89] In Ireland, he was sought out by important visitors from England, such as Hygebald of Lindsey, already mentioned. He prepared by political contacts abroad and financial resources at home a highly effective mission from Ireland to the Low Countries and the Rhineland, vigorously manned by able English, Irish-trained priests and missionaries. His disciple Willibrord became Archbishop of Utrecht with the cooperation of the Franks and the papacy.[90] The books and other liturgical gear of these priests and missionaries (such as the Hewalds' portable altar, mentioned by Bede) will not have been a matter of afterthought. Willibrord founded Echternach in 698, two years after his consecration as archbishop. The Echternach Gospels comes from that foundation, but was not necessarily written there. The Continental mission must have been equipped for its important role by its intelligent, well-connected manager.

The coincidence of the date of Echternach's foundation, 698, with the date of the elevation of St Cuthbert, his enshrinement, led Julian Brown to the reasonable suggestion that the Lindisfarne community prepared the Lindisfarne Gospels for that occasion for their own house, and, as an act of

133 View of the site of the monastery at Old Melrose, in a loop of the River Tweed with the Eildon Hills in the background

public relations, at the same time prepared the Echternach Gospels as a gift for Echternach.[91] The style of Echternach is the style of Corpus MS 197B and the Durham Gospels. But as we saw, the main corrector of the Durham Gospels' text is identified by Brown and Verey as a minor corrector of the Lindisfarne Gospels; so one man had access to both. Beyond this, the recorded connections of Echternach to Lindisfarne are not particularly impressive. Bede's *Life of St Cuthbert* contains a posthumous miracle of the saint, *c.* 700, where the beneficiary is a priest belonging to Willibrord's entourage who comes from abroad and stays for a few days as a guest at Lindisfarne.[92] He falls ill, but is cured by intercession at the new tomb of Cuthbert. 'A few days later when he was fully himself again he set off on his intended journey' – not, obviously, to Lindisfarne; so where was he going? To Melrose, linked by hints in Bede to Iona and Pictland? To Iona itself, or to visit Egbert, either in Ireland or on Iona? The connection with Lindisfarne which emerges from the story is only incidental, although the cured illness redounded to the reputation of St Cuthbert. In the Low Countries Willibrord remained, on Bede's evidence, a devotee of St Oswald as we have seen; the followers of St Columba believed that Oswald himself had acknowledged the power and sanctity of St Columba as his patron and guardian.

The Echternach Gospels shows expertise and conventions that are evident also in the Durham Gospels and Corpus MS 197B. A Gospels in Willibrord's hands seems most likely to derive from the milieu of Egbert; it is in the context of Egbert's activities, battling on, until 718, for the acceptance of the Roman tonsure on Iona, that the rare and peculiar feature of the Roman-tonsured *Imago hominis* of the Echternach Gospels makes *102* sense. It is in the context of Egbert's activities in Pictland that we can understand a most interesting element in the design of the Echternach and Corpus Gospels, namely the largely unadulterated Pictish character of their calf and eagle symbols. Pictish elements are probably already evident in Durrow's

134 The text of *De Abbatibus* referring to Eadfrith and Egbert, Cambridge University Library MS Ff.1.27, *f.* 205. Twelfth century

traditional Pictish animal art was a strong and direct source of inspiration to him,[93] with nothing but his own artistic selectivity preventing pure Pictish forms from appearing in his pages.

The Cologne volume of canons parallels the *127* Echternach Gospels in having a generally assumed origin in Northumbria, and in being overseas in the eighth century. It belonged to Cologne at an early date. Its presence in north-west Germany may connect with the Frisian mission. Bishop Swithberht, one of the Englishmen from Ireland on the mission, was later established at a monastery at Kaiserwerth,[94] seven miles north of Düsseldorf. Bede reports that after their martyrdom the two Hewalds were enshrined with much splendour in the church of the city of Cologne, perhaps in the original church on the site of the present cathedral.

It is apparent that a number of trained scribes were in Willibrord's entourage or secretariat. Why would Willibrord's mission depend particularly on Lindisfarne for a model Gospel-book? A larger monastic confederation, even one not exclusively of Northumbrian houses – a confederation of scriptoria, with itinerant scribes and correctors sharing and manipulating a powerful common tradition – seems a feasible explanation for the many variants and similarities that we see in this particular set of books.[95]

I have referred a number of times to the evidence of the poem *De Abbatibus*. This Northumbrian Latin poem, which was composed by a monk named Aethelwulf between 802 and 821, celebrates a monastic cell belonging to Lindisfarne, founded by a nobleman, Eanmund, in the reign of King Aldfrith's son Osred (705–16).[96] Under pressure from the tyranous King, Eanmund had retired from the world with some companions. He sought advice from Eadfrith, Bishop of Lindisfarne, and *134* also, at much greater length, perhaps at Eadfrith's suggestion, from Egbert in Ireland. He asked Egbert to consecrate and send him an altar.[97] (In this context we remember the Hewalds' portable altar, which could well have been consecrated by Egbert for the use of his missionaries to Frisia.[98]) The portable altar of St Cuthbert is still extant in *135-6* Durham, and it is dedicated to St Peter, as was the altar sent by Egbert to Eanmund.[99] Eanmund also asked Egbert to send him instructions as to where his church should be raised – extraordinary testimony to Egbert's involvement, even though from a distance, in Northumbrian affairs. The appeal to Egbert seems quite likely to have been

symbols, the calf and lion; but the full quality and conventions of Pictish animal art emerge only in these two pages, the calf of Echternach and the eagle of Corpus. We may interpret the Pictish features in the two Gospels as reflecting, although at a distance, a total and coherent Pictish Gospels, a book responding to local secular taste in Pictland, just as Durrow reflects local secular taste in Northumbria. Or else we may suggest that the Pictish features are deliberately presented selectively. If the Echternach eagle does not display the Pictish idiom, it is because of the artist's creative desire for variation. But it is self-evident that also for recruits, coming as it did soon after the time when Willibrord's overseas mission had been furnished by Egbert. Eanmund had endowed a new monastery, and was getting the best people to advise him. The fame of the cell impelled many to enter monastic life. Ultán was one such. He was 'a blessed priest of the Irish race, and he could ornament books with fair marking, and by this art he accordingly made the shape of the letters beautiful one by one, so that no modern scribe could equal him' (*ut nullus possit se aequare modernus scriptor*) – so says the ninth-century poet, looking back to events of the early eighth century.[100] It is reasonable to assume that this remarkable scribe was provided by Egbert to supply splendid sacred texts for the wealthy new house. Thus it again seems possible that Egbert was able to exert influence on elaborate manuscripts, of at least part-Northumbrian provenance.

135 Portable altar of St Cuthbert. Second half of seventh century

136 Portable altar of St Cuthbert, from C. W. Battiscombe, *Relics of St Cuthbert*, 1956

137 Carpet-page, the Lindisfarne Gospels, *f.* 2v

138 *Novum opus* preface, the Lindisfarne Gospels, *f.* 3

4 The Lindisfarne and Lichfield Gospels

Design

The Lindisfarne Gospels, British Library Cotton MS Nero D.IV,[1] contains 258 folios measuring 34 cm by 24 cm. It starts, like the Book of Durrow, *137* with a carpet-page. This features a cross with square terminals, and stands opposite a very brittle and elegant set of ornamental letters, the opening *138* words of the *Novum opus* preface, now raised to the decorative importance of a Gospel *incipit* in *10* Durrow (for example the *Initium* initial to Mark). The cross-design on *f.* 2v recapitulates themes from three Durrow carpet-pages – the eight-part cross *2* with a background of interlace (*f.* 1v), the border *42* with the broad spread of chequers or *tesserae* (*f.* 2) and the neatly displayed rectangular applied *12* ornaments of the Luke carpet-page (*f.* 125v). In Lindisfarne, the background to the cross is very finely drawn, with shifts of colour from block to block of interlace. The six-part cross is filled with the sideways-set maze- or *tesserae*-pattern. Four rectangular ornaments stand in the four corners of the design: two square, like abstracts of angels over the arms of the cross, and two, long uprights, like figures in attendance on Christ Crucified. These rectangular ornaments are filled with step-patterns, organized in diamond-shaped radiating compartments. A new motif, not even tentatively suggested by Durrow, is the outer border of birds queuing in a compressed space. Beast-heads – small complacent-looking dog-heads – rest their chins on the four corners, and crests or lappets spring back from their brows to enclose a small area of thick interlace, forming the finial at the corner of the page. There is in this motif a connection with the creatures resting their chins, and skirting the sides of the letter with their mane-like lappets, at the top

139 *Plures fuisse* preface, the Lindisfarne Gospels, *f.* 5v

140 Canon-table, Canon X, the Lindisfarne Gospels, *f.* 17v

141 Canon-table, Canon IV, *Codex Amiatinus, f.* 799. *c.* 700

83 of the *In Principio* initial in the Durham Gospels. The strangeness and sense of spontaneity of design notable in the Durham Gospels is not apparent in Lindisfarne; the effect here is slightly synthetic, exquisitely refined though the techniques of drawing and painting are. The balance maintained between all the motifs in Lindisfarne is absolute; the formulae are all spun out on a delicate scale, one motif giving way to another in a series of elegant, poised, rather constrained permutations.

The *Novum opus* opening is written in ornamental letters which, for all the beast- or bird-head flourishes, scrolls, and interlaces, are stately and *163* clear-cut like a classical inscription, such as Jarrow in these years was bent on imitating.[2] *Novum opus* is *139* followed by the serpentine initials of *Plures fuisse*, a Gospel preface derived from a general introduction to St Matthew's Gospel attributed to St Jerome;

and then comes another example of the scribe-artist's tendency to solidify his letters on the page by background dotting – a preface consisting of Eusebius of Caesarea's own explanation of the canon-tables in a letter addressed to Carpianus, used as a preface also in the sixth-century Greek Rossano Gospels. Lindisfarne has, therefore, a different, more elaborate, system of prefaces than that which we have met hitherto in Insular Gospels.[3]

The canon-tables occupy *ff.* 10–17v; they use a *140, 142* consistent system of lists of numbers between architectural columns, supporting a minor arch over each column and a giant arch over the whole series of columns on the page. The architectural members are flattened and filled with interlace and other ornaments, including in Canon X diagonal fret, a motif very popular with the designer of the

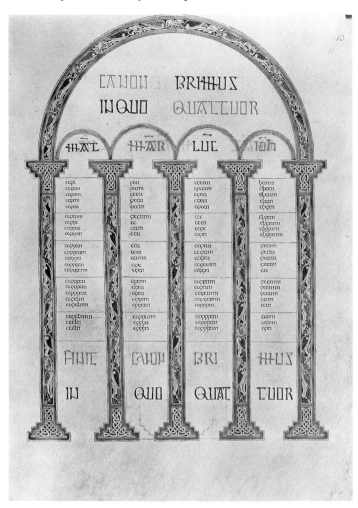

142 Canon-table, Canon I, the Lindisfarne Gospels, *f.* 11

143 Persian bird-textile, *c.* 600, in a relief-sculpture from Takibostan, after O. von Falke, *Kunstgeschichte der Seidenweberei*

somewhat later Lichfield Gospels. The model for Lindisfarne's canon-tables was an Italian or Byzantine one; Jarrow's magisterial version of the
141 Vulgate, the *Codex Amiatinus*,[4] was copied in part or as a whole from an Italian model or models, and its canon-tables are formal and architectural in much the same fashion. In Lindisfarne the chains of
142 birds walking up the arch and columns in Canon I are perhaps adapted from bird-decorated canon-tables and arches in Eastern Christian Gospels, such as the Syrian Rabbula Gospels of 586, reflected later in the tenth-century Armenian Etchmiadzin Gospels.[5] Syrian and Persian textiles with bird-processions are a possible alternative source of inspiration. The appearance of such
143 textiles is known from relief-sculptured reproductions in the monument of the Persian king Khosros II, erected *c.* 600 in a grotto at Takibostan.

144 Beginning of *argumentum* to St Matthew, the Lindisfarne Gospels, *f.* 18v

After the canon-tables comes a list of liturgical feasts, another new element. The inclusion of Neapolitan saints in this list suggests that this and other features of Lindisfarne were imitated from an admired south Italian exemplar.[6] Next comes the *argumentum* to Matthew, featuring an initial quite close in spirit to the Durham Gospels or Cotton MS Otho C.V (compare the *Marcus argumentum* of Durham); and following this, the *capitula* to Matthew – an inversion of the order followed in Durrow, where the *capitula* comes first. The *capitula* starts *Generationum*, on *f.* 19, in its text different from Durrow, which starts *Nativitas*. Whereas Durrow uses the 'Old Latin' prefaces, the prefaces in Lindisfarne are those regularly associated with the Vulgate Gospels. Lindisfarne's Gospel-texts represent the Vulgate in a very pure and authentic form.

Lindisfarne, like Echternach, is written *per cola et commata*, with two columns to the page, except for the great initial pages. St Matthew is represented on *f.* 25v along with his symbol, an angel sounding a trumpet, and also accompanied by a mysterious grey-haired man who looks in from behind a curtain. A second carpet-page on *f.* 26v features vase-shaped arms extending from a central disc. The cross-motif of this page is set off against a mesh of animals.

Lindisfarne's animal ornament shows two discrepant tendencies – on the one hand detailed specific description of the beasts or birds involved, and on the other, maximum abstract pattern-making, so that the animals' haunches and limbs obey the flow-chart of a trumpet-spiral or the swathing and blending of strands of interlace. Birds and long-bodied beasts are woven together into

102

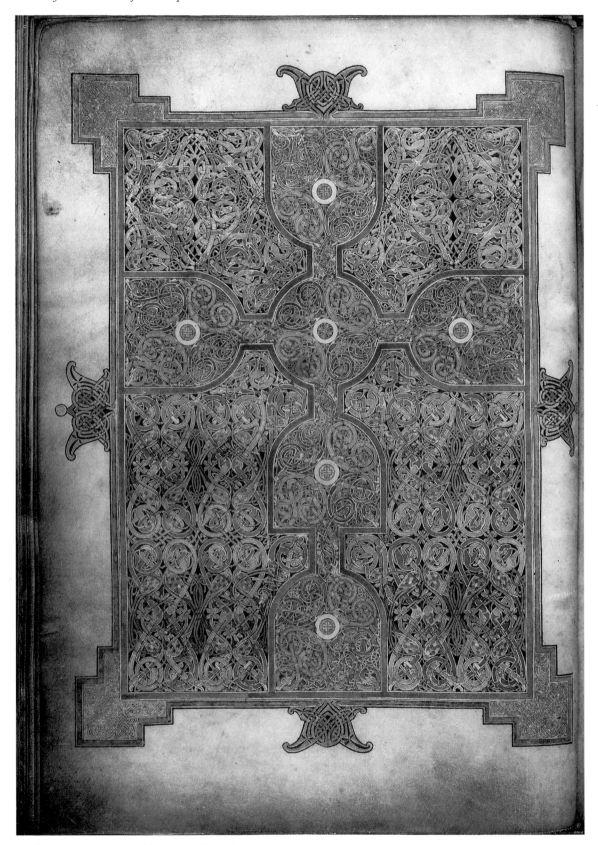

145 Cross carpet-page, the Lindisfarne Gospels, *f.* 26v

146 Beginning of St Matthew's Gospel, *Liber Generationis*, the Lindisfarne Gospels, *f.* 27

ornamental patterns, the birds being the winged
92 birds of the *In Principio* initial in Corpus MS 197B,
and the beasts, slim curvaceous quadrupeds, in
movement like the animals in Corpus MS 197B but
in their faces not dragonish but like dogs, and also
with padded feet and claws, not tendrils or flippers.
It is diagnostic that Corpus MS 197B keeps its birds
and beasts in quite separate compartments. The
very first symptom in that particular workshop of
the mixing of motifs is the one bird that we noted

set in among the swimming creatures on the top 127
frame of the Cologne canons.

Opposite the carpet-page (on *f.* 27) is the grand
opening of St Matthew's Gospel, *Liber Generationis*, 146
followed on *f.* 29 by the inflated *Christi autem* initial 147
of Matthew 1, 18. There is no emphasis on the
Baptism or Temptation of Christ at that section of
Matthew's text (*f.* 32v). We find a very slightly
larger verse-opening at the beginning of the
Passion narrative, *Et factum est*, Matthew 26, 1, but

104

147 *Christi autem* initials, the Lindisfarne Gospels, *f.* 29

no visual emphasis is given to verse 30, *Et hymno dicto*, and the account of the Crucifixion is also without any emphasis, for example at the words *Tunc crucifixerant* (*f*. 86v). *Vespere* (*f*. 88), the beginning of the Resurrection narrative at Matthew 28, 1, on the other hand, is given a larger initial.

The close of St Matthew's Gospel (*f*. 89v) is followed by the *argumentum* to Mark (*f*. 90); this is again a massively blocked-in minor initial. The *capitula* to Mark follows on *f*. 91, the portrait of St Mark accompanied by his lion symbol on *f*. 93v, and then a carpet-page, *f*. 94v, featuring a central disc motif, like Durrow's St John carpet-page, framed, but linked to other portions of the design by interlace, as on the Durrow St Mark carpet-page. Lindisfarne makes out of the coloured interlaces beyond the central disc a short-armed cross, with steep diagonal spread. Its proportions are like those of the seventh-century south English Wilton pendant cross,[7] not at all like St Cuthbert's

169
148
41
11
149, 174

148 (*left*) Carpet-page, the Lindisfarne Gospels, *f.* 94v

149 (*above*) Gold and garnet pendant cross, Wilton, Norfolk. Seventh century

152 own pectoral cross. The *Initium* initial on *f.* 95 has interlacing strands of dots, making linear meshes or forming grotesquely proportioned prancing animals. They are as if traced with a punch on metal. The interlacing strands of dots which ornament the
150 Pictish bowl 7 in the St Ninian's Isle Treasure are
151 very similar, as also is the zig-zag pattern on bowl 6.[8] The *Initium* initial has a stiff double right-angled bar between the main upright stems, like the *In*
92 *Principio* initial in Corpus MS 197B, but the two

pairs of decorated uprights in Corpus MS 197B stand apart, with a bare vellum gap between, whereas this gap has vanished in Lindisfarne; the two vertical portions of the bar are clamped together, exactly as the broad terminals of a true penannular brooch have in the Tara Brooch 153, 154 become bridged and welded together.[9]

Fuit Iohannes in deserto is given a large initial on *f.* 95v, on the reverse of Mark's *Initium*. There is no textual emphasis on the Passion or Resurrection

106

150 Silver bowl 7 from St Ninian's Isle, Shetland. Eighth century

151 Silver bowl 6 from St Ninian's Isle, Shetland. Eighth century

152 (*right*) Beginning of St Mark's Gospel, *Initium*, the Lindisfarne Gospels, *f*. 95

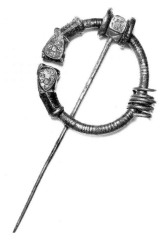

153 Bronze and *millefiori* penannular brooch, from Ballinderry, Co. Offaly. Early seventh century

154 The so-called Tara Brooch, from Bettystown, Co. Meath. Gilt-bronze, gold, silver, glass and amber. *c*. 700

155 *Argumentum* to St Luke, the Lindisfarne Gospels, *f.* 131

156 Carpet-page, the Lindisfarne Gospels, *f.* 138v

narratives. Mark ends on *f.* 130, and a second list of liturgical feasts intervenes. The *argumentum* to Luke on *f.* 131 displays an L of the same scale as Echternach's main *Liber Generationis* initial. The *capitula* of Luke run from *f.* 131v to *f.* 136. The portrait of St Luke with his bull or calf is on *f.* 137v, followed, after a blank recto, by a carpet-pattern on *f.* 138v.[10] This displays rectangular panels floating against a differently ornamented background, in a manner reminiscent of the St Luke carpet-page in Durrow. The *Quoniam* initial on *f.* 139 solidifies the Q and the field to the left of it, and employs dotting to outline the letters NIAM, much as the animal-bodies are created by dots in their background on St Ninian's Isle bowl 2.[11] Interlace made of dotted lines as in the bottom-left corner of Lindisfarne's *Quoniam* page, next to (*ordina*) *re narrationem*, is employed on the base of bowl 4. The motif of the cat having swallowed the birds introduces an

element of humour not met with before in Insular art. The *Fuit in diebus Herodis* initial of Luke 1, 5 is the largest internal initial in the whole Gospel-book other than the *Christi autem*, the second beginning to St Matthew's Gospel; St John the Baptist is thus signalled both in Mark and Luke. On *f.* 148, after the Lucan Genealogy of Christ, there is a fair-sized *Iesus autem plenus spirito sancto* at the start of Chapter 4, which provides a first hint of the ostentatious treatment of that text which we shall meet in the Book of Kells. The *argumentum* to St John on *f.* 203, the *capitula* on *f.* 204, and the table of feast days on *f.* 208, all display initials drawn and proportioned like the lesser initials in the Durham Gospels. St John's portrait and symbolic eagle are on *f.* 209v, with a carpet-pattern on *f.* 210v; this again features rigid vertical and horizontal forms floating on a restless background.

The carpet-pages of Lindisfarne have been

108

likened to antique mosaic floor-patterns, and however indirect the historical connection may be between such culturally remote artistic monuments, the comparison seems justified by the truly classical constraint which the Lindisfarne carpet-pages display, especially that on *f.* 210v.[12] This 'classicism' marks a transient moment in the development of Insular art. A balanced selection of the different available motifs is made by the scribe-illuminator, in cooperation with, perhaps in obedience to, the tenets of fine metalwork. The so-called Tara Brooch marks the same stage in the history of Insular design.[13] Beast- and bird-heads and fish-tails lift off the minute perimeter of the Brooch just as do heads in Lindisfarne. The most striking similarity lies in the balanced juxtaposition of the various motifs.

154

The *In Principio* initial on *f.* 211 makes use, as do all the great vertical initials in Lindisfarne, of staring-eyed, mask-like groups of trumpet-spirals, fixed at the top and bottom of elaborately segmented multi-coloured interlace stems. The *In Principio* initial of Lindisfarne resembles that of Durrow, Durrow's most splendid initial, in planting the wedge-shaped descending base of the I into a swarm of symmetrically arranged spirals.

160

32

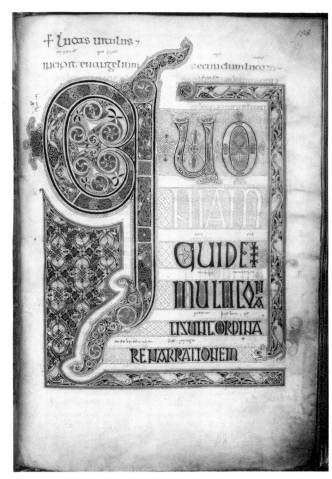

157 Beginning of St Luke's Gospel, *Quoniam quidem*, the Lindisfarne Gospels, *f.* 139

158 Silver bowl 2 from St Ninian's Isle, Shetland. Eighth century

159 Carpet-page, the Lindisfarne Gospels, *f.* 210v

160 Beginning of St John's Gospel, *In Principio*, the Lindisfarne Gospels, *f.* 211

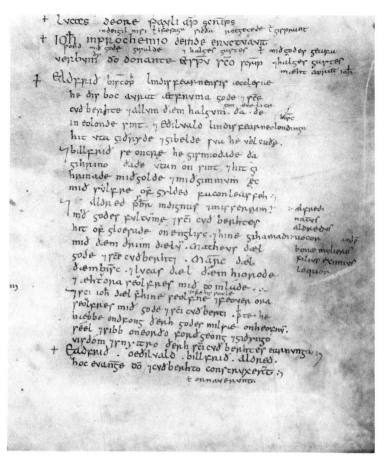

161 Provost Aldred's colophon, the Lindisfarne Gospels, *f. 259*

'Eadfrith Bishop of the Lindisfarne church originally wrote this book for God and for St Cuthbert and jointly for all the saints whose relics are in the island.' Neither Cuthbert's body nor the relics of Oswald and Aidan were any longer on Lindisfarne Island in 970; but in the 700s they *were* still there; so this information has a seventh-or-eighth-century ring to it. 'And Ethelwald Bishop of the Lindisfarne Islanders impressed it on the outside and covered it as he well knew how to do. And Billfrith, the anchorite, forged the ornaments which are on the outside, and adorned it with gold and gems and gilt-silver, pure metal. And I, Aldred, unworthy and most miserable priest, glossed it in English between the lines.'

Why did this information need to be recorded on the last leaf? It may have been oral tradition up to that time, not inscribed anywhere. But the phrase 'are in the island' suggests that an older written record was being transcribed and added to. Was the inscription on the original binding, and did the addition of the gold ornaments (tenth- and eleventh-century Ireland saw much enshrining of older material) cover up an inscription recording the work of the two early eighth-century (or perhaps even late seventh-century) participants, Eadfrith and Ethelwald? On the other hand Billfrith 'the anchorite' has a religious profession very much part of the original scene. In Ethelwald's time as Abbot of Melrose the anchorite Dryhthelm (of the vision of Purgatory fame) flourished; and Bede's informant about Dryhthelm, Haemgisl, was afterwards a hermit in Ireland. St Cuthbert was himself a hermit, and maintained a spiritual relationship with other hermits in his lifetime.

The Gospels were written 'for God and St Cuthbert', not for the church of Lindisfarne, or for St Peter, to whom the church was dedicated. This could mean that it was written literally for him, before his death in 687, or in specific celebration of his cult, inaugurated officially with his elevation in 698, although the evidence of Bede's prose *Life* points to Cuthbert's supposition – perhaps edited into the *Life* – that pilgrims would flock to his grave;[15] we also hear that preparations were in train before 698 for the accommodation and display of the relics. The cult, centred on Lindisfarne, then on Chester-le-Street, and finally on Durham, flourished without a break until the end of the Middle Ages.[16]

Cuthbert entered monastic life as a youth in 651,

Provenance and date

We shall now consider where and when the Lindisfarne Gospels were made. The book contains 161 a colophon on its last leaf (*f. 259*), not, like the 162 colophons of Durrow or Echternach, simply copied from older exemplars. The Lindisfarne colophon was written by the author of the 'Old English' translation added between the lines of the original Latin text. He was Aldred, Provost of Chester-le-Street, the place where the community of St Cuthbert was stationed between 883 and 995, before moving to Durham.[14] The colophon mentions four participants in the physical fabric of the Gospels, the last being Aldred himself. Thus the information that the book contains was recorded later (*c.* 970) than the information recorded on the *cumtach* of the Durrow Gospels relating that book to St Columba. Some of the information, however, sounds older than 970.

soon after Bishop Aidan's death, while Boisil was prior of Melrose and Eata was abbot. Cuthbert presumably came from further north or further west. He was already a devout Christian before entering religion, although recalcitrant pagan peasants feature in one of the first stories told in his *Life*.[17] In spite of a vision of angels carrying Aidan's soul up to heaven – after the vision he was soon to hear, while travelling, the news that Aidan had died – Cuthbert did not proceed to Lindisfarne but presented himself at Melrose, inland, to the north-west of Lindisfarne.[18] Boisil had evidently a powerful reputation for sanctity, both then and posthumously – witness his appearance in a vision, as messenger of Christ, to a companion of Egbert in Ireland, *c.* 690. The Melrose community was called upon, *c.* 660, to man the new royal foundation at Ripon, established by Oswy's son Alchfrith, with Eata as abbot – Eata was a protegé of Aidan – and Cuthbert as guest-master.[19] But then Alchfrith fell under the persuasions of Wilfrid to become a champion of the Roman party; and around the time of decisions at the Synod of Whitby the Melrose contingent at Ripon resigned, and Wilfrid began his work at Ripon which transformed it into a major Roman centre with stone buildings, splendid Continental fabrics and furniture, a golden Gospels, and eventually, Wilfrid's own tomb and epitaph.[20]

Neither Eata nor Cuthbert, however, made any moves to leave Northumbria. Their conciliating presence is a continuing factor in the post-Synod, post-Wilfrid settlement of the Church in Bernicia. King Egfrith, Oswy's successor, quarrelled with Bishop Wilfrid of York and drove him into exile.[21] Archbishop Theodore now intervened to re-organize the Northumbrian Church. In place of Wilfrid he consecrated Eata in 678 as Bishop in Bernicia, while Bosa was placed in York.[22] Bosa had been taught by Abbess Hild at Whitby, and so was Irish in sentiment. Theodore had evidently to make do with locally trained clergy, but of course these men were ready to conform to Roman practice.[23] Theodore came north again in 680 to consecrate Tunberht as Bishop of Hexham, which signalled the division in two of the Bernician See, Eata obviously offering no resistance.[24] It is interesting to think of all these bishops needing Gospel-books, and the splitting of the Sees would perhaps mean a new show-piece Gospels each time. As bishop, Eata in 678 brought Cuthbert from Melrose to be prior of Lindisfarne.[25] Tunberht, the

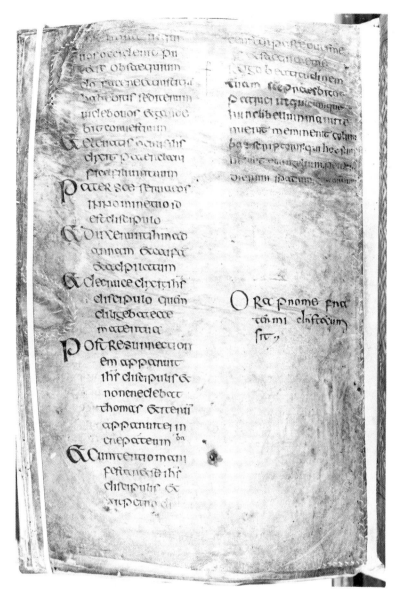

162 *Capitula* to St John's Gospel and colophons, the Book of Durrow, *f.* 247v

bishop of Hexham, had been abbot of Gilling, founded by Oswy in atonement for his murder of King Oswine, Aidan's friend.[26] Tunberht was a kinsman of Ceolfrith, who had left Gilling and gone to Ripon at Wilfrid's invitation;[27] later Ceolfrith transferred again, to Benedict Biscop's monastery at Wearmouth.[28] Tunberht may be the Bishop of Hexham missing from the Jarrow dedication plaque of 684 or 685; the omission from the inscription of a reference to the local bishop may be due to embarrassment at Theodore's deposition of him around that time. Alternatively,

163 Dedication inscription, St Paul's Church, Jarrow. 684/5

Eata would have been the presiding bishop at the dedication service, were he invited.[29] All these appointments and transfers helped to weave together the disparate strands, Roman and Irish, of the Northumbrian Church, on the eve of the consecration as bishop of Cuthbert, the greatest of the Northumbrian saints.

In 680, along with Tunberht, Theodore consecrated Trumwine as Bishop to the Picts, under Egfrith's control. Then, according to Bede, Theodore in 684 called a synod 'of no small size', gathered in the presence of King Egfrith on the River Alne in Northumbria, and deposed Tunberht of Hexham. So he needed a new bishop, and presumably Eata, Bishop of Lindisfarne, suggested Cuthbert. Trumwine of Abercorn was also strongly in favour of Cuthbert, and accompanied *165* King Egfrith personally to persuade him to take episcopal office.[30] As we have seen, during his residence at Melrose Cuthbert visited and worked among the Picts, and Trumwine will have valued him in this connection. In Cuthbert's advancement to episcopal office in 685 the person of Boisil, his old master, is recalled in Bede's *Life*, as having prophetically foreseen (before 664) that Cuthbert

would become a bishop.[31] Cuthbert was consecrated at York by Theodore, but it was agreed that Eata should move to Hexham so that Cuthbert might remain in Lindisfarne. The wheel of Eata's fortunes had come full circle, from being ousted from pre-Wilfrid Ripon, to being placed in control of his stone church at Hexham. In the same year, 685, Egfrith was killed in battle against the Picts. *164* Cuthbert anticipated this disaster, and he also foreknew the likely succession of Egfrith's half-brother Aldfrith, then resident at Iona. Cuthbert, the saint in whose honour the Lindisfarne Gospels was written, was immersed in the political and cultural cross-currents of his time.

Cuthbert died in 687 and was not replaced for a year, Wilfrid having charge of Lindisfarne. Then Theodore intervened again, and consecrated Eadbert Bishop of Lindisfarne in 688. He is called by Bede *vir scientia scripturarum divinarum insignis*[32] – distinguished for his knowledge of holy writ; Theodore's successor Berhtwald, Abbot of Reculver, archbishop of Canterbury from 692, is called very similarly by Bede *vir scientia scripturarum imbutus*,[33] whereas Wihtbert, Egbert's associate, sent as bishop to the Frisians, who failed as a missionary and returned to Ireland as a hermit, was according to Bede *doctrinae scientia insignis*,[34] that is, perhaps, exegete. In those years 688–98, Eadbert of Lindisfarne would have had plenty of opportunity to know the Scriptures in a new way. That was the time of the first large-scale scribal activity and editing of texts of the Bible at nearby Jarrow. Bede quotes from Eadbert's verse-celebration of the miracle of Cuthbert being found incorrupt after eleven years in his grave; the verses show that Eadbert was familiar with the kind of typology – Old Testament images symbolizing the life and Passion of Christ – which was displayed in pictures at Jarrow in the 680s.[35]

Was Eadbert the planner of the Lindisfarne Gospels? Eadbert, Bede tells us, removed Finan's thatch roof from the church at Lindisfarne and covered the walls and roof with sheets of lead. Was that something which Archbishop Theodore could have suggested, or urged, at the time when he dedicated the church of Lindisfarne to St Peter?[36] It seems a likely move in the improvement and fortification of the church as the repository of the relics of St Cuthbert. Eadbert's other reputation with Bede was for his observance of the law, canonical observance in respect of charity. A tenth

164 Battle scene, reverse of a cross-slab at Aberlemno, Angus. Early eighth century

165 King Egfrith urges St Cuthbert to accept the bishopric. Illustration of Bede's prose *Life*, British Library, Add. MS 39943, *f*. 51. *c*. 1200

part of beasts, corn, fruit and clothing on his estates was annually given to the poor.[37] Does that strike a more formal note than Bede's warm references to the spontaneous charities of Aidan and Finan – more like Wilfrid than Aidan? It was with Eadbert's authorization that the translation of St Cuthbert was undertaken. When, on his retreat, not on Farne but at some other remote spot, he was found by the excited monks who reported that the body of St Cuthbert had been found miraculously incorrupt, he spoke of the coffin 'which you have prepared' (*arca quem parastis*), so that object had been manufactured in anticipation of the disinter-

166 (*above left*) Sts Peter and Paul and two other Apostles, detail of the side of St Cuthbert's coffin. 698

167 (*above*) Symbols of St Matthew and St Mark, detail of the lid of St Cuthbert's coffin. 698

168 (*left*) Symbols of St Luke and St John, detail of the lid of St Cuthbert's coffin. 698

169 (*right*) Portrait of St Mark, the Lindisfarne Gospels, *f.* 93 v

ment.[38] The coffin's date is not later than 698, therefore, and perhaps somewhat earlier. The *166-8* classicizing figurative art of the coffin, whether added hastily in 698, which is unlikely, or prepared carefully in advance, is related to that of the *169* Lindisfarne Gospels. The Gospels improves the *179* intelligibility of the coffin Evangelist symbols, as David Wright has suggested,[39] by rationalizing the way the bull and lion hold their books with one hoof or paw placed behind the book. So in that

respect, the Gospels design should be after the coffin. Eadbert died in 698, and was buried in the former grave of St Cuthbert, below the coffin which was elevated on the floor of the church.[40]

Eadfrith succeeded Eadbert as Bishop of Lindisfarne and ruled until 721. Bede addressed his prose *Life of St Cuthbert* to Eadfrith as 'Lord Bishop and holy father'[41] but says nothing at all about him, whereas, as we have seen, he remarks on Eadbert's knowledge of Scripture and his charity, and reports

his speech and panegyric of Cuthbert. Where did Lindisfarne get its bishops after Cuthbert? The control of Canterbury will not have been so strict after Theodore's time, and even he had to make the best of the situation in the north, presumably under royal pressure. Control must have been even more local in the time of Archbishop Berhtwald whom Bede somewhat disparages.[42] Françoise Henry suggested that Eadfrith was the man called Eahfrid to whom Aldhelm wrote in around 690 when Eahfrid had just returned from six years study in Ireland, complaining that the number of English scholars resorting to Ireland was like 'a swarm of bees'.[43] Whoever this Eahfrid was, we may assume that he will have known Egbert and his English companions and followers. We can surmise from Aethelwulf's *De Abbatibus* that it was Eadfrith of Lindisfarne who suggested that Eanmund in seeking guidance and recruits for his new foundation should turn to Egbert. As we saw (p.

134

97), the coming of Ultán is the probable consequence of that: a distinguished scribe, and presumably illuminator. Ultán's work should represent the next generation, *after* Eadfrith, since Eanmund's foundation took place in the reign of Aldfrith's son and successor.

King Aldfrith (685–705) is likely to have taken a close interest in Northumbria's Irish and Ionan connections. In 686 and 688 his friend Adomnán came for political negotiations with the Northumbrian king, and Jarrow entertained him and successfully persuaded him to conform with Roman practice. The whole of Ireland and northern Britain in these years were involved in

171 Portrait of Esdras, the *Codex Amiatinus, f.* V. *c.* 700

170 Portrait of St Matthew, the Lindisfarne Gospels, *f.* 25 v

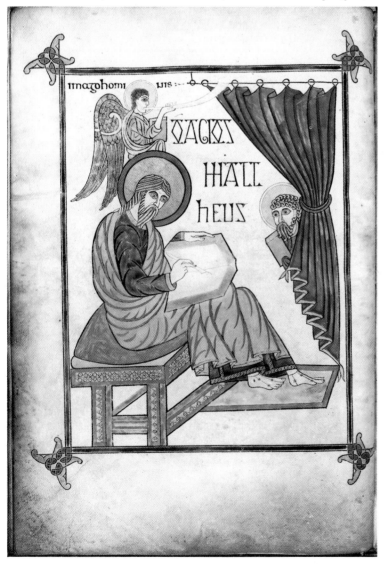

positive moves towards accepting Roman observance. The spiritual message to Egbert, *c.* 690, from Boisil, Cuthbert's mentor, former prior of Melrose, must in some way reflect the general Anglo-Irish situation, and perhaps King Aldfrith had some influence in that matter. On Bede's evidence he was a frequent visitor to Melrose.

According to Prior Aldred's colophon, Eadfrith was the scribe of the Lindisfarne Gospels. A Melrose connection in the completion of the Gospels is certain, in the person of the man who eventually became Eadfrith's successor as Bishop of Lindisfarne, Ethewald. Aldred says that Ethelwald *bound* the Gospels. He was Abbot of Melrose at the time when Dryhthelm had his visions.[44] In his *Life of St Cuthbert* Bede reports a miracle which represents Ethelwald, then a young man, as a member of Cuthbert's entourage as Bishop of Lindisfarne (685–7).[45] It may be that Eadfrith, an older man, also had a Melrose career, directly connected with Boisil, Eata and Cuthbert.

172 Mother and child, sculptured grave-slab from Murrell Hill, Cumberland. Second or third century

173 Portrait of St Luke, with Evangelist symbol and scenes from St Luke's Gospel. St Augustine's Gospels, Corpus MS 286, *f*. 129v. Sixth century

The imagery of the Evangelists

Whatever his specific Insular connections as scribe-illuminator, Eadfrith makes some consistent moves to modify the text and programme of the Insular Gospel-books as we have seen them up to this stage. In the first place, the prefaces which he employs are different ones. Then again the layout of his book, *per cola et commata*, breaks with the tradition of Durrow and Durham, although it does agree with Echternach. Eadfrith's openness to new influence is also seen in the way he accepts lock, stock and barrel from his examplar the lists of Neapolitan feasts inserted before the Gospels. All this may be due to Theodoran pressure of the sort Lindisfarne may have felt in the 680s, or else to the pressure of the monastery of Jarrow which was currently at work on the *Codex Amiatinus*, 171 containing a figure of Esdras/Cassiodorus similar to the image chosen by Eadfrith for his Evangelist 170 Matthew.[46] The Greek *tituli* of the Lindisfarne

Evangelists suggests an interest in Greek quite likely to be Theodoran in origin.[47] Lindisfarne was perhaps aiming at uniformity with Jarrow in outlook – visual and textual, if not scribal. It is just possible that the appearance of the Lindisfarne Evangelists consciously reflects in some way the tastes, attitudes or susceptibilities of St Cuthbert himself. Cuthbert is associated in Bede's *Life* with Romano-British sculpture at Carlisle.[48] In an atmosphere, in Northumbria, of new scriptural editing, centred on the making of the *Codex Amiatinus*, it might be, in order to emphasize the historical reality of the Gospel writers, that new ways of depicting them, anchoring them substantially, were now sought, using as models admired local antiquities, for example the Romano-British Murrell Hill grave-slab in Carlisle.[49] 172 Incidentally, the Murrell Hill slab has the extra interest of showing a seated figure with a winged genius above its head and a pair of large lions, also overhead – the juxtaposition of man and symbol

174 Gold and garnet pectoral cross of St Cuthbert. Seventh century

175 Portrait of St Matthew, Copenhagen Gospels, *f.* 17v. Early eleventh century

found in Lindisfarne. The kind of image that otherwise informs the Lindisfarne Evangelists is the sixth-century Italian St Augustine's Gospels depiction, which is of a writer, not a mystical figure *173* – the composer of a narrative, who presides rationally over the events he records.[50] If St Cuthbert was provided by Theodore with a Gospel-book containing author portraits (as well as with a pectoral cross of Kentish or part-Kentish *174* manufacture),[51] the Lindisfarne Gospels might retain, respectfully, some of the forms of that older southern model. An originally southern model for the figures might explain the much later, Anglo-Saxon south-English manuscript which seems so puzzlingly to echo the Lindisfarne Gospels. Bruce-Mitford has postulated a common model of some kind for the late seventh-century Lindisfarne and the early eleventh-century Copenhagen Gospels.[52] *175* That link would be more understandable if Lindisfarne's model had come from or via a southern-English centre.

The interpretation of Lindisfarne's Matthew page requires an *excursus* into ninth-century Carolingian art, as represented by the prefatory pictures to the Book of Revelation in two great Bibles, the Moûtier-Grandval Bible from Tours, of about 840, and the Bible of San Paolo fuori le Mura, Rome, of about 870.[53] In the former, an enthroned *176* figure, seated frontally, grey-haired, bearded, is surrounded by the four beasts of the Book of Revelation. They, particularly the eagle, appear to draw back the cloth which the figure holds behind and above his head. In the upper part of the miniature the four beasts appear again, surrounding the altar on which lies the sealed book. The lamb comes to unseal it, and Christ's other persona, the Lion of Judah, approaches from the right. In the San Paolo Bible the enthroned figure is more *177* venerable-looking, with a gold nimbus. He sits, not below the altar, but alongside it. The verses on the recto of the San Paolo Bible miniature say: 'The innocent lamb which became a victim for us, rising victorious, removes the veil of the Law.' The sense of this comes from St Paul's Second Letter to the Corinthians 3, 13, where the veil that Moses put over his face, and over the reading of the Old Testament, is said to be done away in Christ. The contrast is between the Old Law, and the grace and truth of Christ – institutional regulations deposed by the direct revelation of God in Christ.

The identity of the venerable man in the Carolingian Bibles is disputed by scholars. Plainly

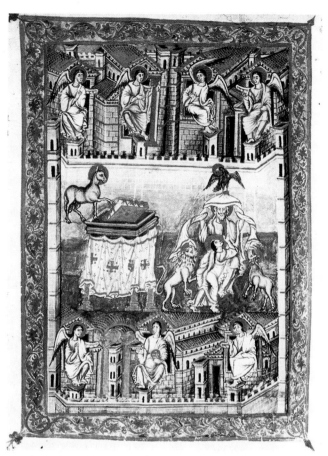

176 Apocalypse miniature, Moûtier-Grandval Bible, *f.* 449. *c.* 840

177 Apocalypse miniature, Bible of San Paolo fuori le Mura, *f.* 307v. *c.* 870

178 The creation of Man and other scenes from the Old and New Testaments, on the 'Dogmatic Sarcophagus', Rome, Vatican Museum. Fourth century

he might be Moses, unveiled. But since the nature of the Father is unveiled by the sacrifice of the Son, so the illustration might derive the enthroned figure from Revelation 4, the One who sat upon the throne who holds the sealed book, which the Lamb alone can open. The images in the two Carolingian Bibles may be different, Moses in the one, the Ancient of Days in the other. That some such iconography was worked out, or known from an earlier model, in Northumbria is suggested by the problem of the grey-haired bearded man, nimbed, but not cross-nimbed, who peers in at St Matthew writing his Gospel in the Lindisfarne Gospels. A curtain is drawn aside to reveal this man. I suggest that he is Moses unveiled, or even perhaps God the Father – God's nature and loving purpose being pre-eminently revealed by the Incarnation, of which St Matthew is the principal witness, with his emphasis on the human genealogy of Christ, and his appropriate symbol, the man or angel. There are, of course, earlier and contemporary parallels for the depiction of God the Father in human form. God the Creator, with the two other Persons of the Trinity alongside, forms Adam in the early fourth-century 'Dogmatic Sarcophagus' in the Vatican *178* Museum.[54] The *Codex Amiatinus* includes in its prefatory matter three diagrams setting out the order of the books of the Bible ordained by three great authorities, St Hilary, St Jerome and St Augustine. Each of these tables has a medallion at the top containing one of the Persons of the Trinity: St Augustine's, the Holy Spirit in the form of a dove; St Jerome's, the Son in the form of the *73* Lamb; and St Hilary's, the Father, a bust-length man.[55] Since St Matthew in Lindisfarne appears to reflect the Esdras portrait in the *Codex Amiatinus*, that same *Codex*, or more probably its model, seems a reasonable source for the postulated image of God the Father alongside the Lindisfarne St Matthew. If on the other hand, as suggested above, the mysterious grey-haired interloper is intended to represent Moses, this would offer some parallel for an interesting part-narrative illustration in the Book of Kells, to which we shall come shortly.

The Lichfield Gospels

A rational historical depiction of the Evangelist is the norm in the Lindisfarne Gospels. However, the interpretation that I have offered of the extra man in the St Matthew page suggests that experiments

179 Portrait of St Luke, the Lindisfarne Gospels, *f.* 137v

were also under way at Lindisfarne, perhaps under Jarrow stimulus, in exploring typological imagery.

The Lindisfarne hint is taken up very strikingly on the St Luke page of the Lichfield Gospels, Lichfield Cathedral Library MS.1.[56] This is a damaged and fragmentary book, paginated, not in folios. It contains 236 pages, measuring 30.8 cm by 23.5 cm. The miniature of St Luke on p. 218 adopts *180* the Lindisfarne iconography of author portrait and *179* Evangelist symbol combined in the same picture-space. But the Lichfield St Luke is no simple author portrait; rather it is an iconographically charged image. The hieratic figure carries a green coiled and budding branch in his right hand and a decorated cross in his left. The Gospel of St Luke, after the short *Quoniam quidem* introduction, Chapter 1, verses 1–4, begins at verse 5, at the words *Fuit in diebus*, to narrate the story of the birth of St John the Baptist, whose father was the priest Zacharias; he executed the priest's office before God: 'His lot was to burn incense when he went into the Temple'. Thus the Gospel opens with the traditional ritual of

180 Portrait of St Luke, the Lichfield Gospels, p. 218

Christ. The Apostles represent the Church, the new institution, which has succeeded and replaced the old Jewish rites, and of which the principal symbol is the cross.

The kinship of the Lichfield artist with Eadfrith of Lindisfarne is very obvious in the design of their Chi-Rho initials to Matthew 1, 18, and again in *181, 147* Lichfield's one surviving cross-page, inserted *182* before St Luke's Gospel. For the cross-shape itself it depends on Eadfrith's design on *f.* 2v of the *137* Lindisfarne Gospels, and for the stirring animal-background it draws inspiration from Eadfrith's design on *f.* 26v. Bruce-Mitford has pointed out a *145* connection between the bird-mesh on the *Quoniam quidem* page of Lindisfarne and the bird-mesh on *157* the fragment of a cross-shaft from Aberlady, *183* Lothian[58] – that is, on the northern coastline of Northumbria as it then was, between Trumwine's church at Abercorn and the royal borough of Dunbar, where Bishop Wilfrid was for a short time imprisoned by King Egfrith.[59] But the Aberlady birds are short-billed, hen-like birds, not the fiercer gannet-like long-beaked birds of Lindisfarne, and they have close parallels in the birds inhabiting the narrow passages on the Lichfield cross-page. The *184* disposition of the interlocked bird-bodies, the scroll on the wing and the intertangled long-toed feet, suggest that the Aberlady sculptor knew a design like that of Lichfield.

In their hieratic quality, their abstract stylization, their rejection of classical values of representation, the portraits of the Evangelist Luke and Mark in *180, 185* the Lichfield Gospels stand rather with the *Imago hominis* page of Echternach than with Lindisfarne's *102* Evangelists. The influence of Lindisfarne, discernible in the Lichfield Luke and Mark pages in the juxtaposition of man and symbol, does not fully *185* account for the form of the Evangelist symbols. The specific design of the Lichfield lion, though he holds his book as in the Lindisfarne version, is much nearer to the flame-skinned lion of the *112* Cotton MS Otho C.V, while St Luke's calf, although he looks out at us as in the Lindisfarne Gospels (and in St Cuthbert's coffin), has shed his *168* book, skips lightly, and has the scaley feathers of a bird all over his hide, in anticipation of those strange ambiguities of form that will meet us in the Book of Kells. Lichfield's St Luke himself, frontal, heavy-headed, strangely robed,[60] clearly adumbrates the solemn human and divine presences that confront us everywhere in the Book of Kells. *223*

A scribe-artist trained in older traditions of

181 *Christi autem* initials, the Lichfield Gospels, p. 5

the Jewish Temple. In the Old Testament Book of Numbers, Chapter 17, the miraculous budding and flowering of Aaron's rod is taken by the Children of Israel as a sign from God that Aaron and his sons and descendants are to be set apart as keepers of the tabernacle, as priests of Israel. Thus St Luke in the Lichfield Gospels displays in one hand the budding rod of Aaron, symbol of the Jewish priesthood, appropriate to the *incipit* of his Gospel. Bede's commentary on St Luke's Gospel helps to explain the presence in St Luke's other hand of a cross.[57] Bede points out that while the Gospel according to St Luke begins with the ministry of Zacharias in the Temple it closes with the description, Chapter 24, verse 53, of the coming of the Apostles to the Temple of Jerusalem with great joy, to praise God after witnessing the Resurrection and Ascension of

124

182 Cross carpet-page, the Lichfield Gospels, p. 220

183 Bird ornament on a cross-shaft from Aberlady, East Lothian. Eighth century

184 Detail of cross carpet-page, the Lichfield Gospels, p. 220

185 Portrait of St Mark, the Lichfield Gospels, p. 142

pictorial design – those of Echternach and Cotton MS Otho C.V – but responding also to the stimulus of Eadfrith's reformed Evangelist portrait/symbol iconography and to his decorative designs generally – a scribe-artist located in Northumbria: such is the artist of the Lichfield Gospels. I would call him Ultán, if I were pressed for a name. As the *De Abbatibus* poem says of Ultán, 'He could ornament books with fair marking, and by this art he accordingly made the shape of the letters beautiful

186 one by one.' The great Lichfield initials in their rectilinear treatment have rightly been compared to

241 Runic inscriptions, perhaps supporting a Northumbrian origin. Wendy Stein in her Doctoral thesis on the Lichfield Gospels has described in detail the character of the Lichfield script, placing it as a

126

development between Lindisfarne and Kells. In his layered painting technique the Lichfield artist moves very close to Kells. Stein nonetheless sees 'provincial' qualities in the book's 'excessively regular script and in the slightly clumsy figures'.

The Lichfield Gospels was in Wales by the early ninth century. An inscription on the last page of St Matthew's Gospel records that 'Gelhi the son of Arihtuid bought this Gospel from Cingal and gave him for it his best horse [or 'an excellent horse', *equ(u)m optimum*], and he gave this Gospel for the sake of his soul to God and had it placed on the altar of St Teilo'. This church has been securely identified as the church of Llandeilo Fawr, *1* Carmarthenshire.[61] Stein disposes firmly of the suggestion that the Lichfield Gospels originated in Wales itself. In the eighth century Wales seems to have been a cultural backwater, unconverted to the Roman Easter and tonsure,[62] cut off from the international contacts enjoyed throughout the rest of Britain. When Stein comes to survey all the possible alternative centres of origin of the Lichfield Gospels – Ireland, Iona, Northumbria – she repeatedly finds, through lack of historical records of contacts with Wales, difficulty in explaining how the Gospels could have moved to Llandeilo Fawr. An origin-centre, therefore, in the Midlands, especially in the West Midlands, appeals to her, because, as she says: 'Border raids between Anglo-Saxon and Welsh were frequent and well-documented, and a church treasure such as an altar-book would have been attractive booty.'[63] Incidentally she regards the later, tenth-century, move of the Gospels to Lichfield as similarly the result of capture, or of a donation forced upon the Welsh under the misfortunes of war.

Stein's hypothetical date of 730 for Lichfield is a compromise between the dates *c.* 698 for Lindisfarne and *c.* 800 for Kells.[64] However, if we think of Lindisfarne, as I have done here, as no later than 698, and Kells as soon after 750, the date of 730 might be replaced by a rather earlier date in the eighth century. As we have seen (p. 15), in 704 the King of the Mercians, Aethelred, husband of King Oswy's daughter Osthryth, resigned his throne and took up residence at Bardney in Lindsey, first as a monk, then as abbot; his successor to the throne, his nephew Coenred, likewise abdicated, in 709, and went to Rome to be tonsured. Like Chad of Lichfield and Lastingham (as Bede depicts him), these kings were moved by a strong sense of the impending Judgment Day; the imagery of the

186 Beginning of St Luke's Gospel, *Quoniam quidem*, the Lichfield Gospels, p. 221

187 Fragmentary relief-sculptured panels at the Church of St Mary and All Saints, South Kyme, Lincolnshire. Eighth century

114 Crucifixion page in the Durham Gospels would have spoken directly to them.

Aethelred's own son Ceolred became king in 709 and died in 716.[65] He earned an evil reputation among clergy at home and overseas for violating monasteries. St Wilfrid's biographer records the part-destruction and attempted looting of St Wilfrid's monastery at Oundle by Mercian dissidents, some time after the saint's death in 709.[66] Until 716 Aethelbald, a claimant to the Mercian throne, was in exile or in hiding for fear of Ceolred. He came clandestinely to consult his kinsman Guthlac, who was quartered, perhaps not without political and strategic purpose, in his hermitage on Crowland Island, in the midst of the wilderness of the Fens.[67] As a youth Guthlac himself was a hostage among the Welsh, and Welsh brigades may have foraged to and fro in the Midlands; at least, according to his biographer Felix's account,[68] they haunted Guthlac's imagination in his island-retreat. Guthlac died in 714. In

716 Aethelbald became King of the Mercians, and rose to great power throughout Britain during a long reign. But the very extent of his wars, and his eventual assassination by his bodyguard in 757, suggests that there may have been an undertow of instability in Mercia, with persistent possibilities of raids and losses within the kingdom. Later again, King Offa of Mercia needed to fortify his Welsh border with the great artificial ramp of Offa's Dyke.[69]

Although Stein sees the transfer of the Lichfield Gospels from western Mercia to Wales in a possible context of pillage, she does not take this element of violent, accidental, appropriation into account in her remarks about the lack of historical links between Ireland and Wales, Iona and Wales, Northumbria and Wales. Surely the Welsh connection is co-incidental, the result of theft. The record in the Lichfield Gospels itself that it was bought for the price of an excellent horse and afterwards given to a Welsh church strongly suggests that its true ecclesiastical owners had lost it. The expensive and stately product of a monastic scriptorium, intended to be placed for safe-keeping on some altar or shrine, it had evidently fallen illicitly into lay hands and become the subject of commercial exchange, at some distance from its real home. Thus the original move, the transfer of the Gospels that we have essentially to envisage, is probably only from Ireland or Iona or Northumbria to some major monastic centre in Mercia. Stein toys with a local Mercian origin for the Gospels, to suit her sense of the provinciality of the book;[70] but her most specific analogies for the Gospels' decoration lie in Northumbria – for example, she recognizes the relationship of the Lichfield birds to those on the Aberlady cross-shaft.

109   I have suggested that the Corpus Gospels, MS 197B, may represent an early gift from a northern scriptorium to St Augustine's, Canterbury, roughly paralleling the transfer of the Echternach Gospels from that same scriptorium to Echternach. The *132* Vespasian Psalter was seen to reflect, in some of its Psalm initials, the art of that scriptorium. The fragments of decorated sculptured slabs that *187* survive at South Kyme in Lincolnshire[71] include a panel of trumpet-spirals set in a rectangular format, *186* as in the head of the Q of *Quoniam* in Lichfield. These sculptures, along with Lichfield, suggest that some idiomatically pure Insular model had come south and was accessible for imitation at an early date in the Midlands. South Kyme is twenty miles south of Bardney. Bardney is celebrated in Bede's *Ecclesiastical History* as the monastery where the revered body of St Oswald was buried. His niece Osthryth originally erected his tomb there and placed his battle-standard over it.[72] Afterwards King Aethelred himself guarded the tomb as abbot. In the third quarter of the eighth century, King Offa beautified St Oswald's tomb still further.[73] In view of Willibrord's devotion to relics of St Oswald in his youth in Ireland and again later in Frisia, as expounded to St Wilfrid, in view of the celebrated northern relics of Oswald, his head at Lindisfarne and his holy hand at Bamburgh, and in view, further, of Egbert's continuous devotion to Oswald's own patron St Columba, there is nothing inherently improbable in the gift of a luxury Gospel-book to Bardney and St Oswald, designed in that same wide creative ambience in which we have placed the Durham, Echternach and Corpus Gospels, and from which features of the Lindisfarne Gospels were also derived. So far as we can

notionally embody them, from the evidence of *De Abbatibus*, the works of Ultán the scribe, Irish by birth and in his maturity resident in Northumbria, are likely to have been of similar character.[74]

The Lichfield Gospels can be recognized as a book made by an artist-scribe of Ultán's generation, after 705, which marks the beginning of Osred's reign in Northumbria. As we have seen, 716 is an interesting date, both in Mercia and Iona: Aethelbald gained his throne; Egbert converted Iona to the Roman Easter. The Lichfield Gospels' later-medieval association with St Chad is of course anachronistic, but not culturally inappropriate in view of Egbert's early acquaintance with Chad, and his interest in Chad's life and holy death, to which Bede bears witness. Whether St Wilfrid's Oundle around 715 could have possessed, and lost by theft, a Gospel-book in this strongly Insular style is doubtful; we are ignorant of the range of Wilfrid's visual taste in his mature years. Many places in the Midlands – Hygebald's monastery at Barrow in Lindsey, Lichfield, where Chad was enshrined – must have honoured the memory of their seventh-century contacts, recorded by Bede, with the now-transformed, widened and flourishing society that had begun long years before with the coming of St Columba's monks to mainland Britain. It is to one or other of these Midland churches, or to an important Mercian figure like King Aethelbald himself, that the Lichfield Gospels could have come from the north or the far west, some time in the first quarter of the eighth century.

According to the poet of *De Abbatibus*, when Ultán's skeleton was disinterred from his grave prior to being translated to a shrine inside the church, two heavenly birds descended on sunbeams on to his bones, their backs shining, 'modulating songs with their beaks'. The bones of Ultán's hands were regarded as especially sacred relics by his community because with them he had inscribed the mystical words of God.[75] That same sense of awe, as before the work of angels,[76] was felt by subsequent generations in respect of the ornament and imagery of the Book of Kells. Ultán may have come to Northumbria from the centre of Egbert's sphere of influence; after 716 that centre was Iona. This is interesting and suggestive, not only because of Lichfield's physical resemblance to Kells, but also because it underlines the importance of Iona as a common factor, already remarked upon, linking our last Gospel Book, Kells, to our first, the Book of Durrow.

188 Glossary of Hebrew names and four Evangelist symbols, the Book of Kells, *f.* 1

5 The Book of Kells

Design

The Book of Kells, Dublin, Trinity College MS A.1.6 (alternatively MS 58)[1] comprises 340 folios measuring 33 cm by 25 cm. Its folio 1 contains the glossary of Hebrew names which occurs in the Book of Durrow after the preface, *Novum opus*, and before the canon-tables; in Kells also the canon-tables are about to begin, on *f.* 1v. So we have evidently lost the preface, *Novum opus*, an important feature not only of Durrow but also of Echternach and Lindisfarne. Lindisfarne and a close dependent of the Echternach Gospels, Trier, Domschatz MS 61, both contain in addition the *Plures fuisse* preface. Kells may also have included the *Plures* text, placed before *Novum opus* as in Trier, or after it as in Lindisfarne. Judging by the beginning of the *208 capitula* to Matthew where the initial of *Nativitas* has swollen to the best *Novum opus* standard, that of *138* Lindisfarne – and indeed outdoes Lindisfarne by adding the decorative border to the block of letters, which Lindisfarne only uses in its main Gospel initial pages – the lost Kells *Novum opus* initial seems likely to have been extremely ostentatious.

Even before the canon-tables, which in Kells provide a particular focus for the Evangelist symbols, the imagery of the four Evangelist *188* symbols is introduced, squashed in on *f.* 1 beside the glossary. The symbols are placed, unusually, at right-angles to the upright page, in the right column, with all four represented upright, animal-headed but with human arms and hands, a genuine example of the imagery wrongly supposed by Werner to exist in the Book of Durrow.[2]

The canon-tables are very sumptuous, with heavy semi-architectural members, bases, block capitals, columns, and arches over the individual

189 Canon-table, Canon III, Harley MS 2788, *f.* 9. Early ninth century

131

190 Canon-table, Canon I, the Book of Kells, *f.* 1v

191 Canon-table, Canon I, the Book of Kells, *f.* 2

numbered lists, as well as a main arch placed over all four lists. This main arch contains the beast-symbols of the Evangelists. The spandrels are squared off. The Kells canon-tables closely resemble the grand weighty canon-tables that *189* appear in Carolingian Court School and related Gospel-books.[3] They likewise have the symbols up in the tympanum of the arch, whereas other Insular canon-tables which feature the symbols – those in *199, 198* the Maeseyck[4] and Rome Gospels[5] – use a different design of beast canons, placing the beasts in an *190* individual arch over a list of numbers. On *f.* 1v, Kells displays the beginning of Canon I, *in quo quattuor*, Matthew, Mark, Luke and John. The symbols appear in the spandrel in that order: the man and the lion, facing right, the calf, winged like a large moth or bird, and the eagle facing left. At the top of the canon-table are seen the head and

shoulders of an angel. On *f.* 2 Canon I continues. *191* This time the man and lion turn towards one another, and so do the calf and eagle. On *f.* 2v *192* Canon II begins, *in quo tres*, Matthew, Mark and Luke. At the top of the canon-table is represented a naked bust-length man, with a nimbus decorated with three crosses, holding the tongues of two cat-masks. The Evangelist symbols are the man, at the left, the lion in the centre, facing right, and at the extreme right a creature with a calf's head gazing back to the left, but with an eagle's body. The head is correctly that of Luke's calf, required by Canon II, but a playful syncopation or fluidity of attributes is already apparent. Exactly what limits the artist set upon himself in this exchanging of attributes among the symbols needs to be assessed cautiously, because it affects our interpretation of the whole layout of the canon-tables.

132

192 Canon-table, Canon II, the Book of Kells, *f. 2v*

193 Canon-table, Canon II, the Book of Kells, *f. 3*

193   On *f.* 3 Canon II continues. The man is at the left, the lion in the middle, looking back towards the right but with its body in a crouching pose, lying from right to left. The lion is followed by the calf, facing towards the left. No shape-shifting occurs.

194   Canon II continues also on *f.* 3v. In this opening, *ff.* 3v–4, the canon-tables alter their format to become true Insular beast canons, with the symbols placed under the arch of the panel devoted to their own text-numbers. We should perhaps have expected this change of design to coincide with a change of canon. However, the change of format occurs while we are still working through the tables of Canon II, and it prepares us for two further changes of format, the well-known change on *ff.* 4v–5, which A. M. Friend[6] regarded as of great art-historical significance, and the change on *ff.* 5v–6, which was for Friend symptomatic of the breakdown of the Kells scriptorium. On *f.* 3v we are visually still with Canon II, Matthew, Mark, Luke, not with Canon III, Matthew, Luke, John. At the left is the man or angel, at the centre the lion, for Mark, and beyond him the calf, for Luke. But the centre lion is lion-headed only; his body is that of an upright, profile calf, while St Luke's calf has the body of a lion. The numbers of Canon III are also included on this page, since the list is very short, presumably to clear the way for the symmetrical treatment of the next pairs of pages. So evidently Canon III is not visualized at all, on *f.* 3v. On *f.* 4 we move to Canon IV, *in quo tres*, Matthew, Mark and John. At the left is the angel, at the right, the eagle of St John, but in the middle there is an ambivalent animal, a frontal splayed lion, ostensibly for Mark as the canon requires, but the head of the creature, as Friend first pointed out, is that of a

194

195

194 Canon-table, Canons II–III, the Book of Kells, *f.* 3v

195 Canon-table, Canon IV, the Book of Kells, *f.* 4

calf. According to Friend the artist confines his decorative shape-changing to the bodies of his creatures. These vary, but the choice of head is strictly dictated by the canon. If so, on *f.* 4 we are looking at the imagery of Canon III, Matthew, Luke, John, with the numbers of Canon IV written under it. The artist and the scribe-compiler of the canon-tables are said by Friend to be out of step. The scribe is getting through the canons faster than the artist.

In his study of the canon-tables of the Book of Kells, Friend argued that Kells was dependent upon a Carolingian model. It was important to him, in establishing his case, that *f.* 4 of Kells should visually be Canon III. Friend had observed that in the ninth-century Carolingian Gospels British Library Harley MS 2788, the pages laid out for the

canon-tables also alter their format; they move to a different system of supporting columns, replacing flat panelled columns by classical marbled ones with spiral ribbons, and have different imagery in the tympanum – an angel upholding an inscribed handled plaque (*tabella ansata*) – after the visual contents of Canon III – Matthew's man, Luke's calf or bull, and St John's eagle – have been displayed. What is written under that set of images, man, bull, and eagle, is, as it happens, the end of Canon III's numbers and the whole of Canon IV; so when the new format appears in Harley MS 2788 the scribe is on to the numbers of Canon V, *in quo duo*, Matthew, Luke. A new model has intruded into Harley MS 2788, suppressing beast canons in favour of the plaque-holding angels of the kind which are the special feature of the Carolingian Lorsch Gospels.[7] *197*

189

196

135

196 Canon-table, Canon V, Harley MS 2788, *f.* 9v. Early ninth century

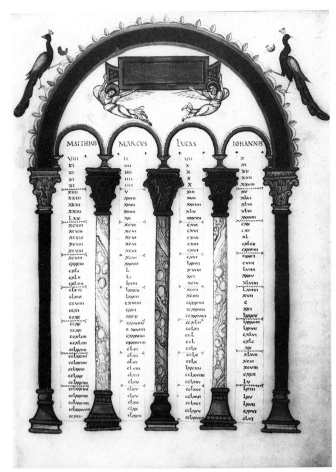

197 Canon-table, the Lorsch Gospels, *f.* 36. Early ninth century

200 As it happens, there are no beasts after *f.* 4 in Kells: we turn to *f.* 4v and the beasts have vanished, and if the visual material provided on *f.* 4 of Kells is indeed expressly conditioned by Canon III, then the break in Kells (if it *is* a break) is at the same point as in Harley MS 2788. Friend's bold conclusion was that these two manuscripts shared a common model, defective after Canon III, with only six paired pages of beasts and then a break. According to Friend the artist of Harley MS 2788 solved the problem posed by his original, defective model by adopting the angel displaying the title of the canon-table from the Lorsch Gospels; that is, he reached up to his library shelf and took down an alternative, equally sumptuous model! Meanwhile the discarded, defective model was shipped overseas, to Iona[8] according to Friend, and used to plan the layout of the Book of Kells, inevitably producing symptoms of the same break at the same place in the canon-table programme. To revert to the Carolingian scriptorium of Harley MS 2788, it seems very odd that the visual system represented in the 'defective' model was not sufficiently understood by observing its extant pages to allow the artist to persevere with the scheme even when his model gave out. It implies, also, very little forethought on the part of the artist that he should be paralysed by a break in his model. This certainly reduces the artist of Harley MS 2788 to a copyist only.

I am not altogether convinced that the 'break' in Kells comes after Canon III, in visual terms, and not after Canon IV. This altogether depends on whether we believe that the artist means Mark by that vivid frontally placed lion's body, or Luke because of the calf's head. Friend's definition of the

136

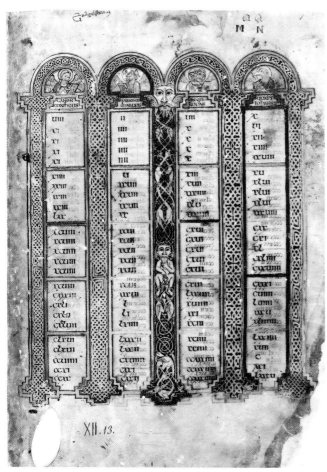

198 Canon-table, Canon I, the Rome Gospels, *f.* 1. Eighth century

199 Canon-table, the Maeseyck Gospels, *f.* 2. Eighth century

Kells artist's intentions may not be right. We may note, incidentally, that there is no sensibility to the actual content of the canon-table in other Insular *198, 199* beast canons; neither the Rome nor the Maeseyck Gospels makes any effort to relate the symbolic creatures to the number-tables below. In addition Friend was wrong not to differentiate between those canon-tables in Kells which put beasts in the tympanum, and those which put them under the *194* individual arches. If we take that pictorial formula into proper account, a break in format occurs in Kells after *f.* 3, that is, midway through the numbers of Canon II. Is it not important that this artist rings the changes in his format several times?

200   Canon V, on *f.* 4v, involves many correspondences between two Gospels, Matthew and Luke. The design of arches, a single arch over two columns, then repeated with a shallow-spandrelled

tympanum in the single embracing arch above, expresses the 'two-ness' of this table. There are no symbols, and it may be that the artist preferred not to represent two only of the four creatures, since his interest had always been in showing all four continuously present, through the use of aspects or attributes. On this leaf, *f.* 4v, only, he would have been reduced to two creatures. He prefers none, and employs instead the motif of a great beast-head running straight up, with a stiff neck, continuous from an ornamental vertical bar, similar to the decoration of the initial page of the Cologne *127* ecclesiastical canons. The circular bases of the columns on *f.* 4v of Kells, seen in plan, are exactly paralleled in the *Codex Aureus* in Stockholm,[9] *201* usually associated with Canterbury.

    In a long series of two-fold comparisons, that of Matthew and Luke is followed on *f.* 5 by Canon VI *202*

137

200 Canon-table, Canon V, the Book of Kells, *f.* 4v

comparing Matthew and Mark, Canon VII, Matthew and John, and Canon VIII, Mark and Luke; these are short lists, involving all four Gospel-writers. The visual imagery very happily expresses this. Matthew and Mark in Canon VI are represented by the angel in the left spandrel and the lion at the left of the tympanum. The man and eagle symbols required by Canon VII appear at the top, in the left and the right spandrels, and the symbols of Mark and Luke, for Canon VIII, are placed inside the tympanum. For the following Canon, IX, which compares passages in Luke and John, the right of the tympanum and the right spandrel on *f.* 5 provide the imagery, but in fact as we turn to

f. 5v we come to a gaunt picture-less grid-system, 203 with *f.* 6 pairing with it.

Writing in *Scriptorium* in 1955 Patrick McGurk[10] pointed out that this same change of format, from arches to grids, takes place in British Library Royal MS 7.C.XII. I have mentioned that these are 96 probably the canon-tables from the dismembered Corpus/Otho C.V Gospels. A model defective at this point was used wherever that now-fragmentary and partitioned luxury Gospel-book was made, and where Kells was made. This is a truly significant link between the Kells canon-tables and another; far more significant that the probably only coincidental link with Harley MS 2788. It seems that there was an archaic traditional format which was preferred, and was maintained for Canons IX and X. Should this not mean that despite the grand visual development of the canons – surely not dependent in any slavish way on models, since lavish variants are confidently undertaken – at the end a venerable sanctified fragment was reproduced exactly as it stood? This

201 Canon-table, Canon II, *Codex Aureus,* Stockholm, *f.* 6v. Mid-eighth century

202 Canon-table, Canons VI, VII and VIII, the Book of Kells, *f.* 5

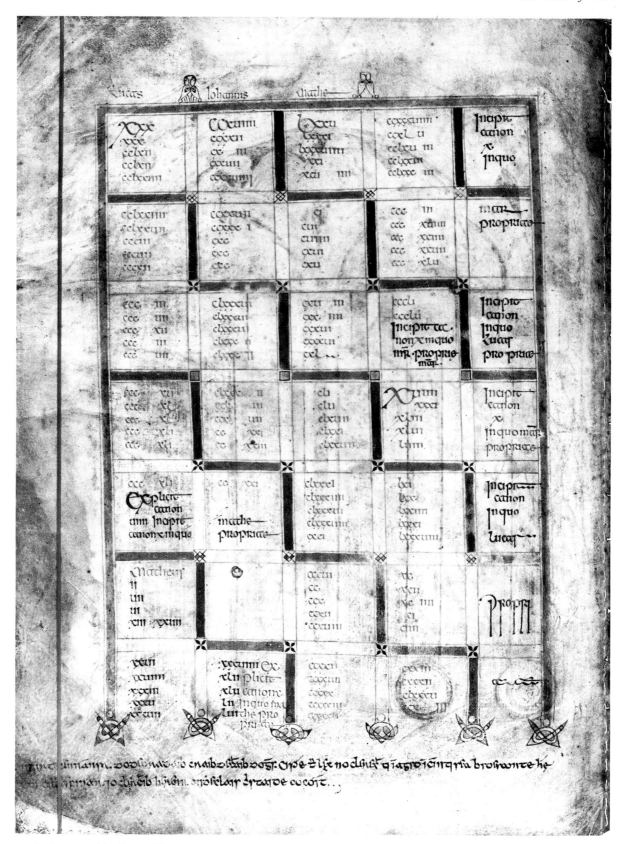

203 Grid canon-table, Canon IX, the Book of Kells, *f.* 5v

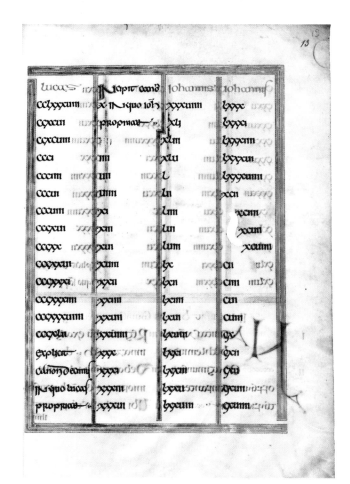

204 Grid canon-table, Canon X, the Echternach Gospels, *f.* 12v

205 Grid canon-table, Canon X, the Echternach Gospels, *f.* 13

original was a primitive type of canon – simple framed tables – whose format was accepted throughout Durrow and Echternach. The designers of these Gospel-books have adopted the format of the fragment to include all the canon-tables. Kells and Corpus/Otho C.V and Royal MS 7.C.XII preserved the original only at the place that it itself was the authority. In Kells, *ff.* 6v–7 were blank, occupied in the twelfth century by copies of charters. Friend's interpretation of these leaves as part of the canon-table layout is disposed of by the pedigree of the break from arch to grid. No impairment such as Friend envisaged is involved. He wrote that 'Kells was completed in some inferior scriptorium after the marvellous artist of the earlier pages was no longer available . . . finished as best they could . . .'.[11] But no collapse of the scriptorium by accident or flight is required to account for the break in format of the canons after Canon VIII.

Folio 7v introduces prefatory pictorial matter, an image of the Virgin and Child Enthroned, attended by angels, placed opposite the text of the *capitula* to Matthew, starting *Nativitas*. The *Nativitas* initial is prettily ornamented with rosettes, a feature of Echternach's *In Principio* initial and of the *Imago hominis* in the same Gospels. This opening of Kells, *ff.* 7v–8, is unified by the use of step-patterns on the Virgin's throne and on the right margin of the *Nativitas* page. In addition, there is a remarkable display of diagonal fret, the hallmark of the Lichfield Gospels,[12] in various sizes along horizontal bands. The lettering of the *capitula* alternates large and small. The D-shaped panels on either side of the enthroned Virgin elaborate on the same motif in the Lichfield St Mark portrait. The Virgin's throne has a fantastic animal-head terminal on its back strut, reminiscent of the zoomorphic throne of St Mark in Lichfield.

The *capitula* occupy *ff.* 8–11v; the *argumentum* to

206 Initial to *argumentum* to St Matthew, the Book of Kells, *f.* 12

207 Initial to *argumentum* to St Luke, the Book of Kells, *f.* 16v

206 Matthew, *ff.* 12–13; the *capitula* to Mark, *ff.* 13–15v, the *argumentum* to Mark, *ff.* 15v–16v. There is no *capitula* to Luke or John; we move straight on to
207 Luke's *argumentum*, *ff.* 16v–18, and John's *argumentum*, *ff.* 18–19v. Only then are the *capitula* to Luke and John introduced, on *ff.* 19v–23v and *ff.* 24–25v respectively. This dislocation of the Luke and John

capitula, together with the fact that these prologues are written in a sequence instead of being placed, as in Lindisfarne, alongside their appropriate Gospel, indicates the close connection of the Book of Kells with the Book of Durrow. Either Durrow itself was Kells' model, or they both followed the same model.

142

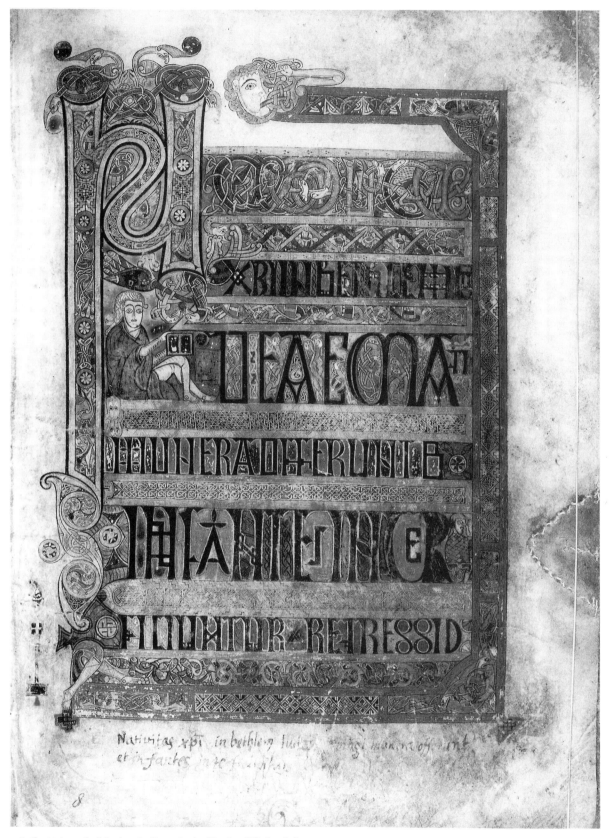

208 *Capitula* to St Matthew's Gospel, the Book of Kells, *f.* 8

209 Annunciation and Visitation. Leaf from the Genoels-Elderen ivory Diptych. Late eighth century

210 Bust-length angel, alongside panel of pelta ornament. St Margaret's Church, Fletton, near Peterborough. Eighth or ninth century

On *f.* 27v the four Evangelist symbols appear *51* again, in a full-page picture opposite a blank page. The symbols are placed in four compartments, with frames all round. Whether the interior frames should be read as a cross is uncertain. The man or angel carries a wand, like the angel in an Annunciation group, for example the Annunciation on the late eighth-century openwork ivory book-cover in the Royal Museum, Brussels.[13] *209* Angels with similar wands occur in eighth- or ninth-century sculptures at Fletton near Peter- *210* borough and Hoddom near Ruthwell in Dumfriesshire.[14] The lion is turned in rampant profile. It stands up in a vertical, not a horizontal space – that is, it has the upright format of the Durrow symbols; but a different visual formula is used. The lion is the leaping, coiled-tailed short-muzzled 'Echternach lion', or perhaps emulates the lion of Cotton MS *105, 112* Otho C.V, since it has a quantity of flame-like hair as well as a curly mane. The calf, too, is the Echternach calf, reversed and turned up on end to *110* fill a vertical space. The eagle is not of the Echternach type: it has the upright stance and half-opened drooping wings of the Durrow penguin- *61* like symbol, but the great scroll on its breast confirms its link with the Corpus eagle. It may *109* reflect the lost eagle of the Durham Gospels. The man or angel is naturalistic compared with the Echternach man. Lindisfarne displayed an angel at *102, 170* this point. Again, the lost *imago hominis* of Cotton MS Otho C.V and of Durham may be invoked. I suggested an Eadfrith-like solution at some point in the programme of the Echternach/Durham/ Corpus scriptorium, in view of the naturalism of the *Imago hominis/imago Mathei* in the Trier *130, 113* Gospels.

Folio 28v displays an upright figure with a *223* nimbus, the right hand concealed in his bosom, the left hand holding a book. This figure is regularly regarded as a portrait of St Matthew. I shall return to the iconography of this page when I attempt an interpretative review of the illustrations in Kells. In Lindisfarne the author portrait is kept isolated from the opening of the text of the Gospel. In Kells *Liber* appears opposite the standing man, on *f.* 29. The *227* Echternach calf is opposite the *Quoniam* initial; in the Lichfield Gospels the Evangelist portraits appear to be intended to be opposite the initials. Kells has a more complex structure, however, because, as we shall see, more figurative pages interrupt the text than was hitherto customary. Kells, however, uses the same simple text layout as

211 Carpet-page, the Book of Kells, *f.* 33

Durrow and Durham, with long lines, and no punctuation.

227   *Liber* is a very elaborately decorated initial-page. It is inhabited by a man holding a book in the margin, a figure above with the effect of a stole, vestments and nimbus, and an angel in the spandrel. There follows the text of Matthew's Gospel up to verse 17 of Chapter 1, comprising the genealogy of Christ, and the pages are framed. A 224 portrait of Christ is then introduced on *f.* 32v.

Opposite, on *f.* 33, is a carpet-page, showing a 211 square design with massive corner-pieces and complex beast-headed and fine interlaced intermediate finials – visual language evolved from the terminals of the uprights of the *In Principio* in 83 the Durham Gospels. Eight circles, linked by narrow bars, decorate the square. The colour-effect – yellow with touches of rose, the whole having a silvery tone because of the minute openwork – outdoes all previous Gospel carpet-pages, but its

212 Text of St Matthew's Gospel, Chapter 26, verse 31, *Tunc dicit illis Iesus*, the Book of Kells, *f.* 114v.

structure can be related to the first and second
2, 3 carpet-pages (*ff.* 1v and 3v) of Durrow. Lindisfarne abandoned the prefatory double-barred cross, before the Gospels open, but placed a cross-page before *Liber Generationis*.

228 On *f.* 34, opposite a blank page, is the large, swelling initial to Matthew 1, 18, *Christi autem*, 'the birth of Christ was in this wise . . .'. The text of Matthew then proceeds conventionally until

Chapter 26. On *f.* 114 the words of verse 30, *Et ymno dicto exierunt in montem oliveti*, are enclosed by a beast-headed arch, supported by columns, framing a picture of the Arrest of Christ. Overleaf, on *f.* 231 114v, at verse 31, is a large framed text: *Tunc dicit* 212 *illis Iesus*, 'Then said Jesus, all of you shall be offended because of me this night . . .'. This same *Tunc* is given emphasis in the Durham Gospels. In the Durham Gospels we also found emphasis at

213 Text of St Matthew's Gospel, Chapter 27, verse 38, *Tunc crucifixerant . . .*, the Book of Kells, *f.* 124

Matthew 26, 1, *Et factum est*. Another large *Tunc*
213 initial occurs on *f*. 124, at Matthew 27, 38, 'Then they crucified with Christ two thieves'. The text here has deep indents, such as we saw at the end of
70 Matthew's Gospel in the Durham Gospels. A snarling lions' head meets its own tail. There are letters at angles. The harsh geometry of the page and the strong diagonal cross-effect somewhat
127 recall the opening of the Cologne canons. The

opposite page, *f*. 123v, is blank. Folio 127v displays a decorated text at the beginning of the Resurrection narrative, at Chapter 28. The V of *Vespere* consists of two serpentine creatures entangled to comprise an upright panel. There appear to be folios missing at this point. At any rate there is no Mark portrait. A four Evangelists symbols page prefaces St Mark's Gospel, on *f*. 214
129v. Four roundels set in rectangles contain the

214 Four Evangelist symbols cross-page, the Book of Kells, *f.* 129v

215 Beginning of St Mark's Gospel, *Initium*, the Book of Kells, *f.* 130

216 Framed and indented end of St Mark's Gospel, the Book of Kells, *f.* 187v

man, lion, calf and eagle, but with many repetitions of the symbols outside the roundel, in the spirit of the first canon-tables. All the creatures hold fans or rods with petals and flowers attached. Opposite, on
215 f. 130, is the opening of St Mark, *Initium evangelii.*

The Durham Gospel enlarges the initial of Mark 14, 27, *Et ait,* the equivalent of the *Tunc dicit,* the Arrest narrative in St Matthew's Gospel. This does not happen in Kells, which enlarges only Mark 15, 25, *Erat autem hora tertia,* 'It was the third hour, and they crucified him.' It is an oddity of Kells that it isolates this phrase, and historiates it, on *f.* 183.

216 Folio 187v has the page split diagonally, containing in an hour-glass-like pair of spaces the end of the text of St Mark's Gospel, and in two triangular spaces an angel with a book and a winged lion of St Mark. The division of the page is made by

elongated and bent lions' legs, as distorted as the animals which form the throne in the Lichfield *185* Mark portrait. Folio 188, opposite, displays the *Quoniam* initial at the beginning of St Luke's *238* Gospel, so we have now no cross- or symbols-page and no Luke portrait. The initial Q is loaded with incidents. The page contains only the single word *Quoniam.*

After the Lucan version of Christ's genealogy, *f.* 200–2, a full-page picture is introduced on *f.* 202v, normally interpreted as the Temptation of Christ, *242* the narrative of which is about to follow, after the large inscription *Iesus autem plenus spirito sancto* on *f.* 203. The picture is crowded with interesting detail, *217* and like the scene of the Arrest of Christ, requires some analysis to bring out its full meaning. Luke's text of the Last Supper and Betrayal and Crucifixion is not given marks of emphasis in Kells. The Durham Gospels emphasized Chapter 22, verse 1, *Adpropinquabat.* Kells signals the Resurrection story, on *f.* 285, with the enlarged text of Chapter 26, verse 1, *Una autem,* inhabited by angels, and the whole framed.

Folio 290v is decorated with a saltire cross, with *218* the four Evangelist symbols in the spandrels. The truncated form of symbol used here is found tucked alongside the Evangelist portraits in Trier MS 61, with wings above and below. The Matthew portrait in St Gall MS 1395 displays the same type of symbol, with wings set stiffly up and down. Folio 291v has a massively framed portrait of an *252* elaborately nimbed seated figure, with pen and book. Opposite him, on *f.* 292, is the *In Principio* *255* initial of St John's Gospel. No other portions of St John's text are given special emphasis in Kells.

To sum up this brief survey of contents, the most complex text is St Matthew's Gospel. It has four figurative pages, quite apart from the Evangelist symbols page, the carpet-page and the great initials. If, as the text opposite blank *f.* 123v might suggest, it was intended to introduce there a picture of Christ Crucified, then the illustrative programme was even larger. Mark has only its Evangelist symbols page – no illustrations, no portrait. Luke has no Evangelist symbols page or portrait but has the Temptation illustration. John has a symbols page and a portrait, but no narrative illustrations survive. Even so, the level of pictorial treatment of the Gospels – the Gospels as an illustrated text – is unrivalled in the Insular tradition, unless by British Library Royal MS I.E.VI in *its* original format as an illustrated Bible.[15]

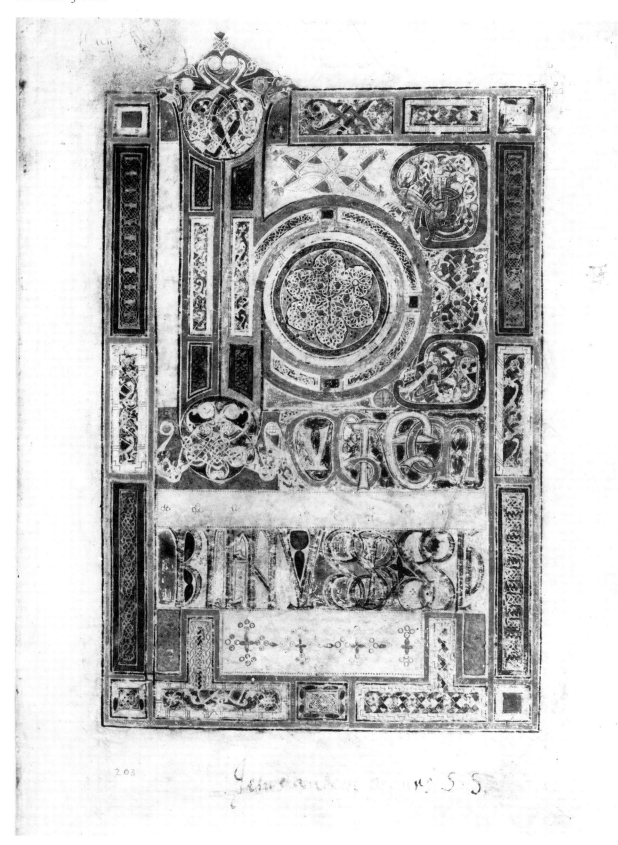

217 Text of St Luke's Gospel, Chapter 4, verse 1, the Book of Kells, *f. 203*

218 Four Evangelist symbols cross-page, the Book of Kells, *f.* 290v

The imagery of the Virgin-page and the Matthean prefaces

219 As we have seen, the Evangelist symbols are given remarkably full play in Kells. They constantly keep company with one another. On a number of occasions in the canon-tables they blend one with another, but normally they appear, even more than once in the same picture, in their own form. In the Evangelist symbol pages which preface the Gospels, the four disparate creatures are clearly represented. There is no tendency in the Book of Kells, therefore, to do what the designer of the

104 Trier Gospels did in his prefatory 'tetramorph', namely to coalesce the four Evangelists into a single figure, to show them, as it were, speaking with one voice. In Kells, their formal visual disparateness comes over at least as clearly as their unity of purpose. They are, in their plentiful appearances, like a primitive litany or spell that evokes their four names, over and over.

I would contrast this Kells device of simple reiteration with the more sophisticated illustration that occurs in the Gospels presented by the Emperor Louis the Pious to an Abbey Church at Soissons in 827.[16] Before the canon-tables in the Soissons Gospels is a picture which unites the witness of the four Evangelists allegorically. The four Gospels are the four streams that jet from a cylindrical spout, in the centre of a splendidly

220 constructed piscina or cistern. This symbolizes the Well of Life, the *Fons vitae* from which Christianity springs.[17] Christ instructed his disciples to 'Go and teach all nations, baptising them in the name of the Father and the Son and the Holy Spirit.' The *Fons vitae*, the baptismal cistern, is also Christ himself, because the blood of redemption and water of baptism flowed from his side on Good Friday, according to St Leo the Great in his programme of inscriptions on the fifth-century Baptistry of St John Lateran. Also in the fifth century, taking an Old Testament image from the history of Moses, as glossed by the Apostle Paul, Paulinus of Nola says: 'Christ is the Rock, from which flow four sonorous streams, the four Evangelists.' St Augustine adds another interpretation: Christ is the new Adam, tending Paradise. Paradise, the Eden of Genesis, is a symbol of the Church. Out of the single spring in Eden, according to Genesis 2, 10, four rivers flowed. These are the four Evangelists. In this interpretation we again come back to the fount of true doctrine, and the spread of Christianity from it

219 Evangelist symbols, detail of the Book of Kells, *f.* 5

220 The Fountain of Life, the Soissons Gospels, *f.* 6v. Early ninth century

221 Virgin and Child, the Book of Kells, *f.* 7v

throughout the world, in the words of the Gospel writers.

In the Soissons Gospels the unity of the Evangelists' message and the benefit which flows from them are celebrated in an allegorical image of the kind that a classicizing, stone-church-building milieu would have appreciated. The Soissons miniature is also topographically well-informed. It literally represents the Baptistry of St John Lateran. The remote provinces where the Book of Kells was

made might well have taken a different approach in visualizing this Gospel unity.

We turn, therefore, with all the more interest to the portrait of the Virgin, inserted in Kells after the canon-tables, on *f.* 7v. Alcuin, with a training in York in Anglo-Irish liturgical practice, calls the Virgin Mary the *Fons vitae*.[18] Again according to St Leo the Great, *Generatio Christi origo est populi Christiani*. The Virgin faces the summary of Matthew's history of the Infancy of Christ,

221

154

Nativitas Christi in Bethlehem Iudeae. This is the account which records the enquiry after the Messiah by the wise men from the East, and their coming to Bethlehem: *Et entrantes domum, invenerunt puerum cum Maria matre eius* . . . . The Kells Virgin in her sideways pose might well be abstracted from an Adoration of the Magi.[19] Angels attend on the enthroned Virgin Mother in the Adoration of the Magi scene in Sta Maria Maggiore. The Sta Maria in Cosmedin mosaic, from Old St Peter's, shows angels accompanying a sideways-placed Virgin. But the Christ-child turning in reverse seems definitely to contradict the use of an Adoration of the Magi as the model. If the image of the Virgin and Child incised on the end of St Cuthbert's coffin[20] represents, as seems likely, the original appearance of the model that was available to the Kells artist, then the turning-back of Christ towards the Virgin was the invention of the Kells artist himself.

222

The gestures of affection are not those of the *Eleousa*,[21] the standard Greek type of tender Virgin who embraces the Christ-child, cheek to cheek with him. The Kells Christ-child places his right hand on the right hand of the Virgin, as she supports him on her knees with both her hands. This gesture is so unusual that the contact of right hands may be seen as deliberately emphasizing the humanity which Christ takes from his mother. The supposition of Kitzinger that the artist of the Kells Virgin is faithful to the model because 'his own taste evidently was in favour of the ornamental and the two dimensional, and it would hardly have occurred to him to show her with her legs crossed if he had not found her thus depicted in his prototype'[22] can be queried on two counts: first, the Virgin's legs are not crossed; and second, crossed legs, as in the figure squatting under the N of *Nativitas* opposite, are characteristic of the twined and entangled idiom employed by Insular artists. The artist of St Gall Codex 51 even makes the fingers of Christ's blessing hand plait through one another.[23] Freedom to rehandle the model is quite within the competence of the Kells artist.

208

119

The leftwards gaze of the Christ-child concentrates attention on the role of the Virgin, her authority as *Fons vitae*, from which spring the Christian people, briefly indicated by the congregation of six bust-length profile figures in the adjacent frame. As we shall see, this theme of the *populi Christiani* is elaborated in the later Temptation scene. Just as the Crucifixion image in the

222 Virgin and Child, the end of St Cuthbert's coffin. 698

Durham Gospels can be seen to be retrospective, referring back to the text on the previous recto, so the Virgin page of the Book of Kells, illustrating the mystery of the Incarnation, the portal opening on salvation, can serve to gloss the canon-tables placed before it, as an alternative, more intense and devotional, to the academic or classicizing composition of the architectural *Fons vitae* miniature before the canons in the Soissons Gospels.

114
70

The monumental frontal figure on *f.* 28v of Kells, generally called St Matthew, has been associated by Jonathan Alexander with the tetramorph figure placed in the Trier Gospels before the canon-tables, because of the presence in the Kells picture of more than one Evangelist symbol. The back-rest of the throne behind the

223

104

155

223 'St Matthew', the Book of Kells, *f.* 28v

figure's shoulders is crowned by maned lions' heads. The bench or cushion is draped at thigh level, although the figure does not appear to sit, and at either end of his bench rises a beast's head, the calf at the left, the eagle at the right. These attributes, wider than St Matthew's man, invest the Kells figure with some ambiguity. An enthroned figure surrounded by the beasts of the Apocalypse might reasonably be taken to represent a *Majestas*. The figure has a mauve and scarlet nimbus, the inner circle of which is marked by three triangles touching the hair at right, left and top, giving the effect of a cross-nimbus. The figure occupies exactly the same setting as the undoubted figure of 224 Christ on *f.* 32v, with the same stationing of the figure between two upright posts or strips, which bend at right-angles sideways to meet their square capitals, supporting the semicircular arch overhead. In an Apocalypse cycle, the appearance of Christ, the sacrificed lamb, is preceded by the worship of the Ancient of Days, enthroned but uncommunicating, holding in his hand the sealed book whom no man can open. The crossed-arms pose of the figure is reminiscent of that of the 218 Matthew symbol on *f.* 290v, the Evangelist symbols page before St John's Gospel, but the figure on *f.* 28v is more mysterious in that his right hand is hidden in his bosom. This gesture must be significant. The pose is a focus of attention in Psalm 73, when the Psalmist laments the fallen state of the Synagogue, and at verse 11 says to God: 'why do you not withdraw your right hand from your bosom?' – *dexteram tuam de medio sinu tuo?* In Cassiodorus's *Commentary on the Psalms*[24] the whole sequence of Psalm 73 is related to the passing of authority from the Temple to the Church. The Psalm is divided into sections. The second section starts immediately after the hand-in-bosom reference. The second section, beginning 'For God is my king of old, working salvation in the midst of the earth', refers, according to Cassiodorus, to the coming of Christ, when superstition and iniquity will be done away with.

Bede[25] discusses St John's Gospel, Chapter 1, where Christ, the only begotten of God, is said to be *in sinu patris*, 'in the bosom of the Father'. He alone reveals the nature of the Father. According to Bede 'in the bosom of the Father' signifies the secret places, the councils of God, which are uniquely revealed in the Son. If the first figure on *f.* 28v and the second on *f.* 32v are indeed seen in the same setting – one enthroned, surrounded by

224 Christ attended by angels, the Book of Kells, *f.* 32v

the beasts, the other, certainly Christ, acclaimed by angels – and form a sequence, the Almighty enthroned of Chapter 4, and the Lamb, as it had been slain, of Chapter 5, then the gesture of the concealed hand could represent the hidden counsels of God, not yet revealed – revealed only by the Incarnation about to be expounded in the Gospel of St Matthew. The Apocalypse as a model for the Gospel-book of Kells, either as an illustrated Apocalypse MS on which the illustrations were patterned, or as a source to be exploited intellectually, in a process of visual exegesis, would help to explain the great expansion of illustrative matter in Kells as compared with previous Insular Gospel-books.

On the theme of Apocalypse illustrations or subjects affecting the decoration of a Gospel-book, appears in the midst of the throne, who takes the sealed book from the hand of him who sits upon the throne. So evidently the Apocalypse miniature in the Soissons Gospels got there via the *Plures fuisse* preface, as an illustration of it. Judging by the standard of Lindisfarne and Trier Gospels, Kells may originally also have been equipped with the Apocalyptic *Plures fuisse* preface. In Kells, however, we are not concerned, as in Soissons, with a single Apocalypse prefatory picture. I sense a more pervasive influence of the Apocalypse, giving colour to the Gospels as an oracle, or mystery revealed – a concept of the Gospels made overtly formidable – that sealed book in the Almighty's hand, which the Lamb opens.

The remarkable change in layout of Kells, as compared with Lindisfarne or even Durham, Kells' nearest parallel as an 'illustrated' Gospel-book, suggests that an experiment in book-design was underway in the scriptorium which produced Kells. The initials to the Gospels are treated in a new way; they are historiated, or at least they are inhabited by figures which must have some general or specific meaning. Opposite the image of the man with the concealed hand, whom I interpret as the Almighty of Revelation 4, the *Liber Generationis* initial on *f.* 29 shows a large figure placed in the 227 margin, holding a book. Françoise Henry suggested that this may represent the donor of the Gospels;[28] however, there is no historical basis for such an interpretation. The Welshman who bought the Lichfield Gospels for the price of his best horse donated it to St Teilo's Church, but he did not commission it. The composition of the page, taking the figure of the standing man below, the angel above and the nimbed vested cleric at the top of the stem of the I, offers a rough parallel with a series of illustrations which occur in the early ninth-century Valenciennes Apocalypse, according to Carl Nordenfalk a Carolingian copy of an Insular original.[29] In the early pages of the Valenciennes Apocalypse St John is ordered to write a letter to 226 each of the seven Churches of Asia Minor. Each Church, in the text, is presided over by an angel. The sacred author is represented under divine command to write Christ's words. The Kells *Liber Generationis* could be modelled on some such illustration – the so-called donor corresponding to St John, holding out the book; the angel could have started life as the angel of Smyrna or one of the other Churches, and the cleric at the top of the I corresponds to Christ. The block of text at the

225 Adoration of the Lamb, the Soissons Gospels, *f.* 1v. Early ninth century

there exists the suggestive parallel of the Soissons Gospels, whose Well of Life I have already discussed. As Underwood has pointed out, the first 225 picture in the Soissons Gospels (*f.* 1v) represents the twenty-four Elders of the Book of Revelation adoring the Lamb.[26] Underwood remarks that this picture 'certainly has no place, as scriptural illustration, in a Gospel Book'. It faces the beginning of the *Plures fuisse* preface, originally a prologue by St Jerome to a commentary on St Matthew's Gospel. It contains quotations based on Chapter 4, verses 4–8, and Chapter 5, verses 6–8, of the Book of Revelation,[27] wherein the twenty-four Elders are seen worshipping God round about his throne, along with the four beasts. Then a Lamb

bottom of the Kells page is in the location of a second church in the Valenciennes Apocalypse layout. The historiation of the initials in Kells is a peculiar feature, and we might explain it partly as the consequence of applying Apocalypse illustrative material to a Gospel *incipit*, to emphasize the revelatory quality of what is being written.

The Gospel of St Matthew opens with a genealogy, *Liber Generationis*, the Book of the Generation of Jesus Christ, the son of David, the son of Abraham: Abraham begat Isaac, Isaac begat Jacob, and so on, through forty-two generations up to Jesus, 'who is called the Christ'. At that point, solemnly, on *f.* 32v, the full-page image of Christ is introduced, with a cross pendant from the arch above his head. Christ is enthroned, accompanied by angels, and by peacocks, an Early Christian and Byzantine symbol of immortality; the divine flesh is immortal, since peacock's flesh was believed to be incorruptible. The sense is of the Apocalyptic Lamb, 'who was slain, and is alive for evermore'. The blood shed in the sacrifice of the Lamb is represented by the chalices, from which vines, symbol of the Eucharist, emerge at either side.

224

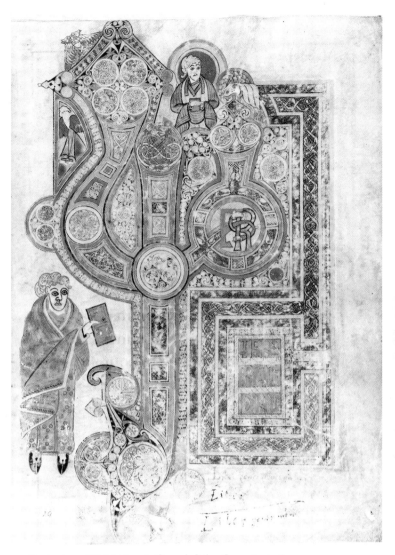

226 St John writing to the Churches of Smyrna and Pergamon, the Valenciennes Apocalypse, *f.* 7. Early ninth century

227 Beginning of St Matthew's Gospel, *Liber Generationis*, the Book of Kells, *f.* 29

Opposite, on *f.* 33, is placed the only carpet-page in Kells. The page is dominated by eight discs. In Christian number symbolism, eight is important. Eight is associated with baptismal cisterns, from at least the time of the Lateran Baptistry. St Leo associated Baptism with the Passion. The Soissons Gospels *Fons vitae* miniature shows the Lateran Baptistry with its eight columns and its octagonal basin. The famous Baptismal cistern in the Baptistry at Pisa is octagonal in shape.[30] It has eight sides because there are eight days in Passion week, from Palm Sunday to Easter Sunday. The cross in Kells, with eight points of focus, could have the same significance. On *f.* 34, opposite a blank – that

211

220

228

228 *Christi autem* initials, the Book of Kells, *f.* 34

is, covered by the carpet-page – is displayed the inflated text of Matthew 1, 18, *Christi autem generatio sic erat* – the mystery of the incarnation revealed. An awful sense of the sanctity of the holy name of Christ is achieved by covering it with the cross carpet-pattern.

The sacred monogram, Chi, Rho, Iota, dominates the page. Alcuin, in a letter to Paulinus, Patriarch of Aquilea, thanking him for a treatise on the Christian faith, speaks of 'the four rivers of the virtues [St Jerome's interpretation] flowing out of one bright and health-giving paradise, irrigating the whole breadth of the Christian church', and perceives in the treatise 'golden whirlpools (*aurivomos gurgites*) of spiritual meaning'.[31] This vocabulary can be very happily applied to the form of this initial, the four curves of the Chi flowing out into estuaries and eddies of swirling energy. As an image of the world irrigated by the four rivers, flowing from their source, Christ, the Kells Chi-Rho page makes good sense, since the elements of air, earth and water are differentiated and characterized. A twelfth-century Irish poem represents the speech of a holy hermit, inhabiting a lonely island: 'I bless the Lord who has power over all, Heaven with its pure host of angels, earth, ebb, flood-tide'.[32] Heaven, air, is represented in the Kells initial by the great angels which perch like strange angelic harpies on the long strand of the letter. But air is also wittily characterized, and the artist's intention revealed, by the two moths or butterflies, equally creatures of the air, tucked in under the shoulder of the upper strand. At the base of the great letter two cats sit cosily curled up with four mice – the peace between the creatures a contrast to the sinister cats of Muiredach's Cross at Monasterboice,[33] swallowing birds and frogs. In Kells they are creatures of the earth, eating cheese or wafers, products of the earth. The watery element is adroitly represented under the stem of

230

the I, where a fish is caught by an otter. Both are creatures of the sea, the fish obviously, and the other equally obviously when we remember the sea-otters which in Bede's *Life of St Cuthbert* come ashore and wipe the saint's feet with their fur, and after receiving his blessing, return to their 'native habitat'.[34]

229

Into this world comes the incarnate Christ. A human head, with golden (orpiment and scarlet) hair and a golden glory round it – similar to the glory that blazes around the figure at the top of the *In Principio* initial – occupies the very centre of the initial. This is the face of Christ, young and beardless, just as it is represented in the so-called Temptation scene on *f*. 202v.

255

242

229 (*above*) St Cuthbert's feet dried by otters, illustration of Bede's prose *Life*, Oxford, University College MS 165. Early twelfth century

230 Detail of the base of the west face of Muiredach's Cross, Monasterboice, Co. Louth. (?) Tenth century

231 The Arrest of Christ, the Book of Kells, *f.* 114

The imagery of the 'Arrest' and 'Temptation' pages, and of the Marcan and Johannine prefaces

The last strong piece of iconography in St Matthew's Gospel is the full-page picture of the Arrest of Christ (*f.* 114). The immediately *231* preceding text deals with the institution of the Eucharist. Christ says: 'Take, eat, this is my body'; and taking the cup: 'Drink ye all of it. For this is my blood of the New Covenant which is shed for many for the remission of sins. But I say unto you, I will not drink henceforth of the fruit of the vine until that day when I drink it new with you in my Father's Kingdom.' And when they had sung a hymn they went out into the Mount of Olives – *Et ymno dicto exierunt in montem Oliveti*. These last words are written above the picture. Overleaf, after the initial *Tunc*, Matthew 26, 31, the text continues *212* with Christ's prophecy of his betrayal and death. He asks Peter and the two sons of Zebedee to watch with him, *Vigilare mecum*, and they subsequently fail the test to do so. Nordenfalk has suggested that the foliage at the top of the illustration represents the Mount of Olives,[35] but it is less likely to be topographical than to refer to the sacred vine of the newly instituted Eucharist, like the chalice- and vine-images of *f.* 32v. An ironical contrast may be intended between the praises and songs of the angels and angelic birds in that previous miniature, and the Apostles' hymn, sung in the circumstances of Christ's imminent betrayal. Christ's figure in the Arrest is not unlike the stiffly upright, large-headed, squat-bodied Evangelist or God/Christ images of the Gospel preface pictures, with similar architectural columns and an arch above. Christ's pose is the ancient *orans* one, as in the catacombs *233* and on sarcophagi, the attitude of prayer and intercession.[36] In this respect the picture implies the prayerful vigil of Christ in the Garden of Gethsemane, to which he invites Peter and the other two disciples. Christ's prayer (Matthew 26, 39) is 'Let this cup pass from my lips. Nevertheless not as I will . . .'. Occurring immediately after the institution of the Eucharist, the scene of the Arrest has strong potential as a Passion image. The west face of Muiredach's Cross, of the tenth century or *232* perhaps earlier, shows in its bottom panel the Arrest of Christ, or alternatively the *Ecce Homo*. In the upper arm, above the scene of the Crucifixion, is an Old Testament subject, from Exodus 17.[37] Moses stands on the mount, watching the contest between the Children of Israel and Amalek, 'against whom the Lord has sworn that He would have war with Amalek from generation to generation'. Amalek is evidently a type of the old enemy, Satan, defeated by Christ; and Moses, holding up his hands 'until the going down of the sun' (Exodus 17, 10–12) is a type of the Crucified Christ. The image is also one of heroic warfare. Moses's hands were heavy, and Aaron and Hur, his attendants, 'stayed up his hands, the one on one side and the other on the other side, and his hands were steady'.

232 Muiredach's Cross, Monasterboice, Co. Louth. Tenth century

233 Daniel, Noah and Jonah, ceiling-painting in the catacomb of Peter and Marcellinus, Rome. Fourth century

The *Life of Wilfrid* by Stephen uses this image, in a confrontation with pagans. St Wilfrid and his clergy 'raised their hands to heaven and gained God's help. For just as Moses – Hur and Aaron lifting up his arms – called continually to the Lord for help when Joshua did battle against Amalek, so did this little band of Christians vanquish a fierce and untamed pagan host.'[38] The Arrest of Christ, with the seizure of Christ's hands, as if Christ's hands were being held up like Moses's, is an example, I believe, of visual exegesis; the Agony in the Garden, with Christ in the pose of Moses, emphasizes the failure of the Apostles to watch with him and support him. As we noted earlier, the text opposite the picture contains Christ's foreboding that 'All of you shall be offended because of me this night . . .'.

The indented frame of the Crucifixion text on *f.* 124 contains three groups of bust-length profile *234* men. They look across at the blank *f.* 123v, just as the group of profile men look across at the *Nativitas* initial from the Virgin on *f.* 7v. In that case they *221* represented the *populi Christiani*. The *populi*

234 Detail of snarling animal-heads, Crucifixion text from St Matthew's Gospel, Chapter 27, verse 38, the Book of Kells, *f.* 124

Christiani would be equally attentive to the image or idea of the Crucifixion. Alternative watchers are those who are mentioned in Matthew 27, 36–9: 'and sitting down, they watched him there. And they that passed by reviled him, wagging their heads...'. In the Gospel of St Matthew the piercing of Christ's side with the lance is not mentioned specifically. In St John's Gospel, Christ, after death, is pierced with a spear, to fulfil the prophecy of Psalm 21: 'They shall look on him whom they pierced.' This is the source of the phrase in the Book of Revelation 1, 7–8, about the Second Coming, which is the sense of the 'Crucifixion' *114* picture in the Durham Gospels. It is unlikely that the Kells Crucifixion picture, if such was intended to be painted on *f.* 123v, would have been any more 'historical' than that of Durham. On the whole, the watchers on *f.* 124 are most likely to be the Christians, who in the Good Friday liturgy are called upon to venerate the Cross. The meaning of these heads is also involved with the meaning of the crowd of watchers in the Temptation miniature in St Luke's Gospel.

The *Initium* initial of St Mark (*f.* 130) is not so *215* obviously historiated as St Matthew's initial. Alongside the priest in the *Liber* initial is a frame-terminal, in the form of a nimbed lion's-head. A larger and more ferocious cat-face with a neck and forepaw under it forms the terminal of the frame in the *Initium* page. In ferocity the cat-mask equals those of the *Tunc crucifixerant* initial in St Matthew's Gospel. These wild beasts may bear the meaning of the many Psalm-references to lions, as enemies, or the devil – Psalm 7, 'Lest he tear my soul like a lion, *235* rending it in pieces while there is none to deliver'; Psalm 21, 'They gaped upon me with their mouths, as a ravening and a roaring lion . . .'. The man sitting athwart the lion's throat, contending with the beast by holding its tongue, may stand in general for that situation of the soul in peril, or the Daniel-Jonah image of redemption out of peril.[39] With his other hand the man (naked? tattooed?) plucks his own beard. In the Rome Gospels a naked man sits in the central column of the first canon-table,[40] touching his genitals and plucking his beard. He is not very obviously placed there in reference to the canon entries, unless he stands for those who in Matthew 4, 23–5, are taken with divers diseases and torments, and those who were possessed with devils. The Rome Gospels man is more likely to be, as it were, topographically placed – down in the darkness, below the light of Christ preached by the four Evangelists. He is presumably a tormented soul, sitting in a venom-filled den, or an image of perpetual recalcitrance, Satan himself.

The more-or-less contemporary illustrated Apocalypses show an image of the Last Judgment on Satan, that old serpent, and on the false prophet, bound and cast into the lake of fire. The naked profile man and the fiery dragon bound together in the Valenciennes Apocalypse[41] illustration offer a fair visual parallel for the image on the top-right corner of the Kells *Initium* page. I suggest the more readily that this is a vision of Apocalyptic torment because of the curious imagery of the *Quoniam*

236
198

237

236 Detail of man and animal's head, top of *Initium* initial, the Book of Kells, *f.* 130

235 Illustration of Psalm 7, the Stuttgart Psalter, *f.* 7. Ninth century

quidem page of St Luke (*f.* 188). We are again confronted by men and monsters, down at the very base of the text on the page, in the 'am' of *Quoniam*. This particular juxtaposition of men and monsters, the beasts' jaws closing around the top of the men's heads, is fairly uncommon. It does occur in celebrated metal objects, the so-called Helgö crozier-head,[42] which may rather be the terminal to a piece of church-furniture, and in the related St Germain-en-Laye D-shaped mounts, which I shall refer to more fully in connection with the Kells 'Temptation' miniature. The two men in the 'am' of *Quoniam* are the only ones menaced among all the figures. The large company of figures, in rows – one of whom serves out nourishment with a spoon – have a preoccupied look, as if they were engaged in some narrative situation. We can compare these

238
240

239

246

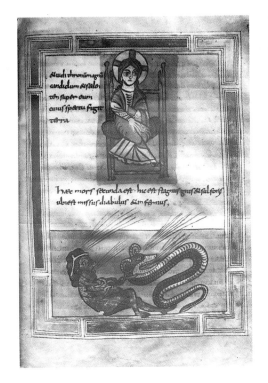

237 (*above left*) God's judgment on Death and Hell, Revelation 20, the Valenciennes Apocalypse, *f. 37*. Early ninth century

238 (*above*) Beginning of St Luke's Gospel, *Quoniam quidem*, the Book of Kells, *f. 188*

239 (*left*) Bronze, glass and enamel crozier-head or chair-terminal from Helgö, Sweden. Eighth century

240 (*above right*) Detail of figures inhabiting NIAM from initials to St Luke's Gospel, the Book of Kells, *f. 188*

241 (*right*) The story of Romulus and Remus, on a panel from the left end of the Franks Casket. Whalebone. First half of eighth century

241 rubbery, long-legged figures to the figures in the Franks Casket, who are certainly in narrative contexts, however obscure.[43] Two men, isolated from a large company of others taking part in some entertainment, recall a situation in the Book of Revelation 11, when the two witnesses are killed by the beast from the bottomless pit. 'And they that dwell upon the earth shall rejoice over them, and make merry, and send gifts to one another because these two prophets (*quoniam hi duo prophetae*) tormented them that dwelt in the earth.' The coincidence of the word *quoniam* cannot be pressed, because it is a word that occurs regularly in the text of the Book of Revelation, not just in Chapter 11. If the tantalizing scene in the Kells *Quoniam* initial does not represent a specific subject, then at least Françoise Henry must be right in suggesting that it represents a generalized scene of torments in Hell.[44]

242 Folio 202v of the Book of Kells displays a full-page picture, opposite the text of Luke 4, 1, *Iesus autem plenus sancto Spirito regressus est ab Iordane*; that is, the end of the Baptism narrative of St Luke, in that Christ returns from the River Jordan. The narrative of the Baptism itself, Chapter 3, verses 21–2, where the Holy Spirit in the form of a dove descends on Christ, is detached from its conclusion, the return from Jordan, 'full of the Holy Spirit', by the text of the Lucan genealogy. This, unlike that of St Matthew, is not arranged to start with Abraham and come forward through the generations to Christ, but instead traces the generations in reverse from 'Jesus [Chapter 3, verse 23] being as was supposed the son of Joseph, which was the son of Heli, which was the son of Matthat', etc., back to 'Adam, which was the son of God'. This juxtaposition of *Adam qui fuit Dei* with the next words *Iesus autem* is deliberate, Jesus at his Baptism having been acclaimed by the heavenly voice: *Tu es filius meus dilectus*. We have in Kells at that juncture in the text a powerful image of Christ as Son of God, full of the Holy Ghost, but in his human condition, chronicled in his genealogy – so a second Adam, and a new beginning. In a previous study I have related the theme of Christ's Baptism to the Kells picture; that was to see the picture in part as retrospective.[45] Bede, discussing Christ's Baptism, speaks of Christ as the new Adam, glorified by the dove of the Holy Spirit, whereas the first Adam was deceived by the unclean spirit. Traditionally there were two chief occasions when Baptism was administered to Christian believers, on Holy Saturday and on the Eve of Pentecost.[46] I

suggested that the crowd of people around the ark-shaped structure where Christ stands in the Kells picture was consistent with the text of Acts 2, relating to Pentecost, when a crowd gathered around the house where the Apostles had met. In view of the groups of men in the Virgin miniature and attached to the text of the Matthean crucifixion narrative, interpreted as *populi Christiani*, this crowd could reasonably be regarded as Christ's redeemed people, gathered around Christ in his Church.

It is possible that the picture bears more analysis yet. Carl Nordenfalk raised the problem of the identity of the crowd of people, but only offered the unlikely explanation that they represent the inhabitants of the monastery in which the Book of Kells was made.[47] They are, I believe, crucial to an understanding of the picture on *f.* 202v. This picture is always called the Temptation of Christ. It is regarded as an illustration of the text that lies ahead, Luke 4, 2–13, when Christ is tempted by the devil. The first Temptation, verses 3–4, is the Temptation to turn stones into bread. The second Temptation, verses 5–8, is the offer of worldly glory and power; this involves the survey of the world and all its kingdoms from a high mountain. The Kells illuminator takes pains to differentiate the crowds in the picture by the colour of their hair and eyes. They might, but not very convincingly, represent the populace of the world over whom Christ is offered control. Christ has a vantage-point at the top of his ark-shaped structure. But this is rightly always seen not as the natural mountain but as an ecclesiastical structure.[48] The scene is interpreted as Christ's third and last Temptation, verses 9–12, when Christ is carried by Satan to the pinnacle of the Temple in Jerusalem, and tempted to throw himself down, to prove the truth of God's promise in Psalm 90: 'He shall give his angels charge over thee, lest at any time thou dash thy foot against a stone.'

The relative scale of Christ and the building makes it perhaps a rather unconvincing image of the precipitous position of Christ on top of the temple.[49] It is partly the large scale of Christ in relation to the building which has given rise to the frequently stated comparison between the building and a house-shrine. The structure has the proportions of a shrine, a short high format and a sloping roof, like a truncated pyramid. The exterior is covered with ornament, again as are the surfaces of shrines – for example, the Emly Shrine now in 243

242 'The Temptation of Christ', the Book of Kells, *f.* 202v

243 Emly Shrine. Silver, enamel. Eighth century

244 Lough Erne Shrine. Bronze. Eighth century

Boston with showy step-patterns of black enamel
87 on silver,[50] and the Monymusk Reliquary in
Edinburgh with the flowing animal-designs. The
Kells structure rings the changes among its
decorative motifs more than these small shrines do,
and it is more continuously ornamented. The roof
is covered with brightly coloured, concave,
tongued roof-tiles or *tegulae*, very loosely spaced;
very much this form of *tegula*, in miniature
imitation presumably of real structures, appears in a
number of hogback tomb-covers at Govan near
245 Glasgow and at Meigle in Perthshire.[51] I mentioned
in a previous chapter that Eadbert, Bishop of
Lindisfarne, had lead sheets placed on the roof and
walls of his wooden church. Perhaps these lead
claddings were elaborate, cut out, like stencils, into

patterns. The walls of the Kells structure have
differently shaped decorative panels, one row
shaped rather like 'clubs' in playing-cards, and
above this a row of inverted birds' heads and necks,
with a short curved parrot- or puffin-like beak.[52]
This parrot-head has its best parallel on the St
Germain-en-Laye D-shaped mount, in the short, *246*
broad birds'-heads which terminate snakes' bodies
at the mount's blunt end. A curious feature of the
Kells structure, which again compares well with
shrines, is the pair of heart-shaped ornaments
which project from the top corners of the structure.
These contain two confronted crested beast-heads
separated by a zig-zag interlace strip, like the
horizontal ornament on the shoulder of the Lough
Erne Shrine.[53] The roof-ridge of the Lough Erne *244*

245 Hogback tomb-cover at
Meigle, Perthshire. Ninth or
tenth century

246 Detail of a gilt-bronze D-shaped mount. St Germain-en-Laye. Eighth century

247 Fragment of a bronze mount from Gausel, Stavanger, Norway. Eighth century

248 Gilt-bronze D-shaped mount. St Germain-en-Laye. Eighth century

Shrine has blunt projecting ornamental finials, and the finials on the Emly Shrine are animal-heads, gilt with green enamel, turning to look back along the roof-ridge. The finials attached to the Monymusk Reliquary project far beyond the ridge, but are narrow, keeping to the profile of the ridge itself. The great finials represented in stone, on the stone imitation of a house-shrine on top of Muiredach's

232 Cross at Monasterboice, are much broader, presenting a flat face to the spectator – heart-shaped, like the finials represented in the Kells picture. These may be turned round at right-angles, so as to enter the viewer's plane of vision, or else are attached differently. The D-shaped plaques in the Museum at St Germain-en-Laye, with another

247 fragment found in Norway, now in Bergen Museum, have been identified by Hunt and Henry

248 as the finials of a large shrine.[54] Each 'finial' is about 20 cm long, massively made, with a strong broad underside, and on the main face, shallow flat-topped projecting bosses. Placed alongside one another, but evidently not immediately conjacent since the edge is elaborately ornamented, they would form a long heart-shaped or blunt pear-shaped projection, very similar in silhouette to the Kells finials. They are remarkably complex structures for non-functioning decorative appendages. The shrine on which they were mounted must have represented the absolute summit of Insular grandeur.

ΚΑΙΕΠΙϹΧΩΝ
ΠΑΛΙΝΕϡΑΠ
ΕΚΤΗϹΚΙΒΩ
ΛΥΤΟΝΗΠΕ
ΕΙΧΕΝΦΥΜΟ
ϹΤΟΜΑΤΙΑΥΓ
ΟΤΙΚΕΚΟΠΑ

X

249 Noah's Ark in the fragmentary Cotton Genesis, Cotton MS Otho B.VI. Fifth century. From *Vetusta Monumenta Rerum Britannicarum*, I, 1747

If the accoutrements of a shrine mimic the shape and structural parts of a wooden, lead-slatted church, then we may suppose that Christ in the Kells miniature is indeed represented on top of a temple or church. He is enormously out of proportion to the building, but people making up the crowd round about and the man in the doorway below are not impossibly large for a small oratory. Christ's proportions in relation to the structure are very much those of Noah in Early Christian representations of the Ark, for example those of the Cotton Genesis,[55] reproduced in the later mosaics *249* in San Marco in Venice, or in wall-paintings in the Roman catacombs.

The largest-scale Noah appears in the catacomb of Peter and Marcellinus. This Noah's incongruous *233* proportions caused a seventeenth-century anti- *250* quary who recorded the painting to identify him as Pope Marcellus preaching from a pulpit.[56] I am tempted to interpret the Kells structure as an ambo or pulpit, in which Christ is in ordinary proportions to the structure he stands in, with the finials intended as lecterns; their broad flanges would serve conveniently for supporting a normal-sized Insular Gospel-book.[57] If Christ were in an ambo or pulpit, we would be able easily to identify the crowd who so oddly accompany him in his Temptation. In Luke 4, 13, the devil ends his Temptation of Christ. At verse 14 Christ returned 'in the power of the Spirit', so still dominated by the words *plenus sancto Spirito*, to Galilee. In Nazareth, from verse 15 onwards, he went into the synagogue on the sabbath day, and stood up to read. 'And there was delivered unto him the book of the prophet Esaias. And when he had opened the book [in the Vulgate he unrolls it – *Et ut revolvit librum*], he found the place where it was written: "The spirit of the Lord is upon me [*Spiritus Domini super me*], because he hath anointed me to preach the Gospel to the poor, deliverance to the captives, and recovering of sight to the blind . . .'. At verse 20 we read: 'He closed [*plicuisset*, folded up] the book, and he gave it again to the minister and sat down. And the eyes of all them that were in the synagogue were fastened upon him.' Medieval readers of the Old Testament Book of Esdras would know that to read the Law of Moses to the Chosen People the priest and lector stood up upon the wooden pulpit 'that was made for the purpose'.[58] Christ would be imagined doing the same in the synagogue as Esdras in the forecourt of the Temple. In his *Liber Officialis*, Amalarius of Metz, the Carolingian

liturgical expert, allegorically connects Esdras'
wooden pulpit with the wood of the Cross, by
which Christ triumphed over Death.[59]

The whole sequence, Baptism, Temptation (full
of the Holy Spirit), reading in the synagogue, in the
power of the Spirit, is united in sense. St Matthew's
Gospel presents the events after the Temptation in
terms different from and more general than Luke,
but the fulfilment of Isaiah's prophecy in the person
of Christ is clearly, and for our purpose
significantly, expressed. We read in Matthew 4, 12:
'Jesus departed into Galilee . . . that it might be
fulfilled which was spoken by Esaias the prophet . . .
beyond Jordan, Galilee of the Gentiles: the people
which sat in darkness saw great light; and to them
which sat in the region and shadow of death light is
sprung up . . .'.

The Church's celebration of Christ as bringing
light to the darkness of the world is concentrated in
the liturgy and rites of Easter. The *Life of St
Patrick*[60] written in the late seventh century by
Muirchú essentially associates the practice and
teaching of Christianity with the lighting of the
Paschal fire. In connection with the solemnities of
the Easter vigil, a hymn of praise established itself
in Christian usage from the fifth century onwards,
centred on the blessing and lighting of the Paschal
candle. The text recalls the mercies of God: 'This
night [the evening of Holy Saturday] is that very
night when the children of Israel were brought out
of Egypt, when a pillar of fire chased away the dark
cloud of sin. The lighting of the candle dispels the
night. Christ rising from the grave sheds his light
over all the children of men.' The hymn
accompanying the lighting of the Paschal candle
begins *Exultet iam angelica turba*, 'now let the
angelic throng rejoice'.[61] The *Exultet* hymn was
especially emphasized in his edition of the Christian
rites by Alcuin.[62] Amalarius of Metz makes plain
the role of the catechumen in the rites of Holy
Saturday. In the scriptural readings which lead up
to his baptism he learns that just as the Israelites
were freed from the hand of Pharaoh, so he is freed
from the grip of the devil by the water of Baptism.[63]
Ceolfrith's letter, quoted by Bede, to the Pictish
King Nechtan about the right calculation and
celebration of Easter refers to the festival of Holy
Saturday:[64] 'after the appropriate solemn Easter rite
of lessons and prayers and Paschal ceremonies, they
offer the mystery of the body and blood of the
Spotless Lamb to God. For it is the night in which
the children of Israel were delivered out of Egypt

250 Noah in the Ark, wall-painting in the catacomb of Peter
and Marcellinus, interpreted by the seventeenth-century copyist
as Pope Marcellus preaching. From G. Wilpert, *Die Katakom-
bengemälde und ihre alten Copien*

by the blood of the Lamb, and also the night in
which, by the Resurrection of Christ, all the people
of God were freed from eternal death. And again,
in which the Lord freed the world with his own
blood from the darkness of sin . . .'. The Stowe
Missal[65] contains the text of a prayer on behalf of
the Christian convert, that 'all blindness of heart
being expelled, the snares of Satan whereby he was
bound fast may be broken, so that the doors of
truth be opened to him'. Satan is called the unclean
spirit, *inmundus Spiritus*. The prayer asks for the
protection of angels 'for the inhabitants of this
house of your servants'.

A representation of Christ expounding the
prophet Isaiah, in illustration of Luke 4, 2–13,
which is what we could reasonably expect the
picture on *f.* 202v of Kells to be, would inevitably
be redolent of the healing grace of baptism, and of
the shedding of the light of Christ over his people at
Easter. It is satisfactory, therefore, that the format
of the Kells illustration should so closely
approximate to that adopted in the eleventh
century in illustrated texts of the *Exultet* hymn,[66] 251
emanating from the ambience of Monte Cassino. In
the Kells miniature, the crowd around the ambo
where Christ rolls up the text of Isaiah which he has

251 *Lumen Christi* scene from Exultet Roll. Eleventh century

initial. The breadth of the ornamental border of the picture, and its division into separate blocks, not the consecutive panels of Lindisfarne but discrete units, with wide frames round each one, closely parallel the treatment of the borders in the two portrait pages in the Durham Cassiodorus,[67] although Kells marks perhaps a later stage in complexity. Emphasis is placed on the motif of the cross, an equal-armed cross being placed at the right and left, and above and below the enthroned figure. The outer arm of the cross emerges beyond the edge of the frame, and is further extended by the hands, head and feet of a second figure spread-eagled behind the whole decorative layout of the picture. The enthroned figure sits with widely splayed knees and feet in profile, each leg viewed as if the figure were seen sitting sideways. The representation of the upper part of the body is stylized even beyond the norm of Kells. The priest-like figure with the stole, for example, in the *Liber 227 Generationis* page is crisply, naturalistically drawn, with an ordinary pair of shoulders and a normal disposition of left and right arms. The frontal 223 figure on *f.* 28v with one hand holding the book and the other hand tucked into his mantle, offers no anatomical problems. But in the St John page the figure's left arm (at the right from the spectator's point of view), holding up the book, grows from the middle of his chest. It is disposed like the single right arm of a sideways-seated figure, such as we 170 see, for example, in the St Matthew portrait in the Lindisfarne Gospels. The head is the same majestic wedge-shaped type of head that we see in the figure on *f.* 28v and in the Christ on *f.* 32v, with masses of splendidly interwoven locks of hair, the human equivalent of the mane of the Echternach lion. 105

Again and again in the Book of Kells we are reminded of the words in which Gerald of Wales in the twelfth century described the Gospel-book of Kildare:[68] 'Here you may see the face of majesty, divinely drawn.' The double mauve, orange and yellow nimbus, and the shapes of the ornaments within the nimbus, together with the three extra attached ornaments, give extraordinary emphasis to this figure. We seem to be approaching the visual equivalent of the literary effort to express divine splendour of the so-called *Vision of Adomnán*.[69] 'There is a great arch above the head of the supreme being, like an ornamented helmet or the crown of a king. If human eyes should see it, they would instantly be melted. There are three circles around him between him and the people, and their nature

read and proved in himself is the crowd of those spiritually reborn by baptism, the *populi Christiani*. The emphasis in the Stowe Missal on the expulsion of the devil by baptism is sufficient in itself to explain the iconography of the Kells picture. It subsumes Christ's 'Temptation' in the general victory offered by Christ to mankind. The art of Kells is symbolical and liturgical, not narrative, anticipating the large symbolic effects achieved in monastic tympana in France in the twelfth century.

A diagonal cross containing the Evangelist symbols on *f.* 290v is followed by a blank page on 252 whose reverse, *f.* 291v, is a full-page picture normally identified as the author portrait of St John. Opposite the picture is the great *In Principio*

174

252 'St John', the Book of Kells, *f. 291v*

253 The Trinity, brass matrix of the seal of Brechin Cathedral Chapter. Thirteenth century

254 Part of the Genealogy of Christ, St Luke's Gospel, Chapter 3, verses 32–36, the Book of Kells, *f*. 201v

cannot be understood by description. There are six thousand thousands with the figures of horses and birds around the fiery chair, as it blazes without limit or end. No one can describe the mighty Lord who is on the throne . . . if anyone should gaze long at him, around him from east and west, from south and north he will find on every side of him a glorious face, seven times as bright as the sun . . .'. This description might suggest something of the reasoning or imagination behind the physical ambiguity that we have noted in the figure on *f*. 291v of Kells. The picture comprises at any rate a remarkably sacred and sumptuous image.

St John was regarded as the most spiritually charged of the Evangelists. As Bede[70] and many other exegetes point out, St John was found worthy to rest on the bosom of Christ at the Last Supper, and drew thence the understanding of the mysteries of God that he displays both in his Gospel and in the Book of Revelation. So St John would be represented in a potent manner, and his resting on the bosom of Christ and drawing inspiration therefrom may well explain the composition of the page, the seated figure and its immediate frame being set off against the figure spread out mystically, with outstretched arms.[71] On the other hand, the majesty of the seated figure makes an identification with Christ not impossible, the book, pen, and ink-pot of the Evangelist making sense in the immediate context of the *incipit* of St John's Gospel, which celebrates Christ as the Word: 'The word was made flesh, and dwelt among us, and we beheld his glory, as of the only begotten of the Father, full of grace and truth.' The act of *writing* God's word endowed Ultán and his hands with special virtue, according to *De Abbatibus*. The relationship of the seated figure to the spread-eagled figure would still be explicable, in similar terms to those used above, since at verse 18 of Chapter 1 of St John's Gospel are the words: 'No man hath seen God at any time: the only begotten Son, which is in the bosom of the Father, he hath declared him.' These words are embodied in later medieval images of the Trinity, where Christ is seated in miniature or as a child upon the Father's bosom, or held out in front, hanging on a cross.[72] *253* In Kells the standing background-figure has a black beard but blond hair. The figure seen in a flaming glory at the top of the Kells *In Principio* initial is *255* similarly coloured. Could this also represent God the Father?

According to the apocryphal *Life of St John*, his

255 Beginning of St John's Gospel, *In Principio*, the Book of Kells, *f. 292*

ineffectual martyrdom involves the proffering to him of a poisoned chalice, from which he drinks without harm, whereas others die of it. In the Late Middle Ages St John is shown holding this chalice as his most familiar attribute, with a dragon or serpent projecting from it symbolizing the venom which had no power over him.[73] The seated figure holding a chalice at the right top corner of the *In Principio* initial seems, however, unlikely to represent St John himself. The context of this most sacred of Gospel passages should demand a more central image. In pose the figure closely resembles a margin figure, on *f.* 201v of the Book of Kells, in the Lucan genealogy, adjacent to the name 'Abraham', and presumably intended to recall the story of Melchisedek who brings bread and wine to Abraham in Genesis 14. Melchisedek's bread and wine became a celebrated 'type' of the Eucharist.[74] In the Epistle to the Hebrews 5, St Paul the Apostle calls Christ 'a priest for ever after the order of Melchisedek, who in the days of his flesh, when he had offered up prayers and supplications with strong crying and tears unto Him who was able to save him from Death . . . Though he were a son, yet learned he obedience by the things which he suffered.' So the resemblance of the two chalice-bearing figures in Kells is a deliberate pointer to that text, and to its meaning, Christ's agony before his Arrest and Crucifixion, referred to in St John's Gospel in two passages, Chapter 12, verse 27, 'Now is my soul troubled', and Chapter 18, verse 11, when Christ says in obedience to the Father's will: 'This cup [*calicem*], which the Father has given me, shall I not drink it?' The proximity of the huge beast-head to the small figure with the cup in the *In Principio* initial will signify the imminent assault of Satan upon Christ. The small figure's back is turned to the consoling divine image which, appropriately housed in the *In Principio* initial, signifies the eternal changeless Father. There are, then, perhaps three occasions[75] when the likeness of God the Father is attempted in the Book of Kells (*ff.* 28v, 291v, 292), as well as a number of images of God the Son – as Incarnate Word in the arms of the Virgin, Apocalyptic Saviour, enthroned Word, and Christ humbly suffering in his humanity.

6 The Book of Kells: the making of a relic

The Irish dimension

As part of the secularization of the old cathedral and monastic libraries of Britain which proceeded desultorily from the sixteenth century on into the seventeenth – essentially the same process which brought the Corpus Gospels to Cambridge and somehow extricated the Lindisfarne Gospels from Durham – the Book of Kells was handed over in the 1660s by Henry Jones to Trinity College, Dublin.[1] Jones also donated the Durrow Gospels, thus bringing together again under one roof two books which had once been housed side by side but which were separated, as I shall suggest, in the late ninth century. In his historical survey of the antiquities of the British churches, published in Dublin in 1639, Archbishop James Ussher records that the Book of Kells was currently revered by the men of Meath, and ascribed to St Columba himself.[2] An independent report dating to 1665 describes the Book of Kells as a large parchment volume in Irish written in Colum Cille's (Columba's) own hand. It was as the Book of Colum Cille that Trinity College received the Book of Kells into safe-keeping.[3]

The Kells association of the manuscript is confirmed by its having inserted on blank pages copies of Irish charters of eleventh- and twelfth-century date relating to the endowments of the church of Kells.[4] The association of the manuscript with Kells and with St Columba himself is principally grounded in the well-known entry in the *Annals of Ulster*, added under the year 1006, *recte* 1007, concerning the wicked theft of the great Gospel (*Soiscelae mor*) of Colum Cille from the western sacristy of the big stone church at Kells, and its retrieval nearly three months later stripped of its gold ornaments.[5] The chronicler calls the Gospel the chief relic (*primh-mind*) of the western world. The word *mind* (plural: *minna*) carries the connotation of 'crown', 'diadem' or 'halidom', so that a precious reliquary as well as relic is implied. The phrase 'of the western world' (*iarthair domain*), although a rhetorical flourish, is not used indiscriminately in the *Annals*. The same phrase is used of the great King Aethelstan when his death is reported in 939, two years after his famous victory at Brunanburh over the Norse of Dublin and their confederates. Aethelstan was 'pillar of the dignity of the western world'.[6] So it is evident that the chronicler had a very high opinion of the relic at Kells. According to one interpretation of the Irish text the Gospels had this prime status on account of its man-made (?) embellishment, or cover (*ar ai in comdaigh doendai*). According to another interpretation, the Gospels had this status of itself, and the phrase 'on account of its cover' merely gives the cause of the theft.[7] We can probably reconcile these two interpretations by emphasizing that it was gold that was stripped off the book, not merely silver-gilt ('silver under gold') or silver.[8] I shall argue that the Gospels and its cover are likely to have been true equivalents of one another, in status and artistry.

The great Gospels of Colum Cille (which we now know as the 'Book of Kells') with its gold cover, represented fundamentally a status symbol, both material and spiritual. By the known standards of the day the Book of Kells is an extraordinarily ambitious and splendid work. The precondition for its manufacture was obviously a mature scriptorium, lavishly equipped with technical expertise. It is technically a very complex book, employing a great range of pigments.[9] The painters' workshop which produced Kells was deeply rooted in Insular artistic achievements, and was at a stage of design beyond, but not far beyond, Lichfield. We may assume that intellectually the illustrations and overall visual character of the Book of Kells reflected both generally and also in particular ways the cult of the saint with whom the 1007 *Annal* entry so emphatically associates it. We know what the community of Iona thought of Columba – what image of him was being officially promoted and promulgated in the period of Adomnán and Egbert – from the *Life* written by Adomnán.[10] When I discussed the Book of Durrow I quoted from Adomnán's *Life of St Columba* not only to establish facts about the Columban mission to Northumbria, but also to savour the spiritual interpretation which the Columban community offered of these historical events. Inevitably, to serve its contemporary purpose, Adomnán's *Life* is not a factual biography.

In the interpretation of Columba offered by Adomnán there are several leading ideas. In the first place his association with the Holy Spirit of God is repeatedly stressed. His name Columba (or dove) was the result of divine inspiration; the Holy Spirit took the form of a dove, according to the Gospels, when it descended on Christ at his baptism. Columba offered himself as a dwelling place for the Holy Spirit.[11] It is significant that, as

242, 217 we have seen, the Book of Kells pauses over, and gives decorative and pictorial emphasis to, the idea of Christ 'full of the Holy Spirit'. Through visitation of the Holy Spirit Columba was an exegete of remarkable insights. At Hinba, for three days and nights continuously the Holy Spirit was poured upon him 'abundantly and in an incomparable manner. Everything that in sacred Scriptures is dark and most difficult became plain.'[12] A number of specific interpretations of the sacred books were revealed to him. The Book of Kells is not a work of editorial excellence, but as an illustrated Gospels it gives typological and other interpretative modes very free play, and in this seems truly to express the insights which Columba is reported to have achieved.

In addition, Columba is likened to Christ. His birth was anticipated by prophecies, and the event itself was accompanied by shining light. Columba turned water into wine. He calmed storms, repulsed demons, and healed the sick. In his major miracle, he raised a boy from the dead. That miracle

of power placed him, Adomnán says, in the same categories as the prophets Elijah and Elisha, and the Apostles Peter, Paul and John. He had earned a glorious eternal place in the heavenly Kingdom, in both companies of prophets and apostles, as a man 'prophetic *and* apostolic'.[13] Adomnán was of course making the conventional moves of the hagiographer. When he drew on the Apocalypse (Revelation 7) at the end of his *Life*, to set Columba among the thousands of white-robed saints who have washed their robes in the blood of the Lamb and who follow the Lamb as their leader, he is merely imitating a letter written by Sulpicius Severus early in the fifth century about St Martin of Tours.[14] But what mattered was the atmosphere created by these sentiments, even if they were derivative. It was important for a spokesman of the Columban community, around 700, to affirm that Columba was a saint of universal validity.[15] His fame, Adomnán states in his closing sentences, has reached throughout 'our Ireland' and also far afield, to the city of Rome (*civitatem Romanum*) which is the chief of all cities (*caput est omnium civitatum*).[16] When the *Annals* record the building of Kells by Columba's community, it is called *nova civitas*,[17] so the reference to Rome by Adomnán was not secular and rhetorical; the sense was of an ecclesiastical city. Adomnán, in advance of the adoption by Iona of the Roman Easter, was stating the case for the pre-eminence of Columba in the universal Church, and the vocabulary and analogies that he deploys were part of a deliberate exercise.

So far as St Columba's homeland of Ireland is concerned, the claims made for him in Adomnán's *Life* must be seen against the claims advanced in the seventh century on their patrons' behalf by the devotees of the two 'senior' saints of Ireland, Patrick, of Armagh, and Brigit, more genuinely of Kildare. The *Life of St Brigit*, written in Latin by Cogitosus in the 670s or 680s,[18] asserts that her church is not just of local importance but is the 'head of almost all the Irish churches and the pinnacle excelling all the monasteries of the Irish, whose *parochia* [a combination of jurisdictional authority and proprietorial rights] is spread throughout the whole land of Ireland and extends from sea to sea'. The Bishop of Kildare is represented as chief bishop (*Archiepiscopus*) of the Irish bishops, and the Abbess of Kildare is the venerated superior of all abbesses, in a calculated bid for social and spiritual primacy.[19] At the same time, and with more political potential, the

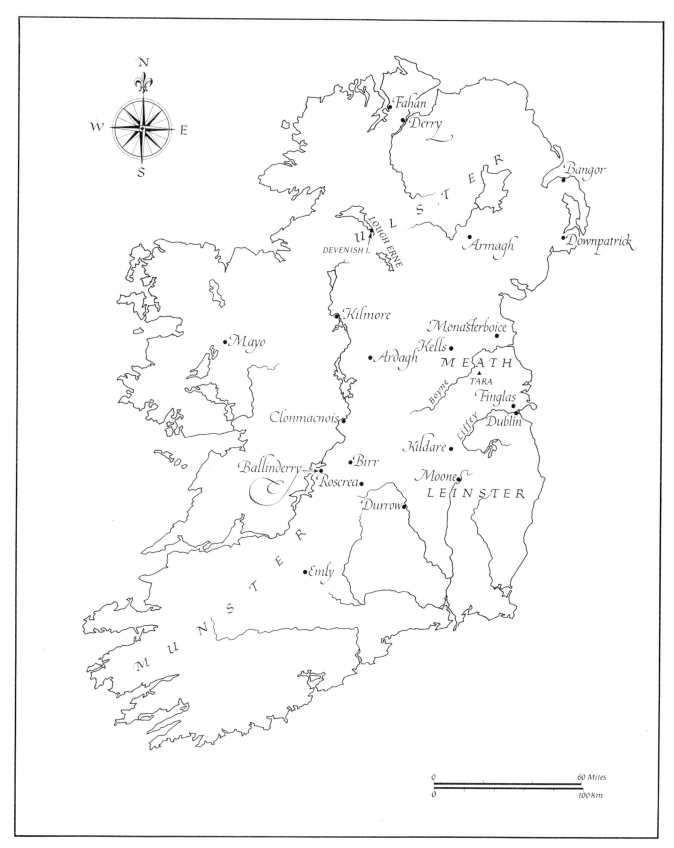

N

W   E

S

Fahan

Derry

U L S T E R

Bangor

LOUGH ERNE
DEVENISH I.

Armagh

Downpatrick

Kilmore

Monasterboice

Mayo

Kells

Ardagh

M E A T H

Boyne

▲ TARA

Finglas

Clonmacnois

Liffey

Dublin

Kildare

Ballinderry

Birr

Moone

Roscrea

L E I N S T E R

Durrow

M U N S T E R

Emly

0   60 *Miles*

0   100 *Km*

256 Map showing relevant sites in Ireland

ecclesiastical lawyers of Armagh were advancing the legal and metaphysical claims of St Patrick. These are stated at their most extreme in the mid-seventh-century *Liber Angeli*.[20] Because St Patrick was the Apostle of the Irish, God rewarded him and his church of Armagh with precedence over all the churches and monasteries of Ireland. Armagh, unlike Iona, had no chink in its armour in respect of recognition of the Roman Easter, and its orthodoxy was vouched for by its claim to possess relics of the princes of the Apostles, Peter and Paul; also a relic of the Roman martyr St Lawrence, and 'by a secret dispensation', a linen cloth stained with the blood of Christ. So equipped, St Patrick was appointed Judge of all the Irish on the great day of terrible Judgment, in the presence of Christ.

Armagh claimed a special union with episcopal foundations throughout Ireland, and added to this an assurance that all monks who 'returned to Patrick' were not to be thought of as denying their original monastic vows. The author of the *Liber Angeli* was not unaware of the practical benefits and prestige enjoyed by Iona as head of the widely scattered Columban confederation of monasteries. But it would not have helped his propaganda to acknowledge or even allude to the 'apostolic' authority of St Columba. Armagh was more immediately concerned to put a check on the jurisdictional and territorial claims of St Brigit of Kildare. In a short addendum to the *Liber Angeli*, St Patrick and St Brigit are declared to be 'the two pillars of the Irish, linked by friendship of charity'. After the definition of his and his successors' authority, St Patrick is made to address St Brigit in affectionate but also briskly businesslike terms: 'O my Brigit, your *paruchia* in your province will be reckoned unto you for your monarchy, but in the eastern and western part it will be in my dominion.'[21] After Cogitosus's *Life of St Brigit*, no more claims to exclusive ecclesiastical overlordship were advanced for the bishops of Kildare, and in the face of Armagh's aggression, Kildare seems literally to have lost ground.[22] Though her cult was deeply rooted in the folk and social psychology of Ireland, St Brigit's devotees were unable to quote a supernatural *Diktat* to support an enlargement of her ecclesiastical role. The lawyers of Armagh were more crafty, on the lookout for the main chance. The main chance lay outside Armagh's immediate home-province of Ulster, and involved latching on to the steadily growing authority, in the secular sphere, of the Uí Néill kingdoms, whose rulers as

Kings of Tara claimed rights of sovereignty over Ireland.[23] In their status-seeking, the 'High Kings' and the patriarchal saints were mutually dependent.

The claims of Columba in the ecclesiastical-political sphere were quietly stated by Adomnán in his *Life*. Later Columban literature was more overt, not to say crude, and in this, reflects the measure of practical success which the Columban community had achieved. The Life of St Columba contained in the fifteenth-century *Lebar Brecc*[24] differs from Adomnán's *Life* in laying claim to a great number of monastic foundations in Ireland, in the form of a narrative of the saint's itinerary through Ireland, a device also employed in the *Life of St Brigit* in the same collection. The account of Columba is full of anachronisms, deliberately contrived; for example, it represents the saint himself choosing Kells (founded in 804) as the site of his chief church.[25] Interestingly enough, the same concession and wish to conciliate St Brigit which we met in the addendum to the *Liber Angeli* of Armagh can be seen in the Middle Irish *Life of St Columba*. This narrates a fantastic incident at Swords, just north of Dublin, where Columba is reported to have founded a monastery. The narrative suddenly shifts to St Brigit, who died two or three years after Columba was born. At one time, while wandering through the Plain of Liffey, the thought strikes her that if the Plain were hers, she would offer it all to God. Then Columba, in his cell at Swords, is reintroduced; he has heard her thought, and in a loud voice he gives St Brigit credit for the idea and evidently confirms the validity of her offer. Then at once the writer reports that St Columba founded many churches among the men of Leinster, for example Moone. St Columba's actions do not encroach, therefore, upon the essential authority of St Brigit.[26]

The tactical exercise which is recorded here was real and practical. The monks of the Columban confederation (*familia Iae*, or *familia Columbae Cille*) were able to integrate their founder as one of the *three* pillars of the Irish – Patrick, Brigit and Columba. In the later literature Patrick and Brigit are given roles like those of Simeon and Anna in the Gospels, prophesying or welcoming the birth of Columba: 'A man child shall be born, sage, prophet, and poet,' says Patrick. Enthusiastically Brigit takes up the theme: 'He will be Colomb Cille, without blemish. It was not over soon, to perceive him . . .'.[27] The most extraordinary evidence of Columba's increased importance is found in the

Book of Armagh, a copy of the New Testament (preserved in Trinity College, Dublin) which also contains an important collection of texts relating to the life of St Patrick and to the rights of his church at Armagh. The *Book of Armagh* was written in 807 at the orders of Abbot Torbach.[28] One of the documents that it contains involves St Columba deeply in the affairs of St Patrick. It was St Columba who by inspiration of the Holy Spirit (*Spirito Sancto instigante*) revealed the place where Patrick lay buried, namely Saul near Downpatrick in County Down.[29] One is tempted to see this conciliatory tampering with evidence, or creation of evidence, as a parallel to the curious reference by 'Columba' to a 'Patrick' in the dedicatory palimpsests on the last leaf of the Book of Durrow.[30]

Before the tactical unity of Patrick, Brigit, and Columba was established and, as legend would have it, they all lay comfortably in the same grave at Downpatrick, under a single coverlet woven by Brigit,[31] the extents and limits of their financial and political 'empires' must have been defined in a series of moves and countermoves. The material basis and motive of this rivalry is betrayed in one specific instance by Bishop Tírechán's complaint, in a catalogue of Patrician churches drawn up about 670[32] and later incorporated into the *Book of Armagh*, of an encroachment by the *familia Columbae Cille* on a Patrician property in Donegal.[33]

In the Irish *Annals*[34] – brief records of accessions, 'hostings', battles, and sudden or occasionally peaceful deaths – it seems possible to discern the outline of the manoeuvres of Armagh and Iona to establish or confirm their influence and prestige in a very volatile political environment. These manoeuvres and the loyalties that they engendered and reflected are directly relevant to the making, and to the subsequent fortunes, of the Book of Kells and related works of art.

The first reference to the movement of relics from Iona to Ireland appears in the *Annals of Ulster* in 727. The relics were brought to Ireland by the abbot of Iona, called Cilléne Droichtech, in association with the 'renewal' or promulgation in Ireland of the Law of Adomnán. This Law, protecting women, children, and men in religious communities against acts of violence, was first drawn up in 697 between Adomnán and Irish lawyers, and was guaranteed by leading laymen in Ireland and Scotland.[35] Among the provisions of the Law was payment of tax by the Columban churches in Ireland to Iona. To validate the

'renewal' of the Law in 727, the relics of Adomnán went on circuit.[36] A later source represents these relics of Adomnán as a heterogeneous collection of relics of various saints, similar to the collection which St Wilfrid of Ripon put together and carefully labelled during his extensive travels.[37] However, it seems more likely that the relics were the bones of Adomnán himself, disinterred after a decent interval like the bones of Fursey or of the scribe Ultán, and encased in a portable shrine. The enshrining, and the transport of the relics to Ireland, must have been the deliberate decision of Cilléne Droichtech.

The relics of Adomnán remained in Ireland for three years, returning to Iona in 730.[38] The objective must have been to have the Law and the payment of tribute money to Iona officially backed by the leading Irish secular authority, the Uí Néill overlord, the holder of the 'High Kingship' of Tara. The Kingship had in the first years of the eighth century been in the control of one or other of the two branches of the Northern Uí Néill, the Cenél Conaill, the rulers of Tyrconnell, the family to which St Columba himself belonged, and the Cenél nEógain, rulers of Tyrone. In 722 they lost the Kingship to a candidate from the Southern Uí Néill, and squabbled bitterly with one another. Their private war reached its climax in 727 when the Cenél Conaill defeated the Cenél nEógain. The Cenél Conaill candidate, Flaithbertach, then went on to defeat and kill the Southern Uí Néill King of Tara. The accession of Flaithbertach vexed the Cenél nEógain, and they continually harried their successful rival.[39] The activities of Cilléne Droichtech are set against this unsettled background. As we have seen, Armagh was equally looking for support from the Uí Néill kings. The special relationship which we should have expected Columba's churches to have with the Northern Uí Néill may have existed as long as the Cenél Conaill, his own kinsmen, had the upper hand, but the interests of the Cenél nEógain appear to have turned elsewhere.[40] By harassment they forced Flaithbertach to resign the kingship in 734, and he was hurried away into religion, not in any Columban monastery as his family ties would suggest, but at Armagh.[41] It is as the champion of Armagh that the new Uí Néill overlord, Áed Allán of the Cenél nEógain, presents himself, going at once to avenge some supposed profanation offered to Armagh by the King of Ulster. In the year of Áed Allán's accession as King of Tara the *Annals of*

162

Ulster report the '*commotatio*' of the relics of Peter and Paul and Patrick to fulfil, or enforce, the Law (*ad legem perficiendam*),[42] that is, an official parade, in circuit, of the *vexilla* of Armagh, coming fast on the heels of the relics of Adomnán. In 737 Áed Allán, after a conference arranged between himself and the King of Munster, promulgated the 'Law of Patrick'. The *Annals* says: 'The Law of Patrick held all Ireland.'[43] This took all the clerics of Ireland under the protection of Armagh, superseding the law of Adomnán. This 'Law of Patrick', and fines for its infringement, no doubt redounded to the legal and financial advantage of Armagh.[44] In obscure circumstances, but perhaps in a bid to change the unpropitious drift of events, Cilléne Droichtech is reported to have *given* the relics of Adomnán to Ireland, to make 'peace and a covenant' between the Cenél nEógain and the Cenél Conaill. 'Droichtech' may mean simply *pontifex*, 'bishop', or it may mean literally 'bridgemaker'.[45] Certainly bridge-building and diplomacy were necessary to regain the united interest and loyalty of the dominant Northern Uí Néill. But the Abbot's conciliatory efforts were in vain.

In 743 Áed Allán was attacked and killed near Kells by Domnall, the King of Meath, of the Southern Uí Néill. Domnall is recorded as having 'entered religion' on two occasions, in 740 and 744,[46] and yet unlike Aethelred of Mercia, at Bardney forty years earlier, he remained an active ruler until he died peacefully in 763. Perhaps he accepted ascetic regulations for himself, such as would appeal to the monks and anchorites of Iona. In 753 Domnall Mide, so called because he was the first of the Meath branch of the Southern Uí Néill to become King of Tara, is recorded to have promulgated the 'Law of Colum Cille', evidently on his own initiative.[47] The gesture and the practical rewards must have been welcome to Iona, for in the following year Sléibéne, Abbot of Iona, came to Ireland, and in 757 Sléibéne is recorded as promulgating the 'Law of Colum Cille' again.[48] The Columban interest was now focussed on a new ally, among the Southern Uí Néill. Domnall Mide died in 763, having managed to survive persistent trouble-making by the Cenél nEógain clan of the Northern Uí Néill. Domnall's Columban commitments are confirmed by his being buried with honour and veneration in St Columba's foundation at Durrow. His ancestors will have been buried in the cemetery of Clonmacnois, and it has been suggested that the extraordinary pitched battle fought between Clonmacnois and Durrow in 764, when two hundred of the *familia* of Durrow were killed, was the result of Clonmacnois' resentment at the loss of prestige and revenue involved in Durrow's burial of King Domnall.[49] It is a useful reminder of how close material benefits and sources of income were to the heart of the great monastic institutions at the end of our period.

At Domnall's death Niall Frossach, the Cenél nEógain candidate, seized the Kingship of Tara. Four years later, in 767, the *Annals of Ulster* again note the promulgation of the 'Law of Patrick'.[50] Presumably tribute was flowing officially to Armagh. But the Southern branch of the Uí Néill, ruled by Domnall Mide's son Donnchad, was restless. Donnchad took an army to the north, and menaced and coerced the Northern Uí Néill. By the early 770s he was king of Tara in all but name. What was done with Flaithbertach in 734, but involving no doubt a stricter and more wearing routine, was done with Niall Frossach. His death as a monk at Iona in 778[51] probably indicates not so much a personal tribute to the sanctity of Iona by a former Cenél nEógain overlord, as the result of the political muscle of the Southern Uí Néill in collaboration with the Columban establishment. In the very same year, 778, as if impatient to do so, Donnchad, now King of Tara, and Bresal, Abbot of Iona, jointly promulgated the 'Law of Colum Cille'.[52] The asceticism which was presumably one of the strengths and appeals of the Columban confederation may have been the central theme of the Synod of the Irish Church which was held at Tara in 780.[53] This was the first general synod to be held in Ireland since 697, when the Law of Adomnán had been promulgated. Those who attended were scribes and anchorites, comprising 'the synods of the Uí Néill and the Leinstermen', presided over by the Abbot of Finglas, a famous ascetic. In 789 the *Annals of Ulster* record what appears to be an overtly anti-Armagh gesture by King Donnchad, at a fair at Rathairthir, when he 'dishonoured' the *Bachall Ísu*, a famous crozier-relic of St Patrick, and others of his relics.[54]

The Tara synod did not have occasion to discuss the matter that was to become the dominant concern from the closing years of the eighth century onwards: the destructive incursion of the Norsemen, which brought to an end the great creative period of Insular monastic culture. The first plundering raid on Iona (*vastatio Iae Coluimcille*) is recorded in the *Annals* in 795.[55] A second raid took place in 802.[56] In 804 the Columban community, wealthy and well-connected, obtained a site for a new monastery of Colum Cille at Kells in Meath, as the *Annals* says, 'without litigation'.[57] Building was begun at Kells under the personal direction of Cellach, Abbot of Iona, showing the close ties between the new project and Iona.[58] It may be wondered whether a powerful expansion of the Columban community was not part of a long-term plan; location of the new monastery in Meath must reflect the joint interests of the Meath branch of the Southern Uí Néill, Kings of Tara or competitors for the Kingship, and the Columban community. But the atrocity of 806 when the Norsemen again struck at Iona, murdering sixty-eight of the monastic 'family', shows that the need for a new mainland base and for strong local secular support was genuine and urgent.[59] It was not to Derry that the Columban refugees went, although Derry is sentimentally wailed-over in the poetry interspersed among the narrative in Manus O'Donnell of Tirconnel's late *Life of Columba* (1532).[60] In the seventeenth century, as we have seen, the men of Meath were reported to hold the great Gospel of Colum Cille sacred. The historical record of the eighth century allows us to probe the deep groundwork of that devotion.

The 'Law of Patrick' was promoted by a parade of the holy relics of Armagh. The Law of Adomnán was promulgated with a display of the relics of Adomnán, Columba's successor and biographer. If Cilléne Droichtech before his death in 752 did indeed deposit in Ireland the diplomatically and spiritually important relics of Adomnán, what substitute for them did the Abbot of Iona employ, in his formal visitations overseas and in his public relations? What do we know of the relics of St Columba himself, which by implication would be involved in promulgations of the 'Law of Colum Cille'?[61]

The relics of St Columba: Iona and after

Judging by the careful partition of the founder Bishop Aidan's bones by Colman when he quitted Lindisfarne in 664, and by the official veneration in which the body of St Cuthbert was held by later generations of Lindisfarne monks, the principal relic not only of Iona but of the entire Columban community must be assumed to have been the body of St Columba. Bede, writing not long before 731, states that the island monastery in which Columba's body lies (*in quo ipse requiescit corpore*) held pre-eminence over all the foundations of Columba.[62] Iona's possession of the body was important in political and ecclesiastical terms. Where he was expected to rise again at the Last Judgment, he would be a powerful advocate for those whose graves had accumulated around his own. Adomnán, reporting the circumstances of Columba's burial one hundred years after the event,[63] states that the body was laid in a prepared tomb, wrapped in linen, the same word *sindon* being employed as in the account of Christ's burial in the Gospels. A measure of secrecy seems to attach to the grave, since Adomnán makes a point of mentioning that storms cut Iona off from outside visitors over the three-day period while Columba's funeral rites were being performed. Adomnán further states that down to his own day heavenly brightness does not cease to appear at the place where the holy bones repose, as well as frequent visits of angels, 'as is established by being revealed to certain elect persons'. This last phrase might suggest either that those who knew of the celestial visions at the grave were a select group, or that only a select group knew the exact whereabouts of the grave. On the other hand the grave is marked by the stone which Columba used as a pillow, placed 'beside it as an epitaph' (*titulus monumenti*). When Adomnán was writing, around 700, Columba awaited the universal resurrection still in his original grave. So despite the enshrining of St Brigit and Conlaed, the first bishop of Kildare, vouched for by Cogitosus, and also despite Bede's evidence for the enshrining of Chad and Cuthbert in England, and likewise of Fursey and the martyred Hewalds on the Continent, it is certain that no elevation and enshrining of Columba had taken place in the course of the seventh century. The site of Columba's original grave is traditionally located at the south-west of the façade of the medieval abbey church, where fragments of an early structure survive, with *257* buttress-like extensions at the base of the walls. A number of intercessory inscribed slabs, of eighth- and ninth-century date, originally formed the adjacent pavement.[64]

According to Adomnán's account, the immediately accessible portable relics of St Columba preserved at Iona and used to invoke the help of the saint were garments (*vestimenta*), including the white tunic (*candida tunica*) which he was wearing

257 Traditional site of St Columba's grave on Iona, with adjacent inscribed grave-slabs

when he died, and books, unspecified, 'written with his own pen' (*libris stilo ipsius discriptis*). Joint use was made of the garments and books; they were laid together on the altar to procure calm weather when a massive shipment of planks for various construction-works on the island was to be ferried over the Sound of Iona. On another occasion, during a severe drought, the holy tunic was carried and lifted and shaken in a rain-making exercise, while the books were opened and passages read aloud.[65] One of the books owned by the monastery is likely to have been the Psalter which Adomnán records Columba as writing in his last illness. When he reached Psalm 33, at verse 10, at the bottom of the page, he said: 'Here I must stop. Let Baíthéne write what follows.'[66] Baíthéne was Columba's cousin and disciple, and his immediate successor as abbot of Iona. Adomnán represents the drought when Columba's books were ritually used in terms

of Leviticus 26, 19–20: 'I will give you a sky above like iron . . . your labour shall be spent in vain. The earth shall yield no produce . . . .'. To answer Scripture with Scripture, God's curse in Leviticus would be very properly parried with the last Psalm-text that Columba wrote: 'There is no dearth for those that fear the Lord . . . they that seek him shall not lack any good thing.'[67] Of course earlier Psalms in Columba's Psalter also contain passages appropriate for rain-making; nor was the Psalter permanently truncated, since Baíthéne was entrusted with its completion. Adomnán notes that Baíthéne was a worthy successor to Columba, 'not in teaching only but also in writing'. Adomnán's phrase, 'written with his pen', might not exclude books actually written by Baíthéne if he employed Columba's implements. Baíthéne was evidently an expert scribe of the Psalms, since in a story from earlier in Columba's *Life*, Adomnán reports

Columba knowing without checking that a Psalter-text written by Baíthéne was perfect except for the omission of a single letter I.[68]

However, Adomnán makes it clear that Columba's personal contribution to a written text was credited with quite special powers. Adomnán refers to a book of hymns for the week (*ymnorum liber septimaniorum*) written in the hand of St Columba (*sancti Columbae manu discriptus*) which survived accidental immersion in a river in Leinster, from Christmas to Easter. The book-satchel rotted, but the book when at last retrieved was found to be extraordinarily white and clear (*candidissimum et lucidissimum*) – evidently the princely Columba had access to the finest vellum. Adomnán relies on 'trustworthy witnesses' here, so the hymn book was evidently not one of the possessions of the monastery at Iona.[69] In another such incident a boy was drowned in the River Boyne with a book-satchel tucked under his arm. Twenty days afterwards the satchel was recovered and the books were found to be spoilt, all except 'the single page written by the holy fingers of St Columba' (*folium sancti Columbae sanctis scriptum degitulis*) which was dry and undamaged.[70] In both these anecdotes Adomnán makes the interesting remark that St Columba's writings had survived unimpaired as if they had been kept in a 'container', called respectively *scriniolum* and *scrinium*, early evidence in the Iona/Irish context of the custom of totally encasing a valuable book. Adomnán states that he has heard from various quarters similar stories about books written by Columba's hand (*de libris manu sancti Columabe craxatis*). So already by around 700 the tradition was that books written by Columba were scattered in a number of places other than Iona.

St Columba's reputation as an original author may have had a basis in fact. The hymn *Altus prosator*, in praise of God the Father, and its complement *In te Christe*, have been attributed to him, and also *Noli pater indulgere*, a text St Chad may have valued because it was commonly used as an invocation against thunder and lightning.[71] In addition to original composition, Columba was responsible in his role of father of monks for the provision of multiple copies of liturgical and scriptural texts, notably Psalters and Gospels. Many passages in Adomnán's *Life* represent Columba seated writing in his hut (*tegorium* or *tegoriolum*). There he has an ink-horn (*corniculum atramenti*) which in one anecdote he rightly foresees

will be spilt by a clumsy visitor. In another anecdote he gestures a blessing, on request, without moving his eyes from a text that he is busy copying.[72] The late Irish *Life* by Manus O'Donnell, full of legends, depicts St Columba as a compulsive transcriber, who violates copyright by reproducing without permission a Gospel-text loaned to him for study by St Finnian. After wrangling and litigation, the Battle of Cúldrebene was fought over the affair, by the men of Connaught and the Southern Uí Néill against the Northern Uí Néill clans, in which the latter, St Columba's own people, were victorious.[73] St Columba had a genuine reputation for insights into the outcome of battles, but a battle fought over a book makes a strange story. However, as we have seen, the monks of Durrow in the late eighth century went to war over a funeral. The link between a written text and a battle becomes intelligible when a book was used as a relic and *vexillum*, to invoke the holy writer's help and protection.

That dimension of relics of St Columba can be followed through in the case of the Cathach, that is *Praeliator*, or 'Battler', directly associated by Manus O'Donnell with the Battle of Cúldrebene itself. In his *Life of St Columba* he names the Cathach 'the chief relic' (*airdmhind* – a variant of *primh mind*) in the territory of the Cenél Conaill.[74] It is in a silver-gilt box which must not be opened. It is ritually carried around the army, three times, sunwise, to ensure victory. This relic was handed down in the family of the Lords of Tyrconnell until in the nineteenth century curiosity became too much, and it was at last opened.[75] Inside the metal case was a wooden box containing a dilapidated manuscript copy of the Vulgate Psalms – not the text, incidentally, from which Adomnán quotes when he mentions the last Psalm-verse written by Columba. In an earlier chapter we saw that the initials in the Cathach represent a very early stage in Insular decoration.[76] If not actually written by St Columba himself, the Cathach text seems likely to have *258* depended on a Psalter written 'by his holy fingers' or 'with his pen'. Although in his legendary litigation with St Finnian St Columba rejected the ruling that a copy belonged to its exemplar, as the calf belongs to the cow, that zoomorphic concept nevertheless held good in the gradual spread of virtue through all that miraculous library of three hundred 'skilful, noble' books which later credulity attributed to him.[77]

An inscription on the metal cover or *cumtach* of the Cathach asks for prayers for those who

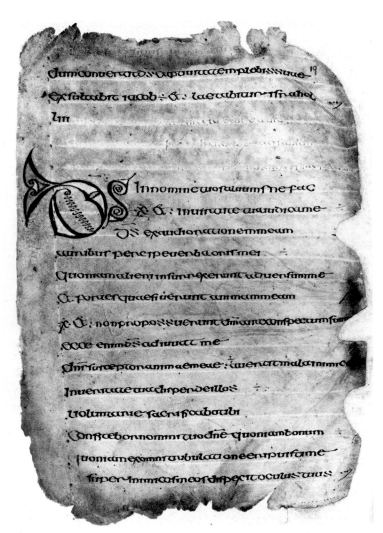

258 Psalm 53, the Cathach of St Columba, *f.* 19. (?) Early seventh century

enshrined the relic. The formula used, *Oroit do Cathbarr* (in Latin, *Oratio pro Cathbarro*), is commonplace in funerary inscriptions. For example it is used on a slab, marked with a cross, formerly incorporated in the pavement in front of the reputed site of St Columba's grave at Iona: *Oroit do Loingsecan* – 'a prayer for Loingsechán'.[78] The donors of the *cumtach* were Cathbarr O'Donnell, King of the Cenél Conaill, who died in 1106, and Domnall MacRobartaig, Abbot of Kells, who died in 1098, and whose name is mentioned among the charters written on the blank leaves of the Book of Kells. This abbot was evidently concerned to draw to the church of Kells relics which it had not had its hands on before. The *Annals of Tigernach* record that in the year 1090 relics of Colum Cille (*minda Colaim chille*), namely the Bell of the Kings, his

flabellum (an implement like a fan for driving flies away from the sacred vessels of the mass), and two Gospels (*in da sosscéla*), were brought out of Tyrconnell, together with 'seven score ounces of silver. And Oengus Húa Domnalláin it was who brought them from the north to Kells.'[79] This Oengus must have been a relation and agent of Cathbarr O'Donnell, and the silver that he brought was used to enshrine the Cathach. We may assume that the verbal usage of the day was loose, and that *soiscél* had ceased to mean specifically the Gospels; one of the two *sosscéla* that Oengus brought to Kells was the Cathach Psalter.[80] There is no chance of the other Tyrconnell *soiscél* being the Book of Kells, for the reference is too casual, and the *soiscéla mór* was already lodged in the sacristy of Kells in 1007. It may well have been another early manuscript closely associated with the saint, not necessarily of the Gospels. In the Middle Irish *Life of St Columba*, the saint is said to have given to Swords a copy of the Gospels 'written by his own hand'.[81] We have seen that the colophon of the stately and official Book of Durrow preserves the text of a note added by Columba to a small private copy of a Gospel-text which had taken him twelve days to write out, or rather, that portion of the days which he set aside for writing. Although it was brought to Kells and enshrined there, the Tyrconnell chieftains retained their rights over the Cathach. Kells might well have made a bid to possess itself of the Tyrconnell *flabellum* as substitute for a lost treasure, since the *Annals of Ulster*, in the year 1034, record the drowning of the Lector of Kells on a voyage from Scotland to Ireland, and the loss in the same mishap of 'the *flabellum* of Colum Cille'.[82]

As already stated, the principal relics of St Columba were, inevitably, his bones. The first literary record explicitly referring to the bodily remains encased in a shrine dates to after the Viking terror had struck Iona, and after the advance party of monks had gone to Kells and built the new monastery. But the holy bones, enclosed in precious metal, are represented as still on Iona. The martyrdom of one Blathmac is recorded in the *Annals* in 825.[83] Walafrid Strabo, Abbot of Reichnau, who died in 849, celebrated the heroism of this Blathmac in a poem, telling how he faced and indeed invited martyrdom, refusing to divulge to the Viking pirates the whereabouts of the shrine of St Columba.[84] According to Strabo, the monks had lifted the precious *Arca* from its footings or pedestal (*de sedibus*) – several slotted stone posts which may help us to visualize these footings survive at Iona[85] – and had hidden it in a barrow. The violation, intended or achieved, of sacred treasures was not unique. Exactly the same happened at Bangor in 824 when the relics of Comgall were shaken out of their shrine by the 'Foreigners'.[86]

The integrity and stability of the principal relics of St Columba at Iona must have been fairly short-lived. A great distribution of official relics is traceable, not without ambiguities, in the ninth-century *Annals*. In 829, four years after the killing of Blathmac, Diarmait, who succeeded Cellach as abbot first of Kells and then of Iona, 'went' to Scotland with the relics, or rather reliquaries, of St Columba – *co minnaib Coluim cille*.[87] This is the earliest reference to enshrined relics of St Columba. The *Arca* of the bones is only mentioned later, in Walafrid Strabo's poem. Presumably Diarmait employed these relics to focus devotion and exact

tribute on a diplomatic-ecclesiastical mission to Scotland, of unknown import. In 831 Diarmait 'came' to Ireland *co mindaibh Coluim cille* – presumably the same relics.[88] A formal partition of Columban relics between Scotland and Ireland took place in 849. Iona, mid-way between Scotland and Ireland, had easily been able to maintain its authority over both. But the new centre of government at Kells was too far off to have the same meaning for the Columban foundations in Scotland, and it was inevitable that mainland Scotland would want its own local focus for the cult of St Columba. In 849, according to the *Chronicles of the Kings of Scotland*, Kenneth, son of Alpin, ruler of the Scots and Picts, transferred relics of St Columba to a church built for the purpose, generally agreed to be at Dunkeld.[89] In the same year Indrechtach, Abbot of Iona, came to Ireland *co mindaibh Coluim cille*.[90] Hints and reports in the *Annals* are difficult to interpret. What, for example,

259 Slotted corner-posts of a shrine, Iona. Eighth century

were the treasures for which Indrechtach suffered martyrdom in 854, at the hands of robbers in England, while on the first lap of a journey to Rome?[91]

What belonged to the portion of St Columba's relics assigned to Scotland in 849 can be deduced in part from subsequent events and evidence. The Scottish *Chronicles* represent the third quarter of the ninth century as a very troubled time. Battles and skirmishes against the Norsemen were constant. For whole years at a time the Norsemen were in Scotland. In 878 Constantine, son of Kenneth, is reported killed by the Norwegians.[92] In the same year the *Annals of Ulster* reports that the Shrine of Colum Cille, *Scrin Coluim Cille*, and the rest of his relics/reliquaries, *a minna olchena*, came to Ireland 'to escape the Foreigners'.[93] The coincidence of the date might suggest that the Scottish Columban relics were being transferred from Dunkeld to Ireland for safety in a period of national turmoil; but this seems on the whole unlikely. The Scottish-Irish partition had been made deliberately thirty years before, and Ireland was not markedly safer than Scotland in the ninth century. Even in comparison with harassed Scotland and Ireland, however, Iona must have been hopelessly vulnerable.[94] The reference to 'the Shrine' (significantly not referred to in the 849 partition) and 'the rest of the relics', suggests that a coherent group of relics, consisting of the Shrine and things integral to it, had finally had to leave Iona and find refuge in the stone churches of Ireland. But the risks of their new location were many. In 920, a year after the High King of Tara of the Northern Uí Néill and the royal heir of the Southern Uí Néill had both been killed in a disastrous battle with the Norsemen, the stone church of Kells was broken into by the 'Foreigners' and many martyrs were made there.[95] Natives and foreigners alike combined to molest the sacred treasures. The church of Skreen, in Meath, so-called from its possession of a (perhaps *the*) Shrine of St Columba, was despoiled in 976 by Donald MacMurcadha. The Danes of Dublin are reported to have stolen the Shrine of Columba in 1127.[96] In 1129 an Irish thief broke open the great altar 'of the stone house' at Clonmacnois and fled with splendid treasures, the gifts of kings.[97] In this context of sacrilege and violence, the theft of the great Gospels from Kells in 1007 can be seen as a commonplace event.

Just as striking as these records of the dangers which confronted the Columban relics are the records of their survival, and of the devotion that they inspired. Early in the tenth century in Perthshire one particular Columban relic became a focus of military and religious zeal. The *Annals of Ireland* transcribed by Duald MacFirbis report the determination in 918 of the Scots to defeat the Norse marauders.[98] In tone the story is very like Adomnán's account of the appearance of St Columba to Oswald of Northumbria on the eve of the battle against Cadwallon, and the story no doubt goes back ultimately to some such source. The Scots fasted and prayed fervently to God and to their Apostle St Columba, and 'with the instruction of their priests they carried the staff [crozier] of Colum Cille in front of their army as their battle standard, and so achieved overwhelming victory. From that time on the relic was called *Cathbuaid*, "victory in battle", and was often carried into war.' The crozier of an Irish bishop or abbot was a prime symbol of the authority he exercised. The *Bachall Ísu* of Armagh was a crozier reputed to be St Patrick's.[99] A crozier is mentioned in Jocelin of Furness's twelfth-century *Life of St Kentigern* as a gift presented to Kentigern by St Columba. Jocelin reports that this relic belongs to the church of Ripon.[100] In the High Middle Ages Dunkeld still possessed the *Cathbuaid*. It is represented in the seal of Dunkeld Cathedral of the late thirteenth *260* century, mounted like a central tower or spire over the 'crossing' of a church-shaped reliquary. The bent-over crozier-head and part of the stem are heavily encased in metal stamped with a diaper pattern. A chain secures the head of the crozier to a small cross on the roof-ridge of the reliquary. In the seal, censing angels are placed at either end of the reliquary, kneeling on shields displaying the royal arms of Scotland, those of King Alexander III. At the base of the seal three clerics are shown at prayer. The church-shaped reliquary was presumably the up-to-date repository of all the relics committed to Dunkeld in the agreement between Iona and Kenneth, son of Alpin, in 849.

Authenticity through continuity of possession is easy to credit at Dunkeld. Perhaps slightly less probable is the fourteenth-century claim of Durham, as Lindisfarne's successor, to possess bones and other relics of St Columba (*de ossibus et reliquiis Sancti Columkelli abbatis*).[101] In the thirteenth century, at the time of cultural expansion and promise represented by the fine artistry of the Dunkeld seal, Iona itself made a move to reassert its special association with its founder. A dispropor-

260 Cast from the original brass matrix of the seal of Dunkeld Cathedral Chapter. Thirteenth century

261 tionately large south transept was begun in the monastic church at Iona, giving access to a dramatically raised presbytery which can only have been intended to display a shrine of some pretension.[102] The war with England in the fourteenth century and its attendant miseries prevented this ambitious scheme from being achieved. What Iona claimed to possess in the High Middle Ages is revealed by the record of a benefaction by Donald, Lord of the Isles, who died in 1421. He gave to Iona lands in Mull and Islay, and also a covering of gold and silver for the hand of St Columba,[103] the holy hand that wrote the noble books. Attitudes of mind had not essentially

changed since the hand of St Columba's devotee, Oswald of Northumbria, was enshrined in metal in the seventh century.

The historical authenticity of Columban relics in medieval Scotland is remarkably demonstrated by the *Brechennoch* or 'blessed shrine'.[104] This object carried an endowment of lands for its hereditary keeper at Forglen, in Banffshire, where there was a church dedicated to Adomnán. Control of these lands, 'given to God and to St Columba and to the *Brechennoch*', was assigned late in his reign by King William I of Scotland to his foundation Arbroath Abbey. After it had remained in the custody of Arbroath for a hundred years, the Abbey disposed

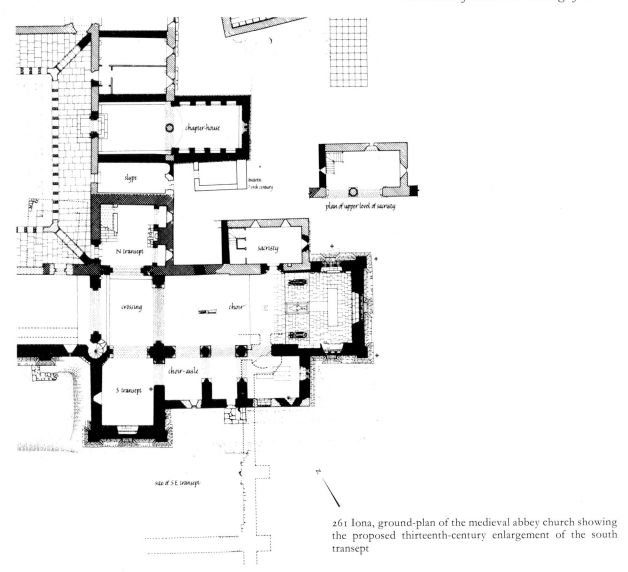

261 Iona, ground-plan of the medieval abbey church showing the proposed thirteenth-century enlargement of the south transept

of it to a lay keeper, Malcolm of Monymusk, the serious military obligations involved in its possession having become irksome. The *Brecbennoch* was yet another *vexillum* or battle-standard. If it had remained on the high altar or in the sacristy at Arbroath, the sixteenth-century sackers of Scottish medieval civilization would have destroyed it. Its having passed into lay custody saved the *Brecbennoch*.[105]

262   Commonly known as the Monymusk Reliquary, it is preserved in the Royal Museum of Scotland. It is a little box hollowed out of solid wood and covered with silver plates, held in place by bronze bands, lavishly decorated with gilded and enamelled mounts. In an earlier chapter we saw that

the tangled dragons engraved on the front panel are 87 close relatives of the dragons that inhabit the *In Principio* initial in the great Gospel-book in Durham, MS A.II.17. That Book is a direct 86 predecessor of Kells in possessing an elaborately framed, indented text and a full-page illustration of weighty symbolic significance. The Monymusk Reliquary, $4\frac{1}{8}$ in (10.5 cm) long and $3\frac{1}{2}$ in (9cm) high, is too small for a book-shrine or *cumtach*. Its function and the origin of its sanctity may perhaps be guessed from references in Adomnán's *Life of St Columba* to a pine-wood box containing a written prayer which the saint sent to the Virgin Maugin, and on another occasion the sending by St Columba of a portion of bread, blessed with the invocation of the name of God. Both these gifts, when dipped in water, worked cures.[106] The wooden core of the Monymusk Reliquary may have been the container of such gifts, or else a simple portable ciborium. Judging by the elegant style of its ornaments, it was enshrined in a major centre of Insular art, in the lifetime of Adomnán or Egbert. How it reached St Adomnán's church at Forglen is unknown, but since it was associated with St Columba in the thirteenth century and had an official role in the royal army, it is presumably one of the Columban relics paraded in Scotland by Abbot Diarmait in 829 and deposited in Scotland by Abbot Indrechtach. Like the Psalter-text in the Cathach preserved by the Tyrconnell O'Donnells, the Monymusk casket belongs to the first stratification of Columban *minna*; its metal casings are nearly four hundred years older than those of the Cathach. When the neat small Monymusk Reliquary was designed, Iona possessed the 'Book of Durrow' but had not yet conceived and undertaken the 'Book of Kells'.

Where, then, does the Book of Kells fit in in the hierarchy of Columban relics, and the history of their distribution? In an earlier chapter I remarked on the close connection between the Book of Durrow and the Book of Kells indicated by shared irregularities in the arrangement of the prefaces. It appears that where Kells was made, Durrow was available as a model. We have to envisage these two books as having, at least for a time, a common history. The great gold cover of the Book of Kells and the *cumtach* of the Book of Durrow are both lost. But Durrow's *cumtach* was still extant in the seventeenth century, and the dedicatory inscription was transcribed then, and has survived. It reads: 'The prayer and blessing of Colum Cille be to Flann son of Maelsechnaill, King of Ireland who had this *cumtach* made' (*Oroit acus bendacht Choluimb Chille do Fhland macc Mailsechnaill*). This compares with the intercessory label on the Cathach, and on the cross-marked slabs round Columba's grave at Iona, and suggests that the prayer asked for in these other cases also was the potent prayer of St Columba, face to face with Christ, on behalf of his devotee.

King Flann died in 916, which is the *terminus* date for the making of the *cumtach* and for the presence of the Book of Durrow in Ireland. But Flann succeeded to the Kingship of Tara in 879,[107] the year after that in which the Shrine of St Columba and 'the rest of his relics' made their final flitting. I suggest that the arrival of these treasures, and their

262 The Monymusk Reliquary. Silver, gilt-bronze and enamel. *c.* 700

being officially welcomed on to Irish soil, was the occasion for the enshrining of the Book of Durrow. Flann is likely to have been an interested party: he was the direct descendant of Domnall Mide, the first Meath Uí Néill to become King of Ireland, who first promulgated the 'Law of Colum Cille'. Domnall's son Donnchad associated himself with Bresal of Iona in the second promulgation. It was through the favour of these Southern Uí Néill kings, presumably, that the church at Kells was eventually founded. The Northern Uí Néill I have presented, relatively speaking, as apostates to the Columban cause. In the last year of King Flann's reign, his brother Aengus, son of Maelsechnaill, royal heir of Tara, died of wounds received in a battle fought resisting an invasion of Meath by the Cenél nEógain clan. Irish vendettas were long-lasting. At the notice of Aengus's death, the *Annals of Ulster* inserts verses rejoicing over this event, seeing it as just vengeance for the killing of Áed Allán by Domnall Mide, as far back as 743![108] If the Northern Uí Néill harboured such memories, then King Flann would remember King Domnall, buried 'with honour' in 764 at Durrow, and could have suggested that the relic which he had particularly adopted, itself a possibly royal manuscript, from seventh-century Northumbria, should be deposited from then on at St Columba's old foundation of Durrow.[109]

If the Book of Durrow came to Ireland with St Columba's Shrine in 878 and only then became the 'Book of Durrow', it is reasonable to suppose that the closely associated manuscript, the 'Book of Kells', also came to Ireland with the Shrine. This is all the more plausible since the phenomenon of the Gospel-book of Kells, as I have described it, makes most sense if we regard it as the Book of the Shrine.[110] The enshrining of St Cuthbert is generally agreed to be the likely occasion for the making of the Lindisfarne Gospels. Although St Wilfrid's burial at Ripon was not the occasion of the writing of his *Codex Aureus*, his biographer Stephen closely associates it with St Wilfrid's body and fame: 'The Gospels in its golden cover is present in our church as a witness to his blessed memory, where also his remains [or relics, *reliquiae*] are resting, and daily his name is recollected in prayer.'[111] In its general ecstatic visionary quality and in the specific slant of its iconography, the Book of Kells is at least consistent with the interpretation of St Columba offered in his official biography. The illustration in the Lucan Ressurrection narrative, where a company of angels sits on the initial letters as upon Christ's tomb, is very suitable in a Book which was preserved as adjunct to the Shrine. As we saw, Adomnán represented the saint as buried like Christ in a linen shroud, with angels regularly visiting his grave. The creation of the Shrine, involving the disinterment and elevation of Columba's bones from their original resting-place, seems likely to have followed the similar treatment of Adomnán and the deposition of his relics in Ireland, and so to date to the period of strong diplomatic activity which marks the abbacy of Sléibéne (752–67). I have interpreted the illumination of the Book of Durrow as a reflection of royal taste and patronage. Although the visual language of the Book of Kells is much more monastic, the scale and ambitiousness of the book and the sumptuous elaboration of its ornaments suggest that royal wealth, flowing freely from Meath and Tara to Iona, contributed to its production.

As we have noted, the gold cover of the Book of Kells was an aspect of its status as 'chief relic' in the record of its theft in 1007. On the evidence of Flann's covering the Book of Durrow, the descendants of Domnall Mide might well have provided the cover of Kells. Such royal gifts quite

certainly had important diplomatic overtones. As is known from the *Annals of . . . the Four Masters,* a *cumtach* was made for the Book of Armagh at the orders of Donnchad, King of Tara, son of Flann, in or around 937.[112] This fact is of great interest. Twice in his reign Donnchad was challenged by his rival, the Cenél nEógain candidate for the suzerainty of Ireland, Muirchertach, son of Niall – once at the Fair of Tailtiu in 927, and again in 938[113] – and on both occasions the *Annals of Ulster* notes that 'God separated them without loss of life', and 'pacified them'; that is, the clergy of Ireland, in face of the appalling problem posed by the Norse invaders, must have managed to insist on unity between the Northern and Southern Uí Néill.[114] It is in this context that we can place the magnanimous gesture of the enshrining of St Patrick's special book, known as 'Patrick's Testament', *Canóin Phátraic*. Armagh had associated itself with the Northern Uí Néill and they were its special champions. When Muirchertach, called 'the Hector of the West of the World', was eventually killed 'by the Foreigners' in 943, Armagh was plundered on the very next day 'by the same Foreigners'.[115] The enshrining of a great book by royal orders, then, was an act of public relations, a political as well as a devotional gesture.

The gold cover of the Book of Kells may have been of ninth- or tenth-century Irish manufacture. It was the precious cover that brought the great Gospels into peril in 1007. The thief may have been tempted by a glimpse of the treasure, when Ferdomnach was installed in the successorship of Colum Cille as Abbot of Kells at the Fair of Tailtiu in that same year, 1007.[116] A date contemporary with the postulated eighth-century date of the book itself is, on the other hand, arguable. According to its colophon, the Lindisfarne Gospels was equipped with a precious cover, and this may have been contemporary. The *bibliotheca*[117] of St Wilfrid's *Codex Aureus* may have been a real factor in the formulation of the Book of Kells as the Shrine-book of Iona. Some time during his abbacy of Iona, between 752 and 767, Sléibéne is known to have visited Ripon to consult historical archives preserved in the monastery.[118] Perhaps it was Sléibéne who donated the crozier-relic of St Columba to Ripon. Such a distinguished visitor would no doubt be shown St Wilfrid's Gospels.

If the Book of Kells was covered as part of the campaign of the manufacture of the Gospels itself, it seems certain that the cover would be pictorial, figurative, in view of the interest in illustration shown throughout the book. The silver, silver-gilt front of the cover of the *soiscél Molaise* in the National Museum of Antiquities of Ireland displays a composition that would have been highly appropriate to the Book of Kells: four upstanding Evangelist symbols placed in the quadrants of a cross. This book-cover is inscribed with the name of its donor, Cennfaelad, who was abbot of St Molaise's monastery on Devenish Island, Co. Fermanagh, between 1001 and 1025.[119] At such a date it is an extremely conservative, not to say archaic design, and may possibly reflect the influence of a famous exemplar, the cover of the Book of Kells, on the very eve of its destruction.

49

The Athlone Plaque, and a number of other surviving Irish openwork book-covers representing the mystical Crucifixion, suggest another possible reconstruction of the lost Kells cover. In the case of the Athlone Plaque, we have evidence for the making of figurative book-covers at an earlier date than that of Kells, around 700.

116

The evidence of Gerald of Wales

Late but valuable circumstantial evidence for the date of manufacture of the Book of Kells itself is provided by the priest and author Gerald of Wales in his entertaining account of a visit to Ireland in 1185, the *Topographia Hibernica*. Gerald's description of a marvellous Gospel-book that he saw in Kildare[120] is often quoted by students of the Book of Kells, but the full implications of the description have not been realized. 'Among the wonders of Kildare,' writes Gerald, 'nothing seems to me more miraculous than that wonderful book which, they say, was written in the time of the Virgin [Brigit] on the directions of an angel. The book contains the harmony of the four Evangelists according to Jerome [the Vulgate] where for almost every page there are different designs, distinguished by varied colours. Here you may see the face of Majesty, divinely drawn, there the mystic symbols of the Evangelists, each with wings, now six, now four, now two; here the eagle, there the calf, here the man, and there the lion, and other forms almost infinite. Look at them superficially, with the ordinary casual glance, and you would think it an erasure and not tracery. Fine craftsmanship is all about you, but you might not notice it. Look more keenly at it, and you will penetrate to the very shrine of art. You will make out intricacies, so delicate and subtle, so exact and compact, so full of knots and links, with colours so fresh and vivid, that you might say that all this was the work of an angel, and not of a man . . .'.

As many commentators have pointed out, Gerald might be describing the Book of Kells.[121] But he perfectly well knew the difference between Meath and Kildare, and the next portion of his account, not so frequently quoted, clearly reproduces the story told to him by the book's owners and guardians, the clergy of St Brigit's church in Kildare:[122]

'On the night before the day on which the scribe was to begin the book, an angel stood beside him in his sleep and showed him a drawing made on a tablet which he carried in his hand (*figuram quandam tabulae quam manu praeferebat impressam*), and said to him, "Do you think that you can make this drawing on the first page of the book that you are about to begin?" The scribe, not feeling that he was capable of an art so subtle, and trusting little to his knowledge of something almost unknown and very unusual, replied "No". The angel said to him, "Tomorrow, tell your lady, so that she may pour forth prayers for you to the Lord, that he may open both your bodily and mental eyes so as to see the more keenly and understand the more subtly, and may direct you in the guiding of your hand." All this was done, and on the following night the angel came again and held before him the same and many other drawings (*eandem figuram aliasque multas ei praesentans*). By the help of the divine grace, the scribe, taking particular notice of them all, and faithfully committing them to his memory, was able to reproduce them exactly in the suitable places in the book. And so with the angel indicating the designs, Brigit praying, and the scribe imitating, that book was composed . . .'

263

One element in Gerald's story can be rejected straight away. St Brigit died in or around 524, and all that we know of Early Christian and Insular art in Britain makes it impossible that the Gospel-book brought vividly before our eyes by Gerald of Wales could have been produced in her time. In the following century Brigit's biographer, Cogitosus, was apparently quite ready to crib phrases from descriptions of the historic churches of Jerusalem, in order to body out his grandiose account of the icon-filled church of St Brigit at Kildare.[123] But he could not have materialized those notional exotic treasures, or somehow have advanced Irish craftsmanship to the peak of intellectual and technical contrivance suggested by Gerald's description of the Book of Kildare. That book was evidently a work of the same date, showing the same artistic taste and verve, as the Book of Kells. Since the designs were inserted in the 'suitable places in the book', and specific images are identified by Gerald, the book was, like Kells, that rare thing, an illustrated Gospels. We have to conclude that the Book of Kildare was a product of one and the same scriptorium and painters' workshop as the Book of Kells itself; that is, of Iona.

Multiple production is not new to us. The *Codex Amiatinus* was one of three great Bibles made concurrently at Jarrow-Wearmouth. In an earlier chapter I discussed the intimate connection one to another of the Durham Gospels, the Echternach Gospels and Corpus MS 197B/Cotton MS Otho C.V. These three books offer subtle variations on a common set of themes. When we describe the initials or Evangelist portraits in one, we begin to visualize the others. The three books, radiating from Egbert's sphere of influence, were created for and distributed among friendly associated churches.[124]

Since in the twelfth century the Gospels of Kildare had been fictionalized into a work of Brigit's own time, it had clearly been a possession of Kildare for many centuries. But how did it get there? Earlier in this chapter, I outlined the difficult situation which developed in Irish ecclesiastical politics after Cogitosus's time. The ambitions of Kildare had gradually to yield to those of Armagh, and the agreement finally patched up between the rivals radically diminished Kildare's *parochia*. Throughout the eighth century the Columban community was making its own presence strongly felt in Ireland, and that presence seems to have been inimical to Armagh. In these circumstances the *familia Iae* might have found it useful to make sympathetic overtures to Kildare, the chief church of Leinster. I suggest that the Book of Kildare is tangible evidence of this contact between Iona and Kildare, a gift from Columba in his brand new shrine to the old-established shrine of Brigit. The Book of Kildare can be interpreted as a sop to Brigit, the counterpart in paint on vellum of that gratuitous affirmation by St Columba at Swords that he readily acquiesced in whatever St Brigit wished to do with the Plain of Liffey.

From this interpretation of the specific circumstances which produced the lost Book of Kildare it follows that the extant Book of Kells dates from the eighth century, the century when the Irish ecclesiastical-political situation was at its most fluid.[125] This date agrees with that suggested by the circumstantial evidence for the making of St Columba's Shrine. The *soiscéla mór* of Colum Cille marks the natural climax of a continuous development from the Book of Durrow onwards. The technical expertise and accumulated information and ideas which inform its pages are totally unshadowed by any inkling of the future *vastatio Iae*.

The hagiography or folklore contained in Gerald of Wales's account of the Book of Kildare is hardly less interesting than his careful observation of its art and imagery. The basic situation is similar to that represented in Armagh's *Liber Angeli*, where the catalogue of Armagh's absolutist claims is prefaced by St Patrick's vision of an angel, who comes to him when he has fallen asleep beside a spring at the east side of Armagh, and brings him God's promise to turn his humble little cell on the open hill-top into the *terminus vastissimus* of metropolitan Armagh. As the legend of the foundation of Armagh grows, Patrick becomes another Moses, who is shown the pattern of Armagh as Moses in the mount was shown the pattern of God's Temple. He lays out his ecclesiastical city as he had seen it in his vision,[126] this copying of a divine model offering some parallel for the story of the Kildare scribe copying the angel's designs. The apparition of an angel holding a book which the visionary is instructed to look at, is paralleled in Adomnán's *Life of St Columba* itself, when at Hinba the saint is shown a glass book (*librum vitreum*) containing the divinely prescribed ordination of the Kings of Dál Riata.[127] By the late ninth century St Columba was associated in legend with yet another book and angel. When he discovered by divine inspiration the burial-place of St Patrick at Downpatrick he found in the tomb three splendid relics (*minna*) – St Patrick's chalice, the 'Angel's Gospel' and the 'Bell of the Testament'. 'An angel distributed the treasures for Colum Cille, the chalice to Downpatrick, the "Bell of the Testament" to Armagh and the "Angel's Gospel" to Colum Cille himself. The reason it is called the "Angel's Gospel" is, because it is from the Angel's hand Colum Cille received it . . .'[128]

If stories like these were told about St Patrick and St Columba, then they could of course have been told about St Brigit. But the odd thing about Gerald of Wales's account of the Kildare legend is

263 The writing of the Book of Kildare, marginal illustration of Gerald of Wales's *Topographia Hibernica*. Early thirteenth century

that the apparition is not to Brigit, but to the scribe. He has the experience, and he has the task. Brigit is given a role, but in an extremely artificial way. She is an extra feature, added to a story involving the writing of a Gospel-book by divine inspiration. Nothing in the early and later *Lives* of St Brigit prepares us for this story. Brigit is more Martha than Mary. She is always busy brewing ale and churning butter and keeping open house. Assisting scribes is not her line at all.[129] The fact that Gerald's story does not appear, independently, in the *Lives* of Brigit suggests that it is late and derivative, contrived to account for the presence of a magnificent venerated book at Kildare, and piously to give St Brigit some initiative in the matter. The original hero, judging by the story-patterns that exist, might well have been St Columba, the obsessive copyist and inspired exegete.

Gerald's report is pseudo-history, but it is not without value in trying to make an estimate of the Book of Kells, since it takes us back to an early stratification of ideas about human actions and their divine inspiration. I have noted that St Patrick was given the dimensions of Armagh, following the theme of Exodus 25, 9: 'Let them make me a sanctuary, that I may dwell among them . . . look that thou make them after their pattern, which was shewed thee in the mount.' St Paul quotes this passage in his Letter to the Hebrews 8, when he refers to 'the example and shadow of heavenly things, as Moses was admonished of God when he was about to make the tabernacle. For see, saith he, that thou make all things according to the pattern shewed to thee in the mount. But now hath he obtained a more excellent ministry, by how much also he is the mediator of a better covenant, which was established upon better promises.' This is Christ, the new 'high priest, who is set on the right hand of the throne of the Majesty in the heavens'. These are doctrinal ideas on a grand scale. But we can perceive in the Irish records a typically medieval capacity for concrete expression and for encompassing the large in the little; I have in mind the mysterious reference in the *Annals of Tigernach* to one of the objects stolen from Clonmacnois in 1129, called the 'model' (literally the 'little stone') of the Temple of Solomon, *cairrecan tempuill Solman* – perhaps a portable altar or antependium of some portentous design.[130] The story of the scribe of Kildare, shown visual exemplars by an angel, fixing them in his mind, and then setting to work to imitate them, is peculiar in that it invokes divine

authority, not for a monastic constitution or enclosure, but for a single illustrated Gospel-book. A Gospel-book was of course the record of the new covenant, laid ceremoniously on the Christian altar. But in the story of the Kildare scribe, inspiration is not involved in the transmission of a perfect canonical text but is concentrated in the visual design, the illustrations placed at the beginning (before the canon-tables?) and throughout the book 'in suitable places'.

The story helps us to grasp the imaginative scope of the Book of Kells, its blending of words and images, its interpretative pictures with their many layers of meaning. The story follows the Apocalypse of St John in placing emphasis on revelationary 'seeing': 'Write the things which thou hast seen', the Son of Man commands St John.[131] *226* The visualization of the text of the Apocalypse takes us a step nearer to actuality. Our period is characterized by illustrated Apocalypses, and I have discerned in the Book of Kells symptoms of the influence of these illustrations. In its visual treatment of the Divine persons, within the rhythm of the Gospel-texts, the Book of Kells is bold and inventive. St Columba came to be associated with hymns celebrating the Persons of the Trinity. The Book of Kells was specially fashioned for St Columba who was for the monks of his community their own particular mediator. On an occasion similar to that when St Columba's garments and books were placed on the altar, when contrary winds were frustrating a building scheme, Adomnán began, as he tells us, 'in a manner, as it were, to upbraid' the saint, 'because we expected some consolation of help in our labours to be given by you, with God's favour, since we imagined that you were in somewhat high honour with God' (*alicujus esse grandis apud deum honoris*).[132] The Book of Kells was made in that conviction, combined with a faith (inherited from the designers of the Durham Gospels and the Lichfield Gospels) in the validity of visual images as signals from man to God, no less acceptable than prayer. It is in this sense that Gerald of Wales is enlightening, when, writing of the Gospel-book of Kildare, Kells' sister manuscript, he says that 'on looking deeply into it, we penetrate to the very shrine of art' – *ad artis arcana*. This is a sensitive and perspicacious comment, all the more so since in Gerald's day the image of the divine sanctuary on earth had long ceased to be the illuminated Gospel-book, and was becoming the Gothic cathedral.

Notes on the Text
List of Illustrations
Index

Notes on the Text

1 Introduction

1 See Bede, *Historia Ecclesiastica*, ed. C. Plummer, Oxford, 1896 [hereafter *HE*], Bk I, ch. 23, p. 42. On the conversion of the Anglo-Saxons, see H. Mayr-Harting, *The Coming of Christianity to Anglo-Saxon England*, London, 1972, Part I, pp. 13–113; J. Campbell, 'The First Century of English Christianity', *Ampleforth Journal*, 76, 1971, pp. 12–29; and J. Campbell, 'Observations on the Conversion of England', *Ampleforth Journal*, 78, 1973, pp. 12–26.

2 K. Hughes, *The Church in Early Irish Society*, London, 1966, pp. 43–4.

3 T. M. Charles-Edwards, 'The Social Background to Irish *peregrinatio*', *Celtica*, II, 1976, pp. 43–59.

4 *HE*, Bk I, ch. 32, pp. 67–8.

5 *HE*, Bk II, ch. 5, p. 90; Bk I, ch. 15, pp. 31–2.

6 *HE*, Bk I, ch. 25, pp. 45–6.

7 A restored Romano-British church according to Bede, *HE*, Bk I, ch. 33, p. 70.

8 *HE*, Bk I, ch. 32, p. 67; also ch. 29, p. 63.

9 *HE*, Bk I, ch. 26; see Mayr-Harting, op. cit., p. 61.

10 *HE*, Bk I, ch. 30, p. 70; Bk II, ch. 7, p. 94.

11 *HE*, Bk II, ch. 6, p. 93; for Mellitus in Rome, see Bk II, ch. 4, p. 88. See also N. P. Brooks, 'The Ecclesiastical Topography of Early Canterbury', in *European Towns, Their Archaeology and Early History*, ed. M. W. Barley, 1977, pp. 487–96.

12 See Pope Gregory's letter to Augustine. *HE*, Bk I, ch. 29, pp. 63–4.

13 *HE*, Bk II, ch. 3, p. 85; Bk II, ch. 15, p. 116.

14 *HE*, Bk II, ch. 1, p. 80.

15 *HE*, Bk I, ch. 34, p. 71, *rex fortissimus et gloriae cupidissimus Aedilfrid*; Bk II, ch. 2, pp. 83–4.

16 *HE*, Bk IV, ch. 23, p. 255.

17 *HE*, Bk II, ch. 12, pp. 108–9. For this see also N. K. Chadwick, 'The Conversion of Northumbria: a Comparison of Sources', in *Celt and Saxon, Studies in the Early British Border*, Cambridge, 1963, pp. 138–66.

18 R. L. S. Bruce-Mitford, 'The Coins and the Date of the Burial', in *The Sutton Hoo Ship-Burial* [hereafter *Sutton Hoo*], 1, London, 1975, pp. 578–677.

19 *HE*, Bk II, ch. 12, p. 110.

20 For a recent review of the evidence, see J. Werner, 'Schiffsgrab von Sutton Hoo. Forschungsgeschichte und Informationsstand zwischen 1939 und 1980', *Germania*, 60, pp. 1–17.

21 *HE*, Bk II, ch. 15, p. 116.

22 See D. P. Kirby, 'Bede and Northumbrian Chronology', *English Historical Review*, 78, 1963, pp. 514–27.

23 *HE*, Bk II, ch. 9, pp. 98, 100.

24 *HE*, Bk II, ch. 10, pp. 100–4.

25 *HE*, Bk II, ch. 13, p. 111, *omnes pariter in fonte vitae Christo consecrarentur . . . .*; see also C. P. Wormald, 'Bede, *Beowulf* and the Conversion of the Anglo-Saxon Aristocracy', in *Bede and Anglo-Saxon England*, ed. R. T. Farrell, B.A.R., Oxford, 1978, pp. 32–95.

26 *HE*, Bk II, ch. 13, p. 112.

27 For Edwin's baptism, see *HE*, Bk II, ch. 14, pp. 113–14; for Honorius's letter, see Bk II, ch. 17, p. 119.

28 *HE*, Bk II, ch. 15, pp. 115–16.

29 On Felix and Sigbert, see P. Hunter Blair, *The World of Bede*, London, 1970, pp. 107–8.

30 *HE*, Bk III, ch. 18, pp. 162–3.

31 *HE*, Bk III, ch. 19, pp. 163–4. For background, see J. Ryan, *Irish Monasticism, Origins and Early Development*, Dublin, 1931.

32 For Columbanus see Jonas, *Vita Columbani*, ed. B. Krusch, *Monumenta Germaniae Historica*, Script. Rer. Merov., IV, 1902; G. S. M. Walker, *Sancti Columbani Opera*, Scriptores Latini Hiberniae, 2, Dublin, 1957; see also Hughes, *The Church in Early Irish Society*, pp. 57–9, 92; also I. Woods, 'The *Vita Columbani* and Merovingian Hagiography', *Peritia*, Journal of the Medieval Academy of Ireland, I, 1982, pp. 63–80.

33 On the Easter controversy see P. Grosjean, 'Recherches sur les débuts de la controverse pascale chez les Celtes', *Analecta Bollandiana*, LXIV, 1946, pp. 200–44; C. Plummer, 'Excursus on the Paschal Controversy and Tonsure', in *HE*, pp. 348–54; see also Hughes, op. cit., pp. 103–5.

34 For St Columba, and literature, see my Chapters 2, pp. 29–31, 54–5, and 6, pp. 179–98.

35 See Hughes, op. cit., pp. 82, 93–4; also D. H. Farmer, *The Oxford Dictionary of Saints*, Oxford, 1978, p. 162.

36 ibid., p. 130.

37 For an interesting interpretation of this scar, see A. P. Smyth, *Warlords and Holy Men, Scotland AD 80–1000*, London, 1984, pp. 97–8.

38 *HE*, Bk III, ch. 19, pp. 164–7.

39 *The Life of Saint Guthlac by Felix*, introduction, text, translation and notes by B. Colgrave [hereafter *Life of Guthlac*], Cambridge, 1956, chs. XXXII–III, pp. 106–7.

40 *HE*, Bk II, ch. 20, p. 124.

41 *HE*, Bk II, ch. 16, p. 117, *ecclesiam operis egregii de lapide fecit*; for the church of St Peter at York, see *HE*, Bk II, ch. 20, p. 125.

42 For Chelles, much frequented by the Anglo-Saxons, see *HE*, Bk III, ch. 8, and Bk IV, ch. 23, pp. 142, 253; for the foundress of Chelles, see Farmer, op. cit., p. 32.

43 *HE*, Bk II, ch. 20, p. 126.

44 *HE*, Bk III, ch. 1, pp. 127–8.

45 *HE*, Bk III, ch. 3, pp. 131–3. For Oswald's patronage of Iona, and its possible political implications, see H. Moisl, 'The Bernician Royal Dynasty and the Irish in the Seventh Century', *Peritia*, 2, 1983, pp. 103–26, especially p. 116.

46 *HE*, Bk V, ch. 12, pp. 303–10. Dryhthelm's story gripped the men of his generation like the Tale of the Ancient Mariner: *etiamsi lingua sileret, vita loqueretur; narrabat autem . . . audivit ab eo repitita interrogatione . . . atque ad eum audiendum saepissime . . . accederet.*

47 *Two Lives of Saint Cuthbert . . . Bede's Prose Life*, texts, translation and notes by B. Colgrave, Cambridge, 1940 [hereafter Bede's

48 *HE*, Bk III, ch. 25, pp. 181–2.
49 See Hughes, op. cit., pp. 105–7.
50 *HE*, Bk III, ch. 25, pp. 183–9, . . . *quia hic est ostiarius ille, cui ego contradicere nolo.*
51 *HE*, Bk IV, chs. 2, 5, 6, 17, 28; pp. 204–6, 214–18, 238–40, 272–3.
52 *The Life of Bishop Wilfrid by Eddius Stephanus*, text, translation, and notes by B. Colgrave, Cambridge, 1927 [hereafter *Life of Wilfrid*]; and Bede, *Historia Abbatum*, ed. along with *HE* by C. Plummer, pp. 364–87. See also Mayr-Harting, op. cit., pp. 129–67; also D. P. Kirby, 'Northumbria in the Time of Wilfrid', in *Saint Wilfrid at Hexham*, ed. D. P. Kirby, Newcastle upon Tyne, 1974, pp. 1–33; and D. H. Farmer, 'St Wilfrid', in the same work, pp. 35–59.
53 See P. Meyvaert, 'Bede and the church paintings at Wearmouth-Jarrow', *Anglo-Saxon England*, 8, Cambridge, 1979; also G. Henderson, *Bede and the Visual Arts*, Jarrow Lecture, 1980.
54 *HE*, Bk IV, ch. 16, p. 241 and Bk V, ch. 20, p. 331.
55 *HE*, Bk IV, ch. 26, pp. 266–7.
56 For Egbert, see my Chapter 3, pp. 91–6.
57 Aldfrith was on Iona immediately before his accession. See *Two Lives of Saint Cuthbert, A Life by an Anonymous Monk of Lindisfarne . . .*, ed. B. Colgrave, Cambridge, 1940, ch. VI, p. 104, *qui tunc erat in insula quam Ii nominant . . .*
58 Bede, *Historia Abbatum*, p. 380.
59 *HE*, Bk V, ch. 20. p. 331.
60 *HE*, Bk V, ch. 12, p. 309, *viro undecumque doctissimo*; see also Bk. IV, ch. 26, p. 268, *vir in scripturis doctissimus.*
61 J. Milton, *Complete Poetry and Selected Prose*, ed. E. H. Visiak, Nonesuch Press, 1948, p. 752.
62 *Life of Wilfrid*, ch. XLII, pp. 84–5.
63 *HE*, Bk V, ch. 7, pp. 292–4.
64 *HE*, Bk IV, ch. 19, p. 249; Bk V, ch. 19, p. 329, and ch. 24, p. 356.
65 *HE*, Bk V, ch. 19, pp. 321–2.
66 See P. McGurk, *Latin Gospel Books from AD 400 to AD 800*, Paris-Brussels, 1961.
67 *HE*, Bk I, ch. 29, p. 63.
68 Corpus Christi College MS 286, for which see F. Wormald, *The Miniatures in the Gospels of St Augustine*, Cambridge, 1954.
69 J. Chapman, *Notes on the Early History of the Vulgate Gospels*, Oxford, 1908; S. Berger, *Histoire de la Vulgate pendant les premiers siècles du Moyen-Âge*, Paris, 1893; also H. W. Robinson, *Ancient and English Versions of the Bible*, Oxford, 1940, pp. 110–15, and Hunter Blair, op. cit., pp. 211–20.
70 For Cummian's letter, see Hughes, op. cit., p. 101; also D. Ó Cróinín, 'Pride and Prejudice', *Peritia*, I, 1982, p. 354.
71 For the Cathach see my Chapters 2, p. 24, 6, p. 187, and notes.
72 A. A. Luce, 'Editor's Introduction', in A. A. Luce, G. O. Simms, P. Meyer and L. Bieler, *Evangeliorum Quattuor Codex Durmachensis*, 2 vols, Olten, 1960 [hereafter *Codex Durmachensis*], pp. 12–14.
73 See G. Henderson, *Losses and Lacunae in Early Insular Art*, University of York Monograph Series 3, 1982. Appendix A, pp. 33–40.
74 Bede, *Historia Abbatum*, p. 379; see also Hunter Blair, op. cit., pp. 221–2.
75 Luce, op. cit., pp. 11–12.
76 *Novum Testamentum Latine Secundum Editionem Sancti Hieronymi*, ed. J. Wordsworth and H. J. White, Oxford, 1911, pp. xiv–xvi.
77 Wordsworth and White, op. cit., pp. xvii–xx.
78 Luce, op. cit., p. 10.
79 For Gospel preliminaries, see Luce, op. cit., pp. 10–12.
80 F. Wormald, op. cit., pp. 6–7.

2 The Book of Durrow

1 For commentary, description and facsimile see A. A. Luce, G. O. Simms, P. Meyer and L. Bieler, *Codex Durmachensis*; see also R. L. S. Bruce-Mitford, 'Lindisfarne and Durrow', in T. D. Kendrick, T. J. Brown, R. L. S. Bruce-Mitford, *Evangeliorum Quattuor Codex Lindisfarnensis*, 2 vols, Olten, 1960 [hereafter *Codex Lindisfarnensis*], II, pp. 255–7. For further bibliography see J. J. G. Alexander, *Insular Manuscripts 6th to the 9th century*, London, 1978 [hereafter *Insular Manuscripts*], p. 32.
2 See Luce, 'Editor's Introduction' in *Codex Durmachensis*, pp. 14–17.
3 Dublin, Trinity College Library MS A.1.6 (58), *f.* 33. For Kells see my chapters 5, pp. 131–78, 6, pp. 179, 188–98; for commentary, description and facsimile see E. H. Alton, P. Meyer, *Evangeliorum Quattuor Codex Cenannensis*, 3 vols., Berne, 1950 [hereafter *Codex Cenannensis*].
4 For the palette in Durrow see H. Roosen-Runge and A. E. A. Werner, 'The Pictorial Technique of the Lindisfarne Gospels', in *Codex Lindisfarnensis*, II, p. 273.
5 See Bruce-Mitford, 'The Hanging Bowls', in *Sutton Hoo*, 3, I, London, 1983, pp. 202–315, especially pp. 263–95; the case for an Irish origin of the hanging-bowls is stated by F. Henry, 'Hanging Bowls', in *Studies in Early Christian and Medieval Irish Art*, I, Enamels and Metalwork, Pindar Press, London, 1983, pp. 115–73.
6 For this dispersal of Insular works of art see J. Peterson, *British Antiquities of the Viking Period, found in Norway*, Oslo, 1940; E. Bakka, 'Some English Decorated Metal Objects Found in Norwegian Graves', *Årbok for Universitetet i Bergen*, Humanistisk Serie 1, 1963. E. Bakka, 'Some Decorated Anglo-Saxon and Irish Metalwork found in Norwegian Viking Graves', in A. Small, ed., *The Fourth Viking Congress*, York, August 1961, London, 1965, pp. 32–40. Also E. Wamers, 'Some Ecclesiastical and Secular Insular Metalwork found in Norwegian Viking Graves', *Peritia*, Journal of the Medieval Academy of Ireland, 2, 1983, pp. 277–306. For the resemblance of the Jaatten bowl to Durrow, see Meyer, 'The Art of the Book of Durrow', *Codex Durmachensis*, pp. 108–9.
7 See facsimiles, *Codex Durmachensis*, ff. 6v–7v; *Codex Cenannensis*, f. 1 and also ff. 26–26v.
8 Dublin, Trinity College Library MS A.I.6, *f.* 8, for which see my Chapter 5, pp. 141, 145; and facsimile, *Codex Cenannensis*.
9 See P. Brown, *The Book of Kells*, London, 1980, p. 75; Luce 'Editor's Introduction', in *Codex Durmachensis*, pp. 33–5.
10 See Luce, 'Editor's Introduction', in *Codex Durmachensis*, p. 9.
11 For the Macregol Gospels see Alexander, *Insular Manuscripts*, No. 54, pp. 77–78. See also E. Kitzinger, 'The Coffin-Reliquary: The Iconography', in *The Relics of Saint Cuthbert*, ed. C. F. Battiscombe, Oxford, 1956 [hereafter *Relics of Saint Cuthbert*], p. 233, note 1; Brown and Bruce-Mitford, 'Authorship and Date', in *Codex Lindisfarnensis*, II, p. 6, note 1; also C. Nordenfalk, 'An Illustrated Diatessaron', *Art Bulletin*, 50, 1968, p. 133 and note 79; p. 134, note 84.
12 See G. Brüning, 'Adamnans Vita Columbae und ihre Ableitungen', *Zeitschrift für Celtische Philologie*, XI, 1917, pp. 241–2; for Adomnán's visits to Northumbria see Bede, *HE*, Bk V, ch. 21, p. 344, and A. O. Anderson and M. O. Anderson, *Adomnan's Life of Columba*, Edinburgh, 1961 [hereafter *Life of Columba*], Introduction, p. 94 and II, 46, pp. 460–3.
13 Bede, *In Lucae Evangelium Expositio, Bedae Venerabilis Opera*, II, *Opera Exegetica*, 3, ed. D. Hurst, Corpus Christianorum Series Latina, CXX, Turnhout, 1960, Prologue, pp. 7–10.
14 See for example Bede on St John the Evangelist in Homelia 9, in *Bedae Venerabilis Opera*, III, *Opera Homiletica*, ed. D. Hurst,

Corpus Christianorum Series Latina, CXXII, Turnhout 1955, pp. 60–7, especially p. 62.

15 See for example Leningrad, State Public Library Cod. F.v.I.8, *f.* 12, reproduced as Frontispiece in Alexander, *Insular Manuscripts*; also the St Andrews Sarcophagus, in J. Romilly Allen and J. Anderson, *Early Christian Monuments of Scotland*, Edinburgh, 1903, III, pp. 351–53. See also I. Henderson, *The Picts*, London, 1967, pp. 149–57; and for cross in interlace see R. B. K. Stevenson, 'Aspects of Ambiguity in Crosses and Interlace', *The Ulster Journal of Archaeology*, 44, 45, 1981–2, pp. 1–27.

16 H. J. Lawlor and W. M. Lindsay, 'The Cathach of St Columba', *Proceedings of the Royal Irish Academy*, 33, 1916, Section C, No. 11, pp. 241–443; F. Henry, *Les Débuts de la Miniature Irlandaise*, *Gazette des Beaux-Arts*, 37, 1950, pp. 19–21.

17 Alexander, *Insular Manuscripts*, Nos 2, 3, pp. 27–8.

18 Alexander, *Insular Manuscripts*, No. 5, pp. 29–30.

19 ibid., No. 1, p. 27; for the Valerianus Codex. Munich, Bayerische Staatsbibliothek Clm. 6224, see E. H. Zimmermann, *Vorkarolingische Miniaturen*, Berlin, 1916, pls 4–10.

20 F. Henry, *Irish Art in the Early Christian Period (to 800 AD)*, revised ed., London, 1965, p. 127.

21 *Life of Columba*, introduction, p. 3; Henry, op. cit., ibid. See also J.-M. Picard, 'The Schaffhausen Adomnán – A Unique Witness to Hiberno-Latin', *Peritia*, I, 1982, pp. 216–49.

22 Henry, op. cit., pp. 125–8 and pl. VII; see also K. Hughes and A. Hamlin, *The Modern Traveller to the Early Irish Church*, London, 1977, p. 91; A. Weir, *Early Ireland: A Field Guide*, Belfast, 1980, pp. 127–8.

23 See D. M. Wilson, *Anglo-Saxon Art from the Seventh Century to the Norman Conquest*, London, 1984, pp. 32–3.

24 Luce, 'Editor's Introduction', *Codex Durmachensis*, p. 31; compare the record of the tenth-century enshrining of a Gospels in Scotland in Andrew of Wyntoun, the *Orygynale Cronykil of Scotland*, Bk VI, ch. 10 under AD 943, ed. D. Laing, *The Historians of Scotland* III (Wyntoun II), Edinburgh, 1872, pp. 91–2.

25 *HE*, Bk III, ch. 4, p. 134.

26 *Life of Columba*, introduction, p. 88, and I, 3, pp. 214–19.

27 By implication; his predecessor Mac Nisi died in 585, he himself in 599; see *The Annals of Ulster (to AD 1131)*, ed. S. Mac Airt and G. Mac Niocaill, I, Dublin Institute for Advanced Studies, 1983, pp. 92–3 and 98–9.

28 Examples of this sort of longsight continue in hagiographical literature into the eighth century. See *Life of Guthlac*, chs XLIII, XLIV, XLVI, XLVIII, pp. 132–6, 142–4, 146–8.

29 *Life of Columba*, I, 29, pp. 264–5.

30 ibid., III, 15, pp. 494–5. The character of this narrative, and the total success of Columba's foresight and intervention, makes an interesting comparison with a story told about St Wilfrid, the Romanizing monk and bishop. The incident is about the building of the church at Hexham in the 670s. During the construction of the highest parts of the walls a young man, one of the bishop's masons, lost his footing on a high pinnacle, fell headlong, and dashed himself on the stone pavement below. 'He broke his arms and legs, every joint was put out. There he lay, gasping his last.' Bishop Wilfrid had him taken outside on a litter, prayed over him and blessed him. 'The breath of life returned to the youth. The doctors bound up his arms and legs and he improved steadily day by day.' Stephen, St Wilfrid's biographer, remarks at the end of this story that the recipient of St Wilfrid's ministrations is still alive to give thanks to God, 'and his name is Bothelm'. This is altogether less miraculous, as well as more circumstantial; common sense and an efficient medical staff play their parts in the young man's recovery. See

Life of Wilfrid, ch. XXIII, p. 46. For Hexham see E. Gilbert, 'Saint Wilfrid's Church at Hexham', in *Saint Wilfrid at Hexham*, ed. Kirby, pp. 81–113.

31 For illustration of this Psalm see also the Stuttgart Psalter, *f.* 107v, in *Der Stuttgarter Bilderpsalter, Bibl. Fol. 23. Württembergische Landesbibliothek, Stuttgart*, I, facsimile (II, contributions by W. Hoffmann, B. Bischoff, F. Mütherich and others), Stuttgart, 1968.

32 *HE*, Bk III, ch. 4, p. 134.

33 *Life of Columba*, I, 21, pp. 250–1, I, 45, pp. 306–7, II, 24, pp. 378–79, III, 5, pp. 472–3, III, 17–18, pp. 500–3, III, 23, pp. 532–3. For Hinba see also Smyth, *Warlords and Holy Men*, pp. 100–101.

34 *Life of Columba*, III, 3, pp. 470–1.

35 ibid., I, 37, pp. 288–9, II, 32, 396–7, II, 33, 400–3, II, 35, 408–9. See also I. Henderson, 'Inverness, a Pictish Capital', in *The Hub of the Highlands: The Book of Inverness and District*, The Centenary Volume of Inverness Field Club 1875–1975, Edinburgh, 1975, pp. 91–108.

36 *Life of Columba*, II, 46, pp. 460–1; M. O. Anderson, 'Columba and other Irish Saints in Scotland', *Historical Studies*, V, Papers read before the Sixth Conference of Irish Historians, ed. J. L. McCracken London, 1965, pp. 26–36; Henderson, *The Picts*, pp. 72–7. On the nature of the Columban confederation of monasteries see D. A. Bullough, 'The Missions to the English and Picts and their Heritage (to *c.* 800)', *Die Iren und Europa im früheren Mittelalter*, ed. H. Löwe, I, Stuttgart, pp. 89–90.

37 *HE*, Bk III, ch. 1, pp. 127–98.

38 *Life of Columba*, I, 1, pp. 198–203.

39 Boethius, *Philosophiae Consolatio, Boethi Opera*, I, ed. L. Bieler, Corpus Christianorum Series Latina, XCIV, Turnhout, 1957, p. 2: *visa est mulier reverendi admodum vultus . . . nunc verso pulsare, caelum summi verticis cacumine videbatur . . .*; compare the apparition of the angel, captain of the host of the Lord, to Joshua, in *Joshua* 5, 13–15. For a thirteenth-century apparition of St Columba, of a threatening rather than beneficent character, see A. O. Anderson, *Early Sources of Scottish History, AD 500 to 1286* [hereafter *Early Sources*], Edinburgh, 1922, II, pp. 556–7.

40 *HE*, Bk III, ch. 2, pp. 128–9.

41 *Life of Columba*, I, 45, pp. 306–7, and III, 23, pp. 522–3.

42 *HE*, Bk III, ch. 3, p. 132; see also my Chapter 1, note 45. For the proximity of Lindisfarne to the royal 'city' of Bamburgh, see *HE*, Bk III, ch. 16, p. 159.

43 See Bruce-Mitford, *Sutton Hoo*, 2, London, 1978, especially pp. 432–611.

44 R. B. K. Stevenson, 'Note on mould from Craig Phadrig', in A. Small and M. Barry Cottam, *Craig Phadrig*: Interim Report on 1971 Excavation, Dundee, 1972, pp. 49–51; Henderson, 'Inverness, a Pictish Capital', in *The Hub of the Highlands*, p. 103.

45 See V. H. Fenwick, 'The Chainwork', in *Sutton Hoo*, 3, II, London, 1983, pp. 511–49, especially p. 535.

46 For suspension techniques see A. Liestöl, 'The Hanging Bowl, a Liturgical and Domestic Vessel', *Acta Archaeologica*, XXIV, 1953, pp. 163–70; also E. Fowler, 'Hanging Bowls', *Studies in Ancient Europe*: Essays presented to Stuart Piggott, ed. J. M. Coles and D. D. A. Simpson, Leicester, 1968, pp. 288–90.

47 *HE*, Bk II, ch. 16, p. 118.

48 See H. R. Ellis Davidson, 'The Smith and the Goddess', *Frühmittelalterliche Studien*, 3, 1969, pp. 216–26; also D. M. Wilson, 'Craft and Industry', in *The Archaeology of Anglo-Saxon England*, ed. D. M. Wilson, Cambridge, 1976, pp. 263–6.

49 *HE*, Bk V, ch. 14, pp. 313–15.

50 Aethelwulf, *De Abbatibus*, ed. A. Campbell, Oxford, 1967, pp. 25–7.

51 *Life of Columba*, III, 9, pp. 484–5.

52 *HE*, Bk V, ch. 19, p. 330; Bk III, ch. 11, p. 148. See also *Life of Wilfrid*, ch. XVII, pp. 34–6.

53 M. Budny and D. Tweddle, 'The Maaseik Embroideries', *Anglo-Saxon England*, 13, 1984, pp. 65–96.

54 Bede's prose *Life*, ch. XLII, pp. 290–5.

55 R. L. S. Bruce-Mitford, 'The Pectoral Cross', in *Relics of Saint Cuthbert*, p. 309.

56 See Bruce-Mitford, 'Comments on the design of the harness', in *Sutton Hoo*, 2, London, 1978, pp. 564–81.

57 *HE*, Bk III, ch. 14, p. 156.

58 . . . *pelliculam vituli . . . clavis affixam violentiis procellarum opposuit . . .* Bede's prose *Life*, ch. XLVI, pp. 302–3.

59 *Argyll: an Inventory of the Monuments*, 4, *Iona*, The Royal Commission on the Ancient and Historical Monuments of Scotland, London, HMSO, 1982, p. 14.

60 R. Powell, 'The Stonyhurst Gospel: the Binding', in *Relics of Saint Cuthbert*, pp. 362–74.

61 *Life of Columba*, I, 50, pp. 322–3.

62 *HE*, Bk III, ch. 5, pp. 135–6.

63 *HE*, Bk III, ch. 6, p. 138.

64 Bruce-Mitford, 'Silver', in *Sutton Hoo*, 3, I, London, 1983, pp. 1–165.

65 *HE*, Bk III, ch. 24, p. 177.

66 *HE*, Bk IV, ch. 1, p. 201.

67 *HE*, Bk III, ch. 25, p. 181.

68 *HE*, Bk III, ch. 23, pp. 174–5.

69 *HE*, Bk III, ch. 26, pp. 190–1.

70 R. Cramp, *Corpus of Anglo-Saxon Stone Sculpture in England*, I, Oxford 1984; part I, pp. 125–6; part II, pls 112–15.

71 *HE*, Bk III, ch. 24, pp. 179–80.

72 *Life of Wilfrid*, ch. VIII, p. 16, *pro animae suae remedio*; ch. XVII, p. 36, *pro animae suae remedio*.

73 *HE*, Bk III, ch. 23, pp. 174–5.

74 *HE*, Bk III, ch. 22, p. 174.

75 *HE*, Bk III, ch. 22, p. 172; ch. 23, p. 174.

76 *HE*, Bk IV, ch. 17, p. 243.

77 *HE*, Bk III, ch. 21, p. 170.

78 *HE*, Bk II, ch. 20, p. 126.

79 *HE*, Bk III, ch. 6, p. 138.

80 *HE*, Bk III, ch. 12, p. 151, and ch. 6, p. 138, *Numquam inveterescat haec manus . . .*

81 *Life of Columba*, II, 45, pp. 452–5.

82 Bruce-Mitford, 'The Coins and the Date of the Burial', in *Sutton Hoo*, 1, London, 1975, pp. 578–677, especially pp. 586–7.

83 Aethelwulf, *De Abbatibus*, pp. 11–15, 19, and 49–53; precious gifts continued to be offered to the church by subsequent members of the community, see pp. 35–9.

84 On small-scale Irish buildings, see F. Henry, *Irish Art in the Early Christian Period (to AD 800)*, London, 1965, pp. 76–91; also Hughes and Hamlin, *The Modern Traveller to the Early Irish Church*, pp. 54–79.

85 *HE*, Bk IV, ch. 17, p. 239.

86 *HE*, Bk III, ch. 25, p. 181.

87 *HE*, Bk II, ch. 14, p. 114; *Life of Wilfrid*, ch. XVI, pp. 32–4, represents Wilfrid as restoring a ruined building.

88 Bruce-Mitford, 'The Pectoral Cross', in *Relics of Saint Cuthbert*, pp. 308–25. But see also the most northerly survivor of gold and garnet jewellery, now in the National Museum of Antiquities of Scotland, in R. Bruce-Mitford, *Aspects of Anglo-Saxon Archaeology*, London, 1974, pl. 87 a, b.

89 *HE*, Bk III, ch. 22, p. 172; Bk III, ch. 25, p. 188. *Life of Wilfrid*, ch. X, p. 22, represents Oswy as in easy control of his contending clergy; he invites their opinion as to the relative power of Sts Peter and Columba 'with a smile', *Oswiu rex subridens interrogavit omnes . . .*

90 *HE*, Bk II, ch. 5, pp. 89–90, and Notes, pp. 85–6. See also Mayr-Harting, *The Coming of Christianity to Anglo-Saxon England*, pp. 18–21.

91 See for example the exile of the sons of Aethelfrith in *HE*, Bk III, ch. 1, p. 127; for Englishmen in Ireland in the days of Finan and Colman, see Bk III, ch. 27, p. 192. See also F. Henry, *Irish Art in the Early Christian Period (to AD 800)*, p. 96.

92 See *Codex Lindisfarnensis*, II, pp. 7–11.

93 Aethelwulf, *De Abbatibus*, p. 21.

94 *HE*, Bk III, ch. 5, p. 136.

95 *Life of Columba*, I, 22, p. 254; see also *The Irish Penitentials*, ed. L. Bieler, *Scriptores Latini Hiberniae*, 5, Dublin, 1963, and K. Hughes, *Early Christian Ireland: Introduction to the Sources*, London, 1972, pp. 82–9.

96 Mayr-Harting op. cit., especially p. 185.

97 See *The Stowe Missal, MS D.II.3 in the Library of the Royal Irish Academy, Dublin*, Henry Bradshaw Society, 32, ed. Sir G. F. Warner, II, London, 1915, p. 24.

98 *Life of Guthlac*, ch. XXXI, pp. 102–3.

99 Bede's prose *Life*, ch. VIII, p. 182, *codex habens quaterniones septem*.

100 On this general theme see H. Richardson, 'Number and Symbol in Early Christian Irish Art', *Journal of the Royal Society of Antiquaries of Ireland*, 114, 1984, pp. 28–47.

101 Genesis 1, 24: *Dixit quoque Deus. Producat terra animam viventem in genere suo, jumenta, et reptilia, et bestias terrae secundum species suas . . .*

102 See my Chapter 3, p. 68.

103 C. Nordenfalk, 'An Illustrated Diatessaron', *Art Bulletin*, 50, 1968, pp. 119–40; M. Werner, 'The Four Evangelist Symbols Page in the Book of Durrow', *Gesta*, VIII, 1969, pp. 3–17; M. Schapiro, 'The Miniatures of the Florence Diatessaron', *Art Bulletin*, 55, 1973, pp. 494–531; C. Nordenfalk, 'The Persian Diatessaron once more', *Art Bulletin*, 55, 1973, pp. 534–46; L. Nees, 'A Fifth-century Book Cover and the Origin of the Four Evangelist Symbols Page in the Book of Durrow, *Gesta*, XVII, 1978, pp. 3–8; M. Werner, 'The Durrow Four Evangelist Symbols Page Once Again', *Gesta*, XX, 1981, pp. 23–33.

104 On the date of the Fahan Cross see R. B. K. Stevenson, 'The Chronology and Relationships of some Irish and Scottish Crosses', *Journal of the Royal Society of Antiquaries of Ireland*, 86–7, 1956–7, pp. 84–96.

105 W. A. Stein, *The Lichfield Gospels*, unpublished Ph.D. Thesis, University of California, Berkeley, 1980.

106 See I. Henderson, *The Picts*, pl. 50. In P. Meyer, 'The Art of the Book of Durrow', in *Codex Durmachensis*, p. 103, Fig. 6, two protruding left feet are shown below the bust-length man symbol; however Meyer states, p. 103, 'the feet are no longer clearly visible . . .'

107 For comment on British Library Cotton MS Otho C.V, see my Chapter 3, pp. 70–1, 76–8.

108 For the context of this textile see O. von Falke, *Kunstgeschichte der Seidenweberei*, Berlin, 1921.

109 J. Romilly Allen and J. Anderson, *Early Christian Monuments of Scotland*, III, Fig. 198 and pp. 183–4; I, Fig. 13, p. lxxiv. See also detail of Aberlemno cross-slab, in Henderson, *The Picts*, pl. 39, where the cut-off neck of the profile animal-head symbol is given terminal decorations. In P. Meyer, 'The Art of the Book of Durrow', *Codex Durmachensis*, Fig. 6, p. 103, hoofs are shown projecting from the base of the bust-length symbol, but Meyer states, p. 104, 'no legs are visible . . .'

110 Bruce-Mitford, 'The Iron Stand', in *Sutton Hoo*, 2, London, 1978, pp. 403–31, especially p. 418.

111 Werner, in *Gesta*, VIII, 1969, p. 7.

112 Catalogue of Exhibition, *Treasures of Early Irish Art 1500 BC to 1500 AD*, Metropolitan Museum of Art, New York, 1977, text by G. Frank Mitchell, Liam de Paor, etc., No. 57, pp. 182–3.

113 London, Lambeth Palace Library MS 1370, for which see Alexander, *Insular Manuscripts*, No. 70, p. 86.

114 See facsimile, *Codex Cenannensis, ff.* 1, 5.

115 R. L. S. Bruce-Mitford, 'The Stag', in *Sutton Hoo*, 2, London, 1978, pp. 332–9. C. Hicks, Appendix A, 'A Note on the Provenance of the Sutton Hoo Stag', ibid., pp. 378–82.

116 R. L. F. Bruce-Mitford, 'A Hiberno-Saxon Bronze Mounting from Markyate, Hertfordshire, *Antiquity*, XXXVIII, 1964, pp. 219–20.

117 Henry, *Irish Art in the Early Christian Period (to 800 AD)*, p. 142.

118 F. Henry, 'Hanging Bowls', in *Studies in Early Christian and Medieval Irish Art*, London, 1983, I, pp. 162–8.

119 The *Genii Cucullati*, for which see J. M. C. Toynbee, *Art in Roman Britain*, London, 1962, Cat. No. 77, p. 156 and pl. 83; also J. M. C. Toynbee, *Art in Britain Under the Romans*, Oxford, 1964, pp. 177–8.

120 *Life of Columba*, III, 1, pp. 464–6. For Celtic cloaks see A. Ross, *Everyday Life of the Pagan Celts*, London, 1970, pp. 46–7.

121 Luce, 'Editor's Introduction', *Codex Durmachensis*, p. 48 'the artist . . . has depicted with care and no little skill the distinctive details of the Celtic tonsure . . .'; see also pp. 49, 58–9.

122 Paris, Bibl. Nat. lat. MS 9389, *f.* 18v; for commentary, see my Chapter 3, p. 95.

123 *HE*, Bk V, ch. 21, p. 344.

124 See *The Annals of Tigernach*, ed. W. Stokes, *Revue Celtique*, XVII, 1896, p. 226, *tonsura coronae super familiam Iae.*

125 *Life of Guthlac*, ch. XX, p. 85.

126 *Bede's Ecclesiastical History of the English People*, ed. B. Colgrave and R. A. B. Mynors, Oxford, 1969, pp. 548–9, note 5.

127 C. Plummer, 'Excursus on Paschal Controversy and Tonsure', *HE*, Notes, pp. 353–4.

128 *Life of Saint Columba . . . written by Adamnan*, ed. W. Reeves, The Historians of Scotland, VI, Edinburgh, 1874, p. cxiv.

129 See N. K. Chadwick, *The Druids*, Cardiff, 1966; Stuart Piggott, *The Druids*, London, 1968. On the question of the Irish tonsure see also J.-M. Picard, 'Bede, Adomnán, and the Writing of History', *Peritia*, 3, 1984, p. 62 and note 5; and E. James, 'Bede and the Tonsure Question', in the same Journal, pp. 86–7.

130 J. J. Tierney, 'The Celtic Ethnography of Posidonius', *Proceedings of the Royal Irish Academy*, 60, 1959–60, Section C, No. 5, pp. 203–7 and p. 249.

131 I. A. G. Shepherd and A. N. Shepherd, 'An incised Pictish figure . . .', *Proceedings of the Society of Antiquaries of Scotland*, 109, 1977–8, pp. 211–17, especially p. 214.

132 See for example the carved relief-figure of a man with an emphatic profile, like the Rhynie man holding an axe, juxtaposed with a Jonah and the whale image, on a Merovingian tombstone fragment in the Schnütgen Museum, Cologne, K.122/K.123; also a Chinese seventh-century glazed pottery figure of a kneeling 'Barbarian', with similarly strong features, in the Musée Cernuschi, Paris, 8971.

133 See Alexander, *Insular Manuscripts*, pls 281, 222, 146.

134 Bruce-Mitford, 'The Gold Jewellery: the Purse Lid', in *Sutton Hoo*, 2, London, 1978, pp. 487–522; and Bruce-Mitford, 'The Shield', ibid., pp. 1–103, especially pp. 55–63.

135 W. F. Volbach, 'Sculpture and Applied Arts', in J. Hubert, J. Porcher, W. F. Volbach, *Europe in the Dark Ages*, London, 1969, pls 240, 242.

136 T. D. Kendrick, *Anglo-Saxon Art to AD 900*, repr. London, 1972, pp. 56–8 and pl. XXVIII, 2.

137 ibid., p. 93; also Bruce-Mitford, *Sutton Hoo*, 3, I, London, 1983, p. 268, Fig. 207.

138 See resistance to the Pictish dimension in Wilson, *Anglo-Saxon Art from the Seventh Century to the Norman Conquest*, pp. 34–5.

139 *HE*, Bk III, ch. 6, p. 138.

140 Henderson, *The Picts*, pp. 52–9.

141 *HE*, Bk IV, ch. 3, p. 206; Bk IV, ch. 12, p. 229; Bk IV, ch. 26 (28), p. 272.

142 Bede's prose *Life*, ch. XI, p. 192.

143 *HE*, Bk III, ch. 26, pp. 189–90, and Bk III, ch. 28, pp. 194–5.

144 *Life of Columba*, Introduction, pp. 19, 91, 104. See also J.-M. Picard, 'Bede, Adomnán and the Writing of History', *Peritia*, 3, 1984, pp. 50–70, especially pp. 53–4.

145 *HE*, Bk III, ch. 26, p. 190.

146 *HE*, Bk III, ch. 13, p. 153.

147 *HE*, Bk III, ch. 12, p. 152.

148 Luce, 'Editor's Introduction', *Codex Durmachensis*, pp. 17–24.

149 *Life of Columba*, III. 44, 45, pp. 450–453. See my Chapter 6, pp. 185–6, for book relics at Iona.

150 *Life of Columba*, II, 8, p. 342.

151 *HE*, Bk III, ch. 21, p. 171; ch. 24, p. 179.

152 Wilson, op. cit. pp. 33, 36.

153 See my Chapter 6, p. 194, for Kells as an Ionan product.

3 The Durham, Corpus and Echternach Gospels

1 *The Durham Gospels (Durham, Cathedral Library MS A.II.17)*, Early English Manuscripts in Facsimile, Vol. 20, ed. by C. D. Verey, T. J. Brown, and E. Coatsworth, with an Appendix by R. Powell, Copenhagen, 1980. For an important review article see Ó Cróinín, 'Pride and Prejudice', *Peritia*, I, 1982, pp. 352–62.

2 Alexander, *Insular Manuscripts*, No. 1, p. 27.

3 For reproductions, see A. Mùnoz, *Il Codice Purpureo di Rossano e il Frammento Sinopense*, Rome, 1907.

4 Alexander, *Insular Manuscripts*, No. 24, pp. 51–2.

5 ibid., No. 25, p. 52.

6 R. L. S. Bruce-Mitford, 'The Art of the Codex Amiatinus', Jarrow Lecture, 1967, *The Journal of the British Archaeological Association*, 32, 1969, pp. 1–25 and pls. A–D, 1–xx. See also Alexander, *Insular Manuscripts*, No. 7, pp. 32–5.

7 ibid., No. 21, pp. 48–50. For Lichfield see my Chapter 4, pp. 122–9, and notes.

8 *Life of Columba*, II, 1, pp. 326–7, *Hujus inquam libelli quasi quaedam lucerna inlustret exordium . . .*

9 J. Romilly Allen and J. Anderson, *Early Christian Monuments of Scotland*, Edinburgh 1903, III, pp. 68–83. See also I. Henderson, 'Pictish Art and the Book of Kells', in *Ireland in Early Mediaeval Europe*, ed. D. Whitelock, R. McKitterick, D. Dumville, Cambridge, 1982, pp. 79–89.

10 For the Monymusk Reliquary see my Chapter 6, p. 191–3.

11 Allen and Anderson, op. cit., III, pp. 179–80.

12 *Life of Columba*, II, 42, pp. 444–5, *Quae . . . prope magnitudine ranarum aculeis permolestae non tamen volatiles sed natatiles erant.*

13 Alexander, *Insular Manuscripts*, No. 12, p. 44.

14 D. M. Wilson in A. Small, C. Thomas, D. M. Wilson, *St Ninian's Isle and its Treasure*, Oxford, 1972, pp. 63–4 and 118–23.

15 Alexander, *Insular Manuscripts*, loc. cit.

16 T. Smith, *Catalogus librorum manuscriptorum Bibliotecae Cottonianae*, Oxford, 1696, p. 72.

17 T. Astle, *The Origin and Progress of Writing*, London, 1784.

18 E. A. Lowe, *Codices Antiquiores Latini*, II, Oxford, 2nd ed. 1972, No. 125, p. 3; see also No. 217, p. 28.

19 See P. McGurk, 'Two Notes on the Book of Kells and its Relation to other Insular Gospel Books', *Scriptorium*, 9, 1955, pp. 105–7.

20 Alexander, *Insular Manuscripts*, No. 11, pp. 42–3.

21 Hunter Blair, *The World of Bede*, p. 127.

22 *Ezekiel* I, 7.

23 J. M. C. Toynbee, *Art in Roman Britain*, London, 1962, No. 35, pp. 140–1.

24 Bede's prose *Life*, Ch. XXVII, pp. 242–8.

25 Alexander, *Insular Manuscripts*, No. 26, pp. 52–4.

26 E. Kitzinger, 'The Coffin-Reliquary', in *Relics of Saint Cuthbert*, pp. 265–7.

27 See my Chapter 2, note 15; also Henderson, 'Pictish Art and the Book of Kells', loc. cit., pp. 101–5.

28 For the seventh-century dating of the Pictish symbol-stones and animal-designs see Henderson, *The Picts*, pp. 115–27.

29 For Pictish figure-sculpture see Henderson, 'Pictish Art and the Book of Kells', loc. cit., pp. 94–5.

30 *HE*, Bk I, ch. 32, p. 69, *praesentis mundi iam terminus iuxta est* . . .

31 *Life of Columba*, preface, pp. 182–3.

32 *HE*, Bk III, ch. 19, pp. 165–7.

33 *HE*, Bk V, ch. 12, p. 309.

34 *HE*, Bk V, ch. 12, p. 310, *ut eius rogatu monasterio supra memorato inditus, ac monachica sit tonsura coronatus* . . .

35 *HE*, Bk IV, ch. 3, pp. 210–11.

36 *HE*, Bk IV, ch. 3, pp. 211–12.

37 Bede, *Historia Abbatum*, in *HE*, p. 370; for discussion see G. Henderson, *Bede and the Visual Arts*, Jarrow Lecture, 1980, pp. 14–15.

38 P. Underwood, 'The Fountain of Life in Manuscripts of the Gospels', *Dumbarton Oaks Papers*, No. 5, Harvard, 1950, pp. 41–138; for St Leo, see especially pp. 54–61.

39 These connect the crucifixion and the New Covenant, to the Ark of the Covenant of the Old Testament, guarded by the cherubim, about which Bede writes in *De Tabernaculo et vasis eius*, I, ed. D. Hurst, Corpus Christianorum Series Latina, CXIX A, Turnhout, 1969, p. 19. *Item per duo Cherubim possunt duo Testamenta figurari quorum unum futuram Domini incarnationem, aliud factam clamat* . . .

40 *Argyll: an Inventory of the Monuments*, 4, Iona, pp. 192–204.

41 *Treasures of Early Irish Art, 1500 BC to 1500 AD*, New York, 1977, No. 29, pp. 91–2. The comment in the Catalogue that the absence of animal-ornament from the Athlone Plaque suggests an early date is, however, not convincing, since it is hard to see where animal-ornament might have fitted in. The chip-carved effect of the decoration suggests Anglo-Saxon technical influence.

42 Alexander, *Insular Manuscripts*, No. 44, pp. 66–7.

43 ibid., p. 67, col. 1.

44 Alexander, *Insular Manuscripts*, No. 61, pp. 80–1.

45 See *Life of Columba*, III, 6, 7, 9, 11, 12, 13, 14, pp. 476–93.

46 *HE*, Bk V, ch. 17, p. 318.

47 C. C. Hodges, 'The Ancient Cross at Rothbury', *Archaeologia Aeliana*, 4th series, I, 1925, pp. 159–68.

48 For discussion of this miniature, see my Chapter 5, pp. 168–74.

49 A. N. Grabar, *Ampoules de Terre Sainte* (Monza-Bobbio), Paris, 1958.

50 J. Beckwith, *Early Christian and Byzantine Art*, Harmondsworth, 1970, pp. 59–60.

51 This analogy was first pointed out by O. K. Werckmeister, 'Three Problems of Tradition in Pre-Carolingian Figure-Style', *Proceedings of the Royal Irish Academy*, 63, Section C, No. 5, 1963, pp. 184–9.

52 *HE*, Bk V, ch. 15, p. 317.

53 Alexander, *Insular Manuscripts*, No. 55, p. 78.

54 A. Gwynn, 'Ireland and Würzburg in the Middle Ages', *Irish Ecclesiastical Record*, lxxxiii, 1952, pp. 401–11.

55 Alexander, *Insular Manuscripts*, No. 13, pp. 44–5.

56 Although parallels are pointed out also with later books, ibid., p. 44.

57 See G. Bonner, 'Ireland and Rome: The Double Inheritance of Northumbria', *Saints, Scholars and Heroes: Studies in Medieval Culture in Honour of Charles W. Jones*, ed. M. H. King and W. M. Stevens, Minnesota, 1979, pp. 101–16.

58 See T. J. Brown, 'Northumbria and the Book of Kells', with an appendix by C. D. Verey, *Anglo-Saxon England*, I, Cambridge, 1972, pp. 219–46, especially pp. 243–5.

59 On this see also Ó Cróinín.

60 See *Matthew Parker's Legacy: Books and Plate*, with introduction by R. I. Page, Corpus Christi College, Cambridge, 1975, and *Matthew Parker and his Treasures*, A Quatercentenary Exhibition, Handlist.

61 Sir Robert Cotton was actively collecting historical manuscripts around 1600, and died 1631.

62 Alexander, *Insular Manuscripts*, No. 12, p. 44.

63 For this book, British Library Cotton MS Vespasian A.i, see D. H. Wright, *The Vespasian Psalter*, Early English Manuscripts in Facsimile, 14, Copenhagen, 1967.

64 Corpus Christi College MS 286, for which see my Chapter 1, note 68.

65 *Hic liber olim missus a Gregorio pp. ad Augustinum archiepz: sed nuper sic mutilatus.* As we have seen *codices plurimos* were sent by Gregory to St Augustine and his fellow missionaries. A fifteenth-century drawing in Thomas of Elmham's History of St Augustine's Monastery, Canterbury (Cambridge, Trinity Hall MS 1) shows books above the High Altar, treasured as relics and inscribed *Libri missi a Gregorio ad Augustinum*. It is in this context that we can read the inscription in Corpus MS 197B.

66 Smith, op. cit., loc. cit., *Dicitur fuisse liber olim S. Augustini, Anglorum Apostoli: sed id mihi nullo modo constare potest. Fortasse folium exscinditur, in quo continebatur traditio.*

67 Bede, *Historia Abbatum*, in *HE*, pp. 379–80.

68 Alexander, *Insular Manuscripts*, No. 11, pp. 42–3. For the connection between the Durham and Echternach Gospels see Brown and Bruce-Mitford, *Codex Lindisfarnensis*, pp. 100–2 and 246–50.

69 For Bede's Homilies see Mayr-Harting, op. cit., p. 175.

70 *HE*, Bk IV, ch. 1, p. 202.

71 *HE*, Bk III, ch. 25, p. 181. For the date 678 see Plummer, Notes, p. 188. It is not clear why the church constructed by Finan should be consecrated long afterwards by Theodore. Eadbert's renovation of the church, mentioned in the same paragraph by Bede, might have seemed a more appropriate occasion.

72 See Acca's evidence for Willibrord's enthusiasm for Oswald, recorded by Bede, *HE*, Bk III, ch. 13, p. 152.

73 For Willibrord at Ripon, see *Life of Wilfrid*, ch. xxvi, pp. 52–3; for Willibrord in Ireland, see *HE*, Bk III, ch. 13, p. 152.

74 Willibrord's relic of St Oswald, a fragment of the wooden stake on which St Oswald's head was fixed 'by the heathen after he was killed' at Oswestry. For this site, see Plummer, in *HE*, Notes, p. 152, and D. P. Kirby, 'Welsh Bards and the Border', in *Mercian Studies*, ed. A. Dornier, Leicester, 1977, p. 36. For Hygebald, see *HE*, Bk IV, ch. 3, p. 211.

75 *HE*, Bk III, ch. 4, pp. 134–5, *At tunc veniente ad eos reverentissimo et sanctissimo patre et sacerdote Ecgbercto, de natione Anglorum, qui in Hibernia diutius exulaverat pro Christo, eratque et doctissimus in scripturis, et longaeva vitae perfectione eximius, correcti sunt per eum, et ad verum canonicum paschae diem translati* . . . *De quo plenius in sequentibus suo loco dicendum est.*

76 *HE*, Bk V, ch. 9, p. 296.

77 *HE*, Bk V, ch. 9, p. 298.

78 *HE*, Bk IV, ch. 4, pp. 213–14.

79 See N. K. Chadwick, 'Bede, St Colman and the Irish Abbey of Mayo', *Celt and Saxon, Studies in the Early British Border*, Cambridge, 1963, pp. 186–205. For a different identification of Egbert's monastery see D. Ó Cróinín, 'Rath Melsigi, Willibrord and the Earliest Echternach Manuscripts', *Peritia*, 3, 1984, pp. 17–42, especially p. 26, note 1.

80 *HE*, Bk V, ch. 10, pp. 298–9. For the subsequent career of Wihtbert, after the failure of his Frisian mission, see now Ó Cróinín, op. cit., pp. 24–5.

81 *HE*, Bk V, ch. 9, pp. 296–7.

82 *HE*, Bk V, ch. 21, p. 332.

83 Bede's prose *Life*, ch. XI, p. 192.

84 *HE*, Bk III, ch. 27, pp. 193–4, *Duxit autem vitam in magna humilitatis, mansuetudinis, continentiae, simplicitatis, et iustitiae perfectione. Unde et genti suae et illis, in quibus exulabat, nationibus Scottorum sive Pictorum, exemplo vivendi, et instantia docendi, et auctoritate corripiendi, et pietate largiendi de his, quae a divitibus acceperat, multum profuit.*

85 D. Kirby, 'Bede and the Pictish Church', *Innes Review*, XXIV, 1973, pp. 6–25. See also A. A. M. Duncan, 'Bede, Iona, and the Picts', *The Writing of History in the Middle Ages*, Essays presented to Richard Southern, ed. R. H. C. Davis and J. M. Wallace-Hadrill, Oxford, 1981, pp. 1–42.

86 See my Chapter 2, note 124.

87 *Life of Columba*, I, 3, pp. 218–19.

88 *HE*, Bk V, ch. 22, pp. 346–7.

89 The fact that Egbert was received by the Iona monks *honorifice . . . et multo cum gaudio* suggests that his authority and prestige were already well established on Iona; see *HE*, Bk V, ch. 22, p. 346.

90 *HE*, Bk V, ch. 11, pp. 302–3.

91 See Brown, 'The Early History of E', *Codex Lindisfarnensis*, pp. 103–4.

92 Bede's prose *Life*, ch. XLIV, pp. 296–9.

93 But see my Chapter 2, note 138.

94 *HE*, Bk V, ch. 11, p. 302.

95 See Ó Cróinín, op. cit., especially p. 359.

96 *Aethelwulf: De Abbatibus*, ed. A. Campbell, Oxford, 1967. See also D. R. Howlett, 'The Provenance and Structure of De Abbatibus', *Archaeologia Aeliana*, 1975, pp. 121–30.

97 *De Abbatibus*, pp. 10–14.

98 *HE*, Bk V, ch. 10, p. 300.

99 C. A. Ralegh Radford, 'The Portable Altar of Saint Cuthbert', *Relics of Saint Cuthbert*, pp. 326–35.

100 *De Abbatibus*, pp. 18–19.

4 The Lindisfarne and Lichfield Gospels

1 See *Codex Lindisfarnensis*; also Alexander, *Insular Manuscripts*, No. 9, pp. 35–40.

2 E. Okasha, *Hand-List of Anglo-Saxon Non-Runic Inscriptions*, Cambridge, 1971, No. 61, pp. 85–6; also J. Higgitt, 'The Dedication Inscription at Jarrow and its Context', *The Antiquaries Journal*, LIX, 1979, Pt II, pp. 343–74.

3 For the preliminaries in Lindisfarne see Brown, in *Codex Lindisfarnensis*, pp. 33–7.

4 See my Chapter 3, note 6.

5 For Lindisfarne's canon-tables see Bruce-Mitford in *Codex Lindisfarnensis*, pp. 186–96.

6 See Brown on the liturgical apparatus in Lindisfarne, *Codex Lindisfarnensis*, pp. 34–7. See also Mayr-Harting, op. cit. p. 175.

7 See Bruce-Mitford, 'The Pectoral Cross', in *Relics of Saint Cuthbert*, pp. 312–13, 317–19.

8 D. M. Wilson in A. Small, C. Thomas and D. M. Wilson, *St Ninian's Isle and its Treasure*, I, Oxford, 1972, pp. 53–5.

9 For this development in Insular brooch design see R. B. K. Stevenson, 'The Hunterston Brooch and its Significance', *Medieval Archaeology*, XVIII, 1974, pp. 31–8.

10 For a study of the subtle mathematical basis of this carpet-page see R. D. Stevick, 'The Design of Lindisfarne Gospels folio 138v', *Gesta*, XXII, 1, 1983, pp. 3–12.

11 Wilson, in *St Ninian's Isle and its Treasure*, I, pp. 47–9.

12 G. Henderson, *Early Medieval*, Harmondsworth, 1972, pp. 98–100.

13 See Bruce-Mitford in *Codex Lindisfarnensis*, pp. 250–2.

14 See Battiscombe, 'Historical Introduction', *Relics of Saint Cuthbert*, pp. 30–5; also *Codex Lindisfarnensis*, pp. 20–3.

15 Bede's prose *Life*, Ch. XXXVII, pp. 278–9.

16 For the visual celebration of St Cuthbert in the later Middle Ages see M. Baker, 'Medieval Illustrations of Bede's *Life of St Cuthbert*', *Journal of the Warburg and Courtauld Institutes*, XLI, 1978, pp. 16–49.

17 Bede's prose *Life*, ch. III, pp. 162–5.

18 ibid., ch. IV, pp. 164–7; ch. VI, pp. 172–4, *Et quidem Lindisfarnensem aecclesiam multos habere sanctos viros, quorum doctrina et exemplis instrui posset noverat, sed fama preventus Boisili sullimium virtutum monachi et sacerdotis Mailros petere maluit.*

19 *HE*, Bk III, ch. 25, p. 183; Bede's prose *Life*, ch. VII, pp. 174–9.

20 See *Life of Wilfrid*, ch. XVII, pp. 36–7.

21 ibid., chs. XXIV–XL, pp. 48–81.

22 *HE*, Bk IV, ch. 12, p. 229; see also Mayr-Harting, op. cit. pp. 149–52.

23 Theodore found one cleric trained in the Irish tradition unsatisfactory, namely Chad's deacon Winfrith, who succeeded Chad at Lichfield but was later deposed by Theodore; after his deposition Winfrith, according to Bede, led a holy life in retirement at Barrow, his monastery in Mercia, so his fault was not lack of spirituality. *HE*, Bk IV, ch. 3, p. 212, and ch. 6, p. 218.

24 *HE*, Bk IV, ch. 12, p. 229.

25 Bede's prose *Life*, ch. XVI, pp. 206–7.

26 *HE*, Bk III, ch. 14, p. 155.

27 See Plummer, HE, Notes, p. 193.

28 *Historia Abbatum auctore Anonymo*, ed. Plummer, in *HE*, pp. 388–91.

29 See Higgitt, op. cit., p. 345.

30 *HE*, Bk IV, ch. 28, pp. 272–3.

31 *HE*, Bk IV, ch. 28, p. 272, *eo maxime victus sermone, quod famulus Domini Boisil, cum ei mente prophetica cuncta, quae eum essent superventura, patefaceret, antistitem quoque eum futurum esse praedixerat.*

32 *HE*, Bk IV, ch. 29, p. 275.

33 *HE*, Bk V, ch. 8, p. 295.

34 *HE*, Bk V, ch. 9, p. 298.

35 G. Henderson, *Bede and the Visual Arts*, p. 16.

36 *HE*, Bk III, ch. 25, p. 181.

37 *HE*, Bk IV, ch. 29, p. 275.

38 *HE*, Bk IV, ch. 30, p. 277.

39 D. H. Wright, 'The Italian Stimulus on English Art around 700', *Stil und Überlieferung in der Kunst des Abendlandes, Akten des 21. Internationalen Kongresses für Kunstgeschichte in Bonn, 1964*, ed. H. von Einem, I, Berlin, 1967, pp. 84–92.

40 *HE*, Bk IV, ch. 30, p. 277.

41 Bede's prose *Life*, Prologue, pp. 142–3, *Domino sancto ac beatissimo patri Eadfrido episcopo . . .*

42 *HE*, Bk V, ch. 8, p. 295, *. . . tametsi praedecessori suo minime conparandus.*

43 F. Henry, 'The Lindisfarne Gospels', *Antiquity*, XXXVII, 1963, pp. 102–3.

44 *HE*, Bk V, ch. 12, p. 310.

45 Bede's prose *Life*, ch. XXX, pp. 254–5; *religiosus presbiter Edilvaldus tunc minister viri Dei, nunc autem abbas coenobii Mailrosensis . . .* See also Plummer, HE, Notes, p. 297.

46 For the Esdras miniature and Lindisfarne, see Bruce-Mitford, *Codex Lindisfarnensis*, pp. 143–9.

47 *O Agios Mattheus; O Agios Lucas; O Agios Iohannis;* but *O Agius*

Marcus. See *HE*, Bk IV, ch. 2, p. 205, for the survival in Bede's time of Theodore and Hadrian's pupils who were proficient in Latin and Greek.

48 Bede's prose *Life*, ch. XXVII, pp. 242–8.

49 Toynbee, op. cit., No. 89, p. 161.

50 See my Chapter 1, note 80.

51 Bruce-Mitford, 'The Pectoral Cross', in *Relics of Saint Cuthbert*, pp. 309–10.

52 See Bruce-Mitford in *Codex Lindisfarnensis*, pp. 149–57.

53 W. Koehler, 'Die Schule von Tours', in *Die Karolingischen Miniaturen*, I, 1933, pp. 136–46; see also J. Hubert, J. Porcher and W. F. Volbach, *Carolingian Art*, London, 1970, pp. 132–41.

54 *Age of Spirituality*, Catalogue of the Exhibition at the Metropolitan Museum of Art, ed. K. Weitzmann, The Metropolitan Museum of Art, New York, 1979, p. 398.

55 For these representations of the divine persons see Bruce-Mitford 'The Art of the Codex Amiatinus', *The Journal of the British Archaeological Association*, 3rd series, XXXII, 1969, pl. C opposite p. 8, and pls IX, X, XI.

56 W. A. Stein, *The Lichfield Gospels*, unpublished Ph.D. Thesis, University of California, Berkeley, 1980; see also Alexander, Insular Manuscripts, No. 21, pp. 48–50; Lowe, op. cit., No. 159, p. 12; and Bruce-Mitford, *Codex Lindisfarnensis*, pp. 257–8.

57 Bede, '*In Lucae Evangelio Expositio*', Corpus Christianorum Series Latina, CXX, ed. D. Hurst, Turnhout, 1960, pp. 424–5.

58 Allen and Anderson, *Early Christian Monuments of Scotland*, III, pp. 428–9. See Bruce-Mitford, *Codex Lindisfarnensis*, p. 255.

59 *Life of Wilfrid*, ch. XXXVI, pp. 72–5.

60 The coils of his flat drapery are reminiscent of the wormy segments which make up the dragon design in the seventh-century cloisonné buckle from Wynaldum, Friesland, for which see R. Bruce-Mitford, *Aspects of Anglo-Saxon Archaeology*, London, 1974, pp. 270–3, Fig. 46c and pl. 88a.

61 M. Richards, 'The Lichfield Gospels (Book of St Chad)', *The National Library of Wales Journal*, 18, 1973, pp. 135–46.

62 *HE*, Bk V, ch. 23, p. 351, *Brettones . . . totius catholicae ecclesiae statum pascha minis recto, moribusque inprobis inpugnent.*

63 Stein, op. cit., p. 140. For her survey of origin centres, see pp. 12–25.

64 ibid., p. 77.

65 *HE*, Bk V, ch. 24, p. 356.

66 *Life of Wilfrid*, ch. LXVII, pp. 144–6. See also *HE*, Bk V, ch. 19, p. 330.

67 *Life of Guthlac*, ch. XLIX, p. 148.

68 ibid., ch. XXXIV, pp. 108–10.

69 F. M. Stenton, *Anglo-Saxon England*, 2nd ed. Oxford 1947, pp. 201–36. See also C. Hart, 'The Kingdom of Mercia', in *Mercian Studies*, Leicester, 1977, pp. 43–61.

70 Stein, op. cit., p. 140, for the provinciality of the script, see p. 131.

71 R. Cramp, 'Schools of Mercian Sculpture', *Mercian Studies*, pp. 205, 218.

72 *HE*, Bk III, ch. 11, p. 148, *. . . vexillum eius super tumbam auro et purpura conpositum adposuerunt . . .*

73 See Plummer, *HE*, Notes, p. 155.

74 For an alternative substantiation of Ultán, as the scribe of the Durham Gospels, see Ó Cróinín, *Peritia*, I, p. 362, where a different time-scale for the Insular Gospel-books is used. See also Howlett, *Archaeologia Aeliana*, 1974, pp. 129–30, where the Book of Kells is ascribed to Ultán's scriptorium.

75 *De Abbatibus*, p. 21, *pingere quo domini iam mistica verba . . .* Ultán is called *deo electus . . . scriptor.*

76 *potius angelica quam humana . . .* (Gerald of Wales); see my Chapter 6, p. 195, note 128.

5 The Book of Kells

1 *Codex Cenannensis*; see also Alexander, *Insular Manuscripts*, No. 52, pp. 71–6.

2 See my Chapter 2, note 111.

3 See this Chapter, note 6.

4 Maeseyck, Church of St Catherine, Trésor, s.n., *ff.* 1–5, s.n., *ff.* 6–132, for which see Alexander, *Insular Manuscripts*, Nos 22, 23, pp. 50–1.

5 Rome, Vatican, Biblioteca Apostolica MS Barberini lat. 570, for which see Alexander, *Insular Manuscripts*, No. 36, pp. 61–2.

6 A. M. Friend, 'The Canon Tables of the Book of Kells', *Medieval Studies in Memory of Arthur Kingsley Porter*, ed. W. R. W. Koehler, Cambridge, Mass., 1939, II, pp. 611–41.

7 The first part of the Lorsch Gospels is preserved in Alba Julia, Roumania; the second part, Luke and John, is in the Vatican, Pal. lat. 50.

8 See Friend, p. 639.

9 Stockholm, Royal Library MS A.135, for which see Alexander, *Insular Manuscripts*, No. 30, pp. 56–7.

10 See my Chapter 3, note 19.

11 Friend, op. cit., p. 639; see also pp. 617–18 for the interpretation of *ff.* 5v, 6, as an 'inglorious close'.

12 It is used, for example, to decorate the frames of both the extant Evangelist portraits, on pp. 142, 218. On this fret-pattern, see Stein, op. cit., pp. 116–19.

13 The Genoels-Elderen Diptych, for which see Catalogue of the Council of Europe Exhibition, *Charlemagne, Oeuvre, Rayonnement et Survivances*, Aix-la-Chapelle, 1965, ed. W. Braunfels, pp. 345–6.

14 For Fletton, see Cramp, 'Schools of Mercian Sculpture', *Mercian Studies*, pp. 210–11. For Hoddom, see Allen and Anderson, *Early Christian Monuments of Scotland*, III, p. 441 and Fig. 463.

15 M. O. Budny, *The Royal Bible, BL MS I.E.VI*, unpublished Doctoral Thesis, University of London, 1985; see also Alexander, *Insular Manuscripts*, No. 32, pp. 58–9.

16 Paris, Bibliothèque Nationale Cod. lat. 8850.

17 For the iconography of the *Fons vitae*, see Underwood, Dumbarton Oaks Papers No. 5, pp. 41–138.

18 *Hic vitae fons est, haec est sapientia vera*; see Underwood, op. cit., p. 49, note 31.

19 On the iconography of the Kells Virgin, see E. Kitzinger, 'The Coffin Reliquary', in *Relics of Saint Cuthbert*, pp. 248–64.

20 On the manufacture of the coffin, see my Chapter 4, note 38.

21 Kitzinger, op. cit., pp. 253–4.

22 ibid., p. 262.

23 In the Last Judgment miniature on p. 267, to echo the looped cord which decorates the frame.

24 Cassiodorus, *Expositio psalmorum*, Corpus Christianorum Series Latina, XCVIII, ed. M. Adriaen, Turnhout, 1958, p. 678.

25 *Homeliarum Evangelii Libri II*, Corpus Christianorum Series Latina, CXXII, ed. D. Hurst, Turnhout, 1955, pp. 11–12.

26 R. M. Walker, 'Illustrations to the Priscillian Prologues in the Gospel Manuscripts of the Carolingian Ada School', *The Art Bulletin*, 1948, pp. 1–10, especially p. 3.

27 For *plures fuisse* see Chapman, *Notes on the Early History of the Vulgate Gospels*, p. 273.

28 Henry, *The Book of Kells*, London, 1974, p. 200 and note 97.

29 C. Nordenfalk, in A. Grabar, C. Nordenfalk, *Early Medieval Painting from the Fourth to the Eleventh Century*, Skira, 1957, pp. 122, 140; For the Valenciennes Apocalypse, Valenciennes, Bibliothèque Municipale, MS 99, see also Alexander, *Insular Manuscripts*, No. 64, pp. 82–3.

30 Completed by Guido da Como in 1246. It is decorated with the

heads of the Evangelist symbols, to associate it with the imagery of the four rivers of Paradise. For the symbolism of hexagonal and octagonal fonts and baptistries, see Underwood, op. cit., appendix, pp. 131–8.

31 J.-P. Migne, *Patrologia Latina*, C, *Alcuini Opera Omnia*, Letter CXIII, col. 341.

32 For the text in translation, see K. H. Jackson, *A Celtic Miscellany*, London, 1951, p. 307. For an interesting interpretation of the Chi-Rho initial in Kells, linking it to the Eucharist and the Resurrection, see S. Lewis, 'Sacred Calligraphy: the Chi Rho Page in the Book of Kells', *Traditio* XXXVI, 1980, pp. 139–59. I agree with Professor Lewis's belief that the illustrations in the Book of Kells are learned and allusive.

33 R. A. S. Macalister, *Monasterboice, Co. Louth*, Dundalk, 1946; also Henry, *Irish Art During the Viking Invasions 800–1020 AD*, pp. 156–94.

34 Bede's prose *Life*, ch. X, pp. 190–1, *Completoque ministerio . . . patrias sunt relapsa sub undas*.

35 C. Nordenfalk, *Celtic and Anglo-Saxon Painting*, London, 1977, p. 124. I do not agree with Nordenfalk when he senses in the 'expressive power' of the picture of the Arrest of Christ – 'a presage, it would seem, of the horrors awaiting the monks with the approaching attack by the Vikings'. See my Chapter 6, p. 196.

36 For example, see *The Age of Spirituality*, Nos 374, 383, 436.

37 See Macalister, op. cit., also Henry, op. cit., p. 157.

38 *Life of Wilfrid*, ch. XIII, pp. 28–9.

39 Compare *The Age of Spirituality*, Figs 51, 52, 59, pp. 397–404.

40 Vatican MS Barberini Lat. 570, *f*. 1.

41 Valenciennes, Bibliothèque Municpale MS 99, *f*. 37. See A. C. L. Boinet, *La Miniature Carolingienne*, Paris, 1913, pl. CLIX D.

42 J. Graham-Campbell and D. Kidd, *The Vikings*, British Museum Publications, London, 1980, pp. 45, 197, No. 263.

43 For the Franks Casket see R. I. Page, *An Introduction to English Runes*, London, 1973, pp. 174–82; see also L. Webster, 'Stylistic Aspects of the Franks Casket', in *The Vikings*, ed. R. T. Farrell, London, 1982, pp. 20–31.

44 Henry, *The Book of Kells*, pp. 200–4 and note 98.

45 Henderson, *Bede and the Visual Arts*, pp. 17–18.

46 Plummer, in *HE*, Notes, pp. 95–6.

47 Nordenfalk, *Celtic and Anglo-Saxon Painting*, p. 123.

48 Henry, *Irish Art During the Viking Invasions 800–1020 AD*, p. 81.

49 This point is partially answered, however, by Nordenfalk, quoted by Lewis, for which see *Traditio*, 1980, p. 156.

50 Catalogue, *Treasures of Early Irish Art 1500 BC to 1500 AD*, No. 31, p. 137.

51 J. T. Lang, 'Hogback Monuments in Scotland', *Proceedings of the Society of Antiquaries of Scotland*, 105, 1972–4, pp. 206–35.

52 This feature is omitted from the drawing of the Kells 'Temple' on p. 204 of Henry, *The Book of Kells*.

53 J. Romilly Allen, *Celtic Art in Pagan and Christian Times*, London, 1904, opposite p. 210.

54 J. Hunt, 'On Two "D"-Shaped Objects in the St. Germain Museum', *Proceedings of the Royal Irish Academy*, LVII, C, 1954–6, pp. 153–7. See also A. Mahr, *Christian Art in Ancient Ireland*, Dublin, 1932, pls 25, 26: F. Henry, 'Deux objets de bronze irlandais au Musée des Antiquités Nationales', *Studies in Early Christian and Medieval Irish Art*, London, 1983, pp. 195–219.

55 For the box-shaped Noah's ark in the 'Cotton Genesis Recension', see G. Henderson, 'Late-Antique Influences in some Illustrations of Genesis', *Journal of the Warburg and Courtauld Institutes*, XXV, 1962, pp. 183–7; for another box-shaped ark, see plaque, Museo Civico, Velletri, No. 371 in *The Age of Spirituality*, pp. 413–14.

56 J. Stevenson, *The Catacombs: Rediscovered Monuments of Early Christianity*, London, 1978, pp. 8–9 and 76.

57 On the related question of desks, see B. M. Metzger, 'When did scribes begin to use writing desks?', *Historical and Literary Studies; Pagan, Jewish and Christian*, Leiden, 1968, pp. 123–37.

58 I Esdras 9, 42.

59 *Amalarius Opera Liturgica*, ed. J. M. Hanssens, Studi e Testi 138–40, Città del Vaticano, 1948–50, II, *Liber Officialis*, Bk III, ch. 17, pp. 305–6.

60 For the *Life of St Patrick* by Muirchú see *The Patrician Texts in the Book of Armagh*, ed. L. Bieler, Scriptores Latini Hiberniae, X, Dublin, 1979, pp. 62–122, and commentary, pp. 1–35 and 193–214. The lighting of fire at Easter occurs in the *Life*, on pp. 84–7. See also the lighting of fire and candles in the Easter ceremonies described in the summary of St Patrick's life by Tírechán, written within a few years of Muirchú's account, also in Bieler, pp. 130–1.

61 See L. Duchesne, *Origines du culte chrétien: Étude sur la Liturgie Latine avant Charlemagne*, 2nd ed., Paris, 1898, pp. 240–6; see also G. B. Ladner, 'The "portraits" of Emperors in Southern Italian *Exultet* Rolls and the Liturgical Commemoration of the Emperor', *Speculum*, XVII, 1942, pp. 181–200; also Mayr-Harting, op. cit., p. 304, note 24.

62 See Duchesne, op. cit., p. 243, note 1.

63 See Amalarius, *Liber Officialis*, Bk I, ch. 12, p. 78, and chs. 18–34, pp. 111–70.

64 *HE*, Bk V, ch. 21, p. 336.

65 See my Chapter 2, note 97.

66 See the *Lumen Christi* illustrations in M. Avery, *The Exultet Rolls of South Italy*, Princeton, 1936.

67 Durham, Cathedral Library MS B.II.30, for which see Alexander, *Insular Manuscripts*, No. 17, p. 46.

68 See my Chapter 6, pp. 195.

69 Kenney, op. cit., No. 226, *Fis Adamnáin*, pp. 444–5. For translation, see Jackson, *A Celtic Miscellany*, pp. 317–25.

70 See my Chapter 2, note 14.

71 Compare the pose with that adopted by the Abbess Ecgburh, in the *Life of Guthlac*, ch. XLVIII, pp. 146–7, *adiurans per nomen terribile ac venerabile superni regis, seque ad patibulum dominicae crucis erigens in indicium supplicis deprecationis extensis palmis . . .*

72 For examples of this imagery, see G. Henderson, 'The Seal of Brechin Cathedral', in *From the Stone Age to the 'Forty-Five: Studies presented to R. B. K. Stevenson*, ed. A. O'Connor and D. V. Clarke, Edinburgh, 1983, pp. 399–415.

73 See for example the right wing of the Donne of Kidwelly Altarpiece by H. Memlinc, in E. Panofsky, *Early Netherlandish Painting*, Cambridge, Mass., 1953, II, p. 316.

74 Henderson, *Bede and the Visual Arts*, p. 16.

75 Henry, *The Book of Kells*, p. 194, interprets what she terms the 'weird, ghostly apparitions' at the top of some of the canon-tables as 'the Trinity or one of its persons . . .'

6 The Book of Kells: the making of a relic

1 A. Gwynn, 'Some Notes on the History of the Book of Kells, *Irish Historical Studies*, 9, 1954–5, pp. 131–61; W. O'Sullivan, 'The Donor of the Book of Kells', *Irish Historical Studies*, 11, 1958–9, pp. 5–7.

2 J. Ussher, *Britannicarum Ecclesiarum Antiquitates*, Dublin, 1639, p. 691.

3 For a useful summary of the history of the manuscript, see P. Brown, *The Book of Kells*, London, 1980, pp. 92–5.

4 For the Kells charters, see G. Mac Niocaill, *Notitiae as Leabhar Cheanannais, 1033–1161*, Dublin, 1961.

5 *The Annals of Ulster (to AD 1131)*, ed. S. Mac Airt and G. Mac

Niocaill, I, Dublin Institute for Advanced Studies, 1983 [hereafter *AU*], pp. 438–9.

6 *AU*, pp. 386–7.

7 See *Annals of Ulster, A Chronicle of Irish Affairs from AD 431 to AD 1540*, I, ed. W. M. Hennessy, Dublin, 1887, p. 519; also Henry, *The Book of Kells*, p. 150 and note 5; see also L. Bieler, *Ireland, Harbinger of the Middle Ages*, London, 1963, p. 113. The translation in *AU*, p. 439, introduces a new ambiguity: 'It was the most precious object of the western world on account of the human ornamentation(?).' Presumably this means 'craftsmanship', of which there is a great quantity, *inside* the Book of Kells!

8 But see *Chronicon Scottorum*, ed. W. M. Hennessy, Rolls Series, 46, 1866, p. 244, under the year 1005, for the statement that gold *and* silver were stolen, *a oir de, ocus a argait*.

9 For the pigments in Kells, see H. Rosen-Runge and A. E. A. Werner, in *Codex Lindisfarnensis*, pp. 273 *ff*; also Henry, *Book of Kells*, pp. 157–8, 211–12.

10 Adomnán's *Life of Columba*, ed. A. O. Anderson and M. O. Anderson, Edinburgh, 1961 [hereafter *Life of Columba*].

11 *Life of Columba*, preface, pp. 180–3.

12 ibid., III, 18, pp. 502–3.

13 ibid., II, 32, pp. 396–9.

14 ibid., p. 539, note 9.

15 J.-M. Picard, 'The Purpose of Adomnán's *Vita Columbae*', *Peritia*, 1, 1982, pp. 160–77.

16 *Life of Columba*, III, 23, pp. 540–2. On this see D. A. Bullough, 'Columba, Adomnan and Iona', Part II, *Scottish Historical Review*, 44, 1965, p. 21, note 2.

17 *AU*, pp. 262–3, *Constructio novae civitatis Columbae Cille hi Ceninnus*.

18 For Cogitosus's *Life of St Brigit*, see *Acta Sanctorum*, Antwerp, 1658, Feb., I, pp. 129–41, and for *Lives* by other authors, ibid., pp. 99–185. See also *Bethu Brigte*, ed. D. Ó hAodha, Dublin, 1978. For studies of the *Lives* of St Brigit, see R. Sharpe, '*Vitae S. Brigitae*: The Oldest Texts', *Peritia*, 1, 1982, pp. 81–106, and K. McCone, 'Brigit in the Seventh Century: A Saint with Three Lives?', in the same Journal, pp. 107–45.

19 For interpretations of these claims see Hughes, *The Church in Early Irish Society*, pp. 83–5, and R. Sharpe, 'Some Problems Concerning the Organization of the Church in Early Medieval Ireland', *Peritia*, 3, 1984, pp. 230–70, especially pp. 260, 262.

20 For the *Liber Angeli* see *The Patrician Texts in the Book of Armagh*, ed. Bieler, pp. 184–91, and commentary, pp. 52–4. See also R. Sharpe, 'Armagh and Rome in the Seventh Century', in *Irland und Europa: Die Kirche im Frühmittelalter*, ed. P. Ní Chatháin and M. Richter, Stuttgart, 1984, pp. 58–72, and R. Sharpe, 'Palaeographical Considerations in the Study of the Patrician Documents in the Book of Armagh (Dublin, Trinity College MS 52)', *Scriptorium*, XXXVI, 1982, pp. 3–28, especially pp. 20–5.

21 The date of this addendum is in dispute. See Sharpe, op. cit., *Scriptorium*, 1982, p. 22; McCone, op. cit., pp. 107–8, 133, 136.

22 McCone, op. cit., pp. 132–45.

23 Hughes, op. cit., pp. 89, 118–19.

24 *Betha Coluim Chille*, in *Three Middle-Irish Homilies on the Lives of Saints Patrick, Brigit and Columba*, ed. W. Stokes, Calcutta, 1877, pp. 90–125.

25 ibid., p. 111.

26 ibid., pp. 114–15; this story is repeated in Manus O'Donnell, *Betha Colaim Chille (Life of Columcille)*, ed. A. O'Kelleher and G. Schoepperle, Illinois, 1918, pp. 100–1.

27 See *Betha Phátraic*, in Stokes, *Three Middle-Irish Homilies*, pp. 40–1; also *Betha Colaim Chille*, pp. 98–9.

28 *Liber Ardmachanus*, Dublin, Trinity College MS 52, for which see *The Book of Armagh*, ed. J. Gwynn, Dublin, 1913; also

29 Although it would obviously have been in Armagh's interests to do so, it was evidently not possible to claim possession of St Patrick's body – hence the emphasis in the *Liber Angeli* on apostolic and other relics. For this see Bieler, op. cit., p. 240. Tírechán turned the problem to good effect by likening St Patrick to Moses, whose burial-place was likewise a sacred mystery, known only to God; see Supplementary Notes, Bieler, op. cit., pp. 164–5 and 44. For Columcille's intervention, see Bieler, pp. 164–5 and 45.

30 R. Sharpe, 'St Patrick and the See of Armagh', *Cambridge Medieval Celtic Studies*, No. 4, Winter 1982, p. 38.

31 Manus O'Donnell, *Bethu Colaim Chille*, pp. 427–8. Compare an earlier version of the burial story, in *Acta Sanctorum*, Feb., I, pp. 163–4.

32 For Tírechán's date, see Sharpe, op. cit., *Cambridge Medieval Celtic Studies*, p. 34; also McCone, op. cit., p. 138, Hughes, op. cit., p. 86, note 1, and Bieler, op. cit., pp. 35–46.

33 See Bieler, op. cit., pp. 140–1; also D. A. Binchy, 'Patrick and his biographers, Ancient and Modern', *Studia Hibernica*, 2, 1962, p. 61; Hughes, op. cit., p. 88 and also p. 113.

34 See K. Hughes, *Early Christian Ireland: Introduction to the Sources*, London, 1972, pp. 99–159.

35 K. Meyer, ed. and transl., '*Cáin Adamnáin*, an Old-Irish Treatise on the Law of Adamnán', *Anecdota Oxoniensia*, Medieval and Modern Series 12, Oxford, 1905; see also M. Ní Dhonnchadha, 'The Guarantor List of Cáin Adamnáin, 697', *Peritia*, I, 1982, pp. 178–215, and J.-M. Picard, 'Bede, Adomnán, and the Writing of History', *Peritia*, 3, 1984, pp. 65–6.

36 *AU*, pp. 180–81, *Adomnani reliquiae transferuntur in Hiberniam et Lex renovatur*.

37 See Anderson, *Early Sources*, I, pp. 240–1, note 5. For St Wilfrid's collection of relics, and their misappropriation, see *Life of Wilfrid*, ch. XXXIII, p. 66, and ch. XXXIV, p. 70.

38 *AU*, pp. 182–3, *Reversio reliquiarum Adomnani de Hibernia*.

39 G. Mac Niocaill, *Ireland Before the Vikings*, Dublin, 1972, pp. 122–3.

40 See Binchy, op. cit., pp. 59–68 and p. 170.

41 Mac Niocaill, op. cit., p. 124.

42 *AU*, pp. 186–7.

43 *AU*, pp. 190–1, *Lex Patricii tenuit Hiberniam*.

44 For this promulgation as Armagh's 'revenge' for the fines previously paid to the confederation of Columba, see Picard, 'The Purpose of Adomnán's *Vita Columbae*', *Peritia*, I, 1982, p. 163. On the relics of Armagh see McCone, op. cit., p. 137. On the circuit of relics, see also Hughes, *The Church in Early Irish Society*, pp. 151–2, 167–8.

45 Anderson, *Early Sources*, I, pp. 240–1, note 5.

46 *AU*, pp. 194–5, *in clericatum Domnall exiit*, and pp. 198–9, *Domnall in clericatum iterum*.

47 *AU*, pp. 206–7, *Lex Coluim Cille la Domnall Mide*.

48 *AU*, pp. 210–11, *Lex Columbae Cille la Sleibene*.

49 *AU*, pp. 216–7. For the interpretation of the cause of the battle, see A. P. Smyth, *Celtic Leinster*, Dublin, 1982, p. 89. For Domnall's death and burial see also Anderson, *Early Sources*, p. 245 and note 1.

50 *AU*, pp. 220–1.

51 *AU*, pp. 232–3.

52 *AU*, loc. cit.

53 *AU*, pp. 234–5.

54 *AU*, pp. 246–7; Donnchad's successor, Áed Ingor ('Ordnide') of the Cenél nEógain, son of Niall Frossach, was given the unprecedented honour of ordination as King by the Abbot of Armagh, a clear gesture of support for his dynasty; see Mac Niocaill, op. cit., p. 34. His ordination did not prevent the

family of Columcille from solemnly cursing him at Tara in 817, for the killing of one of their abbots. See *AU*, pp. 272–3, and Hughes, op. cit., p. 191.

55 See Anderson, *Early Sources*, I, p. 256.

56 *AU*, pp. 258–9, *I Columbae Cille a gentibus combusta est.*

57 *AU*, pp. 260–1; literally, *cen chath.*

58 *AU*, pp. 262–3; see also Anderson, *Early Sources*, I, p. 259.

59 *AU*, loc. cit.

60 Manus O'Donnell, *Betha Colaim Chille*, pp. 180, 190, 192, 194, 292, 294; for Derry's rise to the leading centre of the Columban confederation in the twelfth century, and the continuing alliance of Armagh and the Cenél nEógain antipathetic to Iona, see *Argyll: an Inventory of the Monuments*, 4, *Iona*, pp. 48–9.

61 For a promulgation of the Law of Patrick in association with his own shrine, see *AU*, I, pp. 266–7, under the year 810, *recte* 811, when the Abbot of Armagh went to Connaught 'with the Law of Patrick' and with his shrine, *cum Lege Patricii et cum armario eius.*

62 *HE*, Bk III, ch. 4, p. 134.

63 *Life of Columba*, III, 23, pp. 536–41 and note 6, p. 536. For the stone, as epitaph, see pp. 526–7.

64 For the grave-site and memorial slabs, see *Argyll: an Inventory of the Monuments*, 4, *Iona*, pp. 41–2 and p. 187.

65 *Life of Columba*, II, 45, 44, pp. 450–3.

66 *Life of Columba*, III, 23, pp. 524–5.

67 *Inquirentes autem dominum non deficient omni bono*; Luce, *Codex Durmachensis*, p. 13, states that this text is not Vulgate but 'Old Latin'. We only know, of course, the text as Adomnán recalled it. The Cathach text is Vulgate. On this, see also D. A. Bullough, 'Columba, Adomnan and the Achievement of Iona', *Scottish Historical Review*, 43, 1964, Part I, p. 130.

68 *Life of Columba*, I, 23, pp. 256–7.

69 *Life of Columba*, II, 9, pp. 342–5.

70 *Life of Columba*, II, 8, pp. 342–3.

71 For hymns attributed to St Columba, see J. F. Kenney, *The Sources for the Early History of Ireland*, I, *Ecclesiastical*, New York, 1929, repr. 1966, No. 91, pp. 263–4. For the efficacy of *Noli pater indulgere*, see Manus O'Donnell, *Betha Colaim Chille*, pp. 66–7.

72 *Life of Columba*, I, 25, pp. 258–9; also II, 29, pp. 390–3.

73 Manus O'Donnell, *Betha Colaim Chille*, pp. 176–83. On the battle, see also Smyth, *Warlords and Holy Men*, p. 94.

74 Manus O'Donnell, *Betha Colaim Chille*, pp. 182–5; see also p. 206, for the Cross of Tory as *airdmhind.*

75 *Life of Saint Columba . . . written by Adamnan*, ed. Reeves, p. lxxxvii.

76 See my Chapter 2, pp. 26–7; also Alexander, *Insular Manuscripts*, No. 4, pp. 28–9.

77 See *Betha Coluim Chille*, in Stokes, *Three Middle-Irish Homilies*, pp. 112–13; also Manus O'Donnell, *Betha Colaim Chille*, p. 434.

78 *Life of Saint Columba . . . written by Adamnan*, ed. Reeves, p. lxxxvi; for the Iona slab, see *Argyll: an Inventory of the Monuments*, 4, *Iona*, No. 47, p. 187.

79 *The Annals of Tigernach*, ed. Stokes, *Revue Celtique*, XVIII, 1897, p. 12.

80 Hughes, *Early Christian Ireland: Introduction to the Sources*, p. 255, note 1, assumes that the Cathach was not one of the Cenél Conaill relics brought to Kells in 1090.

81 See *Betha Coluim Chille*, in Stokes, *Three Middle-Irish Homilies*, pp. 114–15, *Soscéla*; Manus O'Donnell, *Betha Colaim Chille*, refers to Columba leaving a book, *lebar*, at Swords. O'Kelleher and Schoepperle translate this as 'missal'.

82 *AU*, pp. 472–3.

83 *AU*, pp. 282–3.

84 Anderson, *Early Sources*, I, pp. 263–5.

85 One massive post and fragments of others, decorated with key-patterns, are made of showy material, deeply textured contorted mica-quartz schist, heavily studded with large garnet crystals. See *Argyll: an Inventory of the Monuments*, 4, *Iona*, No. 104, pp. 216–17.

86 *AU*, pp. 280–1.

87 *AU*, pp. 286–7.

88 *AU*, loc. cit. 'came [back]', p. 287, is unintelligble.

89 Anderson, *Early Sources*, I, p. 288. Ironically the same Chronicle reports the destruction of Old Melrose by King Kenneth. For Dunkeld see also Henderson, *The Picts*, pp. 88–9.

90 *AU*, pp. 308–9.

91 *AU*, pp. 312–13.

92 Anderson, *Early Sources*, I, p. 353.

93 *AU*, pp. 334–5.

94 A. P. Smyth, *Scandinavian Kings in the British Isles 850–880*, Oxford, 1977, p. 257, supports the case that the 878 relics were those from Dunkeld. On the departure of the relics of St Cuthbert from Lindisfarne under similar circumstances see C. F. Battiscombe, 'Historical Introduction', *Relics of Saint Cuthbert*, pp. 36–30, especially p. 28, note 1. See also D. P. Rollason, 'Lists of Saints' Resting-places in Anglo-Saxon England', *Anglo-Saxon England*, 7, 1978, p. 68.

95 *AU*, pp. 368–9, and pp. 370–1.

96 *Life of Saint Columba . . . written by Adamnan*, ed. Reeves, p. lxxxii.

97 *The Annals of Tigernach*, ed. Stokes, *Revue Celtique*, XVIII, 1897, pp. 52–3.

98 Anderson, *Early Sources*, I, pp. 407–8.

99 That is, *Baculus Iesu*, the staff of Jesus. It is mentioned in *Betha Phátraic* in Stokes, *Three Middle-Irish Homilies*, p. 35. It was burnt, unfortunately, in 1538.

100 *Life of Saint Columba . . . written by Adamnan*, ed. Reeves, p. xc.

101 ibid., p. lxxxiv; for a twelfth-century list of Durham relics, which does not include St Columba, see Battiscombe, 'Historical Introduction, Appendixes', in *Relics of Saint Columba*, pp. 112–14.

102 See *Argyll: an Inventory of the Monuments*, 4, *Iona*, pp. 23–4, and p. 85.

103 ibid., p. 145.

104 F. C. Eeles, 'The Monymusk Reliquary or Brecbennoch of St Columba', *Proceedings of the Society of Antiquaries of Scotland*, LXVIII, 1934, pp. 433–8.

105 For lay guardians of relics in medieval Scotland, holding an office that gave rise to the family name Dewar, see *Life of Saint Columba . . . written by Adamnan*, ed. Reeves, p. 242.

106 *Life of Columba*, II, 5, pp. 336–9; II, 4, pp. 330–5. Compare the use of bread blessed by St Cuthbert to work a cure, Bede's prose *Life*, ch. XXXI, pp. 254–6.

107 For the date of Flann's accession see *AU*, pp. 334–5. Luce, *Codex Durmachensis*, p. 32, and Henry, *Irish Art During the Viking Invasions 800–1020 AD*, London, 1967, p. 121, adopt the 877 date given by the *Annals of . . . the Four Masters*; Smyth, *Celtic Leinster*, p. 79, and D. ÓCorráin, *Ireland before the Normans*, by implication, in genealogical table on p. 180, adopt the year 879.

108 *AU*, pp. 362–3.

109 In an important and ingenious Appendix, *Celtic Leinster*, pp. 118–22, Smyth argues for the origin of the Book of Durrow at Durrow itself, in direct association with Adomnán and King Aldfrith. This places the Book of Durrow stylistically too late in the century. Admitting a possible Northumbrian origin Smyth writes that 'the fact that such a magnificent work had been allowed to gravitate towards Durrow at an early stage in its life would in itself be suggestive of the pre-eminent position of the Irish Midlands in the cultural life of the British Isles in the Dark Ages'. My suggestion, above, p. 193–4, brings the

Book of Durrow to Durrow under circumstances very different, more distinguished, than being 'allowed to gravitate'. C. Hicks, 'A Clonmacnois Workshop in Stone', *Journal of the Royal Society of Antiquaries of Ireland*, 110, 1980, pp. 5–35, especially p. 11, argues for the Durrow origin of the Book of Durrow. The arguments of Luce, *Codex Durmachensis*, p. 47, relating to Flann's *cumtach*, are unconvincing.

110 On this point, I agree with the theory first outlined by I. Fisher, *Argyll: an Inventory of the Monuments*, 4, Iona, p. 47.

111 *Life of Wilfrid*, ch. XVII, pp. 36–7.

112 See Reeves, op. cit., *Proceedings of the Royal Irish Academy*, 1891–3, p. 81, and Sharpe, op. cit., *Scriptorium*, 1982, pp. 27–8, and note 83.

113 *AU*, pp. 378–9 and pp. 386–7.

114 These years saw strong action against the Norse in Ireland and England. In 936 King Donnchad attacked and burned Norse Dublin. In 937 Aethelstan won his famous victory over the Norse and Scots in Northumbria. In 938 Donnchad and Muirchertach jointly attacked Dublin. See Ó Corráin, *Ireland before the Normans*, pp. 103–4.

115 *AU*, pp. 390–1.

116 *AU*, pp. 438–9; for a display of relics at the Fair of Tailtiu, in 831, see *AU*, pp. 286–7.

117 See also *HE*, Bk V, ch. 19, where the epitaph of St Wilfrid is quoted, referring to *thecam . . . condignam*.

118 As noted in the earliest known copy of the *History of the Britons* by Nennius, discovered at Chartres late in the nineteenth century, written *c*. 900 but transcribing a text of 801; see A. W. Wade-Evans, *Nennius's 'History of the Britons'*, London, SPCK, 1938, p. 9, . . . *sicut [S] libine abas Iae in Ripum civitate invenit vel reperit . . .*

119 *Treasures of Early Irish Art 1500 BC to 1500 AD*, New York, 1977, No. 57, pp. 182–3.

120 *Topographia Hibernica*, ch. XXXVIII, in *Giraldi Cambrensis Opera*, ed. J. F. Dimock, Rolls Series, London, 1867, V, pp. 123–4.

121 Henry, *The Book of Kells*, p. 165; Brown, *The Book of Kells*, p. 83, and Bieler, op. cit., p. 114.

122 *Topographia Hibernica*, ch. XXXIX, *De Libri Compositione*, loc. cit., p. 124.

123 Bullough, op. cit. II, *Scottish Historical Review*, 44, 1965, pp. 32–3. But see Sharpe, op. cit., *Peritia*, 1, 1982, p. 87, note 3.

124 Gifts of fine manuscripts from one church to another are known in other periods; compare the generosity of Egbert of Trier, for which see C. R. Dodwell, *Painting in Europe 800 to 1200*, Harmondsworth, 1971, p. 56.

125 See McCone, op. cit., *Peritia*, I, 1982, pp. 107–8, for the eighth-century date of the power-struggle between Armagh and Kildare. For the dating of the 'agreement' between Armagh and Kildare to the second half of the eighth century, see also p. 144. The date of the Book of Kells argued by Henry, op. cit., pp. 216–18, and supported by Lewis, *Traditio*, 1980, p. 139, does not take into account the circumstantial eighth-century stimuli to the making of the Book of Kells emphasized above. For the latest statement of a ninth-century date and specifically Irish provenance for the Book of Kells, based on Carolingian and other parallels for the iconography of the illustrations, see P. Harbison, 'Three Miniatures in the Book of Kells', *Proceedings of the Royal Irish Academy*, 85, 1985, C, 7, pp. 181–94.

126 *Betha Phatraic* in Stokes, *Three Middle-Irish Homilies*, pp. 34–5.

127 *Life of Columba*, III, 5, pp. 472–3; for an impressive story about a written roll from heaven, used for the instruction of the Irish, see Hughes, *The Church in Early Irish Society*, p. 179.

128 *AU*, pp. 78–9, *Soiscela inn Aingil*. For the 'traditional' identification of the 'Angel's Gospel' with the Book of Kells, see Anderson, *Early Sources*, I, p. 526, note 6.

129 Although Kenney, op. cit., quotes her reputation as 'the patron of poets and men of learning', p. 358; for a posthumous miracle of St Brigit, involving *artifices*, see Cogitosus's *Life*, Ch. VIII, in *Acta Sanctorum*, Feb., I, p. 141.

130 *The Annals of Tigernach*, ed. Stokes, *Revue Celtique*, XVIII, 1897, pp. 52–3.

131 *Revelation* 1, 19.

132 *Life of Columba*, II, 45, pp. 454–5.

List of Illustrations

134 The text of *De Abbatibus* referring to Eadfrith and Egbert, Cambridge University Library MS Ff.1.27, *f*. 205. 29.5 × 20 cm (11½ × 7⅞ in). By permission of the Syndics of Cambridge University Library.

135 Portable altar of St Cuthbert. Carved oak slab. 5.7 × 3.8 cm (2¼ × 1½ in). Durham, Cathedral Treasury. Courtesy the Dean and Chapter of Durham.

136 Portable altar of St Cuthbert, drawing from C. W. Battiscombe, *Relics of St Cuthbert*, 1956.

137 Carpet-page, the Lindisfarne Gospels, London, British Library Cotton MS Nero D.IV, *f*. 2v. 34 × 24 cm (13⅜ × 9½ in).

138 *Novum opus* preface, the Lindisfarne Gospels, London, British Library Cotton MS Nero D.IV, *f*. 3. 34 × 24 cm (13⅜ × 9½ in).

139 *Plures fuisse* preface, the Lindisfarne Gospels, London, British Library Cotton MS Nero D.IV, *f*. 5v. 34 × 24 cm (13⅜ × 9½ in).

140 Canon-table, Canon X, the Lindisfarne Gospels, London, British Library Cotton MS Nero D.IV, *f*. 17v. 34 × 24 cm (13⅜ × 9½ in).

141 Canon-table, Canon IV, *Codex Amiatinus*, Florence, Biblioteca Medicea Laurenziana MS Amiatinus I, *f*. 799. 50.5 × 34 cm (19⅞ × 13⅜ in).

142 Canon-table, Canon I, the Lindisfarne Gospels, London, British Library, Cotton MS Nero D.IV, *f*. 11. 34 × 24 cm (13⅜ × 9½ in).

143 Bird-textile, Persian, relief-sculpture, Takibostan, after O. von Falke, *Kunstgeschichte der Seidenweberei*, Berlin, 1921.

144 Beginning of *argumentum* to St Matthew, the Lindisfarne Gospels, London, British Library Cotton MS Nero D.IV, *f*. 18v. 34 × 24 cm (13⅜ × 9½ in).

145 Cross carpet-page, the Lindisfarne Gospels, London, British Library Cotton MS Nero D.IV, *f*. 26v. 34 × 24 cm (13⅜ × 9½ in).

146 Beginning of St Matthew's Gospel, *Liber Generationis*, the Lindisfarne Gospels, London, British Library Cotton MS Nero D.IV, *f*. 27. 34 × 24 cm (13⅜ × 9½ in).

147 *Christi autem* initials, the Lindisfarne Gospels, London, British Library Cotton MS Nero D.IV, *f*. 29. 34 × 24 cm (13⅜ × 9½ in).

148 Carpet-page, the Lindisfarne Gospels, London, British Library Cotton MS Nero D.IV, *f*. 94v. 34 × 24 cm (13⅜ × 9½ in).

149 Pendant cross, Wilton, Norfolk. Gold, garnets. 4.8 cm (1⅞ in) wide. London, British Museum.

150 Bowl 7 from St Ninian's Isle, Shetland. Silver. Diameter 12.9 cm (5⅛ in). Edinburgh, Royal Museum of Scotland.

151 Bowl 6 from St Ninian's Isle, Shetland. Silver. Diameter 14.3 cm (5⅝ in). Edinburgh, Royal Museum of Scotland.

152 Beginning of St Mark's Gospel, *Initium*, the Lindisfarne Gospels, London, British Library Cotton MS Nero D.IV, *f*. 95. 34 × 24 cm (13⅜ × 9½ in).

153 Penannular brooch, Ballinderry, Co. Offaly. Bronze, *millefiori*. Diameter 8 cm (3⅛ in). Dublin, National Museum of Ireland.

154 The so-called Tara Brooch, from Bettystown, Co. Meath. Gilt-bronze, gold, silver, glass and amber. Diameter 9.3 cm (3⅝ in). Dublin, National Museum of Ireland.

155 *Argumentum* to St Luke, the Lindisfarne Gospels, London, British Library Cotton MS Nero D.IV, *f*. 131. 34 × 24 cm (13⅜ × 9½ in).

156 Carpet-page, the Lindisfarne Gospels, London, British Library Cotton MS Nero D.IV, *f*. 138v. 34 × 24 cm (13⅜ × 9½ in).

157 Beginning of St Luke's Gospel, *Quoniam quidem*, the Lindisfarne Gospels, London, British Library Cotton MS Nero D.IV, *f*. 139. 34 × 24 cm (13⅜ × 9½ in).

158 Bowl 2 from St Ninian's Isle, Shetland. Silver. Diameter 14.4 cm (5⅝ in). Edinburgh, Royal Museum of Scotland.

159 Carpet-page, the Lindisfarne Gospels, London, British Library Cotton MS Nero D.IV, *f*. 210v. 34 × 24 cm (13⅜ × 9½ in).

160 Beginning of St John's Gospel, *In Principio*, the Lindisfarne Gospels, London, British Library Cotton MS Nero D.IV, *f*. 211. 34 × 24 cm (13⅜ × 9½ in).

161 Provost Aldred's colophon, the Lindisfarne Gospels, London, British Library Cotton MS Nero D.IV, *f*. 259.

162 *Capitula* to St John's Gospel and colophons, the Book of Durrow, Dublin, Trinity College MS A.4.5 (57), *f*. 247v. 24.5 × 14.5 cm (9⅝ × 5¾ in). Courtesy The Board of Trinity College, Dublin.

163 Dedication inscription, St Paul's Church, Jarrow. Stone slab. 52.1 × 64.8 cm (20½ × 25½ in). Photo University of Durham.

164 Battle scene, reverse of cross-slab, Aberlemno, Angus. Sandstone. Height 225 cm (88½ in). Photo Crown Copyright: Historic Buildings and Monuments, Scotland.

165 King Egfrith urges St Cuthbert to accept the bishopric. Illustration of Bede's prose *Life*, ch. XXIV, London, British Library MS Yates Thompson 26 (Add. MS 39943), *f*. 51. 13.5 × 9.8 cm (5¼ × 3⅞ in).

166 Sts Peter and Paul and two other Apostles, detail of side of St Cuthbert's coffin. Oak. Total length of coffin 168.9 cm (66½ in), height 46.4 cm (18¼ in). Durham, Cathedral Treasury. Courtesy the Dean and Chapter of Durham.

167 Symbols of St Matthew and St Mark, detail of lid of St Cuthbert's coffin. Oak. Lid 39 cm (15⅜ in) wide. Durham, Cathedral Treasury. Courtesy the Dean and Chapter of Durham.

168 Symbols of St Luke and St John, detail of lid of St Cuthbert's coffin. Oak. Lid 39 cm (15⅜ in) wide. Durham, Cathedral Treasury. Courtesy the Dean and Chapter of Durham.

169 Portrait of St Mark, the Lindisfarne Gospels, London, British Library Cotton MS Nero D.IV, *f*. 93v. 34 × 24 cm (13⅜ × 9½ in).

170 Portrait of St Matthew, the Lindisfarne Gospels, London, British Library Cotton MS Nero D.IV, *f*. 25v. 34 × 24 cm (13⅜ × 9½ in).

171 Portrait of Esdras, the *Codex Amiatinus*, Florence, Biblioteca

Index